AF477750

The Search for Selfhood in Modern Literature

Also by Murray Roston

PROPHET AND POET: The Bible and the Growth of Romanticism

BIBLICAL DRAMA IN ENGLAND: From the Middle Ages to the Present Day

THE SOUL OF WIT: A Study of John Donne

MILTON AND THE BAROQUE

SIXTEENTH-CENTURY ENGLISH LITERATURE

RENAISSANCE PERSPECTIVES: In Literature and the Visual Arts

CHANGING PERSPECTIVES: In Literature and the Visual Arts, 1650–1820

VICTORIAN CONTEXTS: Literature and the Visual Arts

MODERNIST PATTERNS: In Literature and the Visual Arts

The Search for Selfhood in Modern Literature

Murray Roston

First published 2001 by
PALGRAVE
Houndmills, Basingstoke, Hampshire RG21 6XS and
175 Fifth Avenue, New York, N.Y. 10010
Companies and representatives throughout the world

PALGRAVE is the new global academic imprint of
St. Martin's Press LLC Scholarly and Reference Division and
Palgrave Publishers Ltd (formerly Macmillan Press Ltd).

ISBN 0–333–76334–3

This book is printed on paper suitable for recycling and
made from fully managed and sustained forest sources.

A catalogue record for this book is available
from the British Library.

Library of Congress Cataloging-in-Publication Data
Roston, Murray.
    The search for selfhood in modern literature / Murray Roston.
        p. cm.
    Includes bibliographical references and index.
    ISBN 0–333–76334–3
     1. American literature—20th century—History and criticism.
    2. Self in literature. 3. English literature—20th century—History
    and criticism. 4. Identity (Psychology) in literature. 5. Existentialism
    in literature. 6. Spiritual life in literature. 7. Individualism in literature.
    8. Antiheroes in literature. 9. Humanism in literature. I. Title.
    PS228.S36 R67 2001
    810.9'384—dc21
                                                          2001024589

10   9   8   7   6   5   4   3   2   1
10   09   08   07   06   05   04   03   02   01

Printed and bound in Great Britain by
Antony Rowe Ltd, Chippenham, Wiltshire

Contents

Acknowledgements

I should like to express my thanks once again to the members of the English department at UCLA and especially to their chair, Professor Thomas Wortham, for their unfailing kindness and hospitality on my frequent visits to the department. My home university has been consistently helpful in granting me leave to teach and research there. I am grateful also to Ms Eleanor Birne and Mr Keith Povey for their valuable editorial advice and assistance.

Some of the material in the chapter on Philip Roth was delivered at a Fulbright conference held in India and appeared subsequently in *The Asian Response to American Literature*, published by the Fulbright Foundation.

Finally, as always, my deep affection and thanks to my wife Faith, for her cheerful support, her ever-ready humour, and her delightful company.

Bar Ilan University, Ramat Gan, Israel   Murray Roston

1
The Crisis of Identity

There has rarely been so great a dichotomy as there is in our own century between the public's conception of its condition and that projected by the creative artist and thinker, as the latters' more sensitive cultural antennae detect and decipher the encoded messages of the time. The term 'modern' remains for society at large an essentially heartening, self-congratulatory term, evoking a vision of awesome technological inventions, of break-through techniques in medicine and surgery, of multimedia communication and of exhilarating travel through outer space, such achievements signifying an unprecedented advance over the limited capabilities of previous generations. The predominantly pessimistic mood among the leading poets, novelists and dramatists of this century stands in stark contrast, the sombre tone extending from Conrad's revelation of the horror lurking in the darkness of the human heart, through the intellectual and emotional paralysis of T.S. Eliot's Prufrock, and on to Camus's choice of the tragic Sisyphus as the appropriate paradigm for contemporary man, condemned to the futile task of propelling a huge rock to the top of a mountain only to see it roll back to earth. If Camus did offer a glimmer of hope in that analogy, identifying in Sisyphus's determination to persevere an existentialist assertion of will, the slim margin left for such assertion both in the archetypal legend and in Camus's application of the analogy to his own time evidenced the near-despair motivating his philosophical stance. It is epitomised in the chilling opening sentence of his *Myth of Sisyphus*: 'There is but one truly serious philosophical problem, and that is suicide.'

That statement was less an innovation than the recapitulation of a concept embedded in the literature of the twentieth century, where the theme of suicide had already emerged as a recurrent motif, and was destined to continue as such throughout subsequent decades. Unlike instances of self-immolation in nineteenth-century literature, motivated there by personal misfortune, the unhappy love-affair of Anna Karenina or Melmotte's financial collapse in Trollope's *The Way We Live Now*, in our own era it has taken on the dimensions of a cosmic disillusionment, a consciousness of the inadequacy of humankind in coping with a seemingly indifferent world. Among the manifold accounts of self-immolation in twentieth-century literature may be listed the demise of Quentin in Faulkner's *The Sound and the Fury* lamenting man 'who is conceived by accident and whose every breath is a fresh cast with dice already loaded against him', and Spandrell's programmed death at the conclusion of Huxley's *Point Counter Point* as he is finally convinced that even the *heilige Dankgesang* from Beethoven's A Minor quartet with its seeming proof of the existence of a benevolent and harmonious universe cannot refute the vacuity of a godless cosmos. There is the momentary excitement in *Waiting for Godot* as Estragon proposes that they hang themselves to end the weariness of their lives, Scobie's suicide in Greene's *The Heart of the Matter*, and Seymour's in J.D. Salinger's narrative of the Glass family. John Barth's *The Floating Opera* opens on the day Todd Andrews plans to terminate his life, while James Baldwin's *Another Country* closes its powerful opening section with Rufus leaping from a bridge into the dark waters below. Whether these characters consummate their suicidal plans, as most do, or find some temporary alleviation for their despondency, Vladimir and Estragon unsure if the tree branch will bear their weight, and Todd discovering at the last moment a casuistic reason for postponing the act, such despair at the sterility of the human condition became either the overt or the covert theme for a considerable portion of modernist literature. The writing produced was by no means consistently gloomy. Beckett's play is laced with warmth and humour, Barth's novel has an ebullience and vitality countering much of the underlying melancholy; for the act of writing is in itself a positive assertion, an affirmation that life is not wholly worthless. But even the humour in such productions is for the most part lugubrious, emanating from a mood of despondency, an attempt to discover some mitigating factor, however minimal, in the morass of twentieth-century disillusionment. Nor, one may add, was the mood of depression confined to fiction, as one recalls how many leading writers in this century have committed suicide, among them Hart Crane, Virginia Woolf, Stefan Zweig, Walter Benjamin, Primo Levi, F.O. Matthiessen, Arthur Koestler, Delmore Schwartz, John Berryman, Sylvia Plath and Anne Sexton – with A. Alvarez, after his own failed attempt, composing a full-length study of self-immolation, entitled *The Savage God*.[1]

The darker aspects of the human condition, the frustrations implicit in mortal existence, have been lamented in every generation, from Ecclesiastes's refrain that all is vanity, through the sombre genre of Attic tragedy, to the angst of the Romantic poets and beyond. Yet the motivation for suicide and the form whereby such morbid impulses express themselves have varied significantly from generation to generation, reflecting the anxieties specific to each era. In the eighteenth century, as Michel Foucault has shown, the rationalist suppression of those emotional outlets which might have relieved undue pressures resulted in the prevalence of religious melancholia, William Cowper's attempts at suicide resulting, as with so many of his peers, from a gloomy conviction of his eternal damnation.[2] For the fallen woman of the Victorian era drowning offered escape from an unbearable social stigma, a recourse so frequent at that time as to evoke a plethora of poems, paintings and literary depictions of her fate, including G.F. Watts's canvas *Found Drowned*, Thomas Hood's poem *The Bridge of Sighs*, and the figure of Martha Edell in *David Copperfield*. In an earlier era, Hamlet's suicidal brooding, his longing for death as a consummation devoutly to be wished but forbidden him by Christian canon, functioned no less as a response to immediately contemporary concerns, betraying anxieties fundamentally different from those motivating the pessimism of Camus's day or, indeed, of all other periods. It arose from the growing suspicion that the High Renaissance vision of mankind's infinite potential, the belief in human ability to attain to everlasting prestige, glory and fame in this world was, after all, deeply flawed. The speed with which his father's memory had been forgotten by all but himself confirmed Hamlet's doubt whether the promised renown could in fact survive the putrefaction of the grave and the stench of a rotting skull: 'Dost thou think Alexander look'd o' this fashion i' th' earth? . . . And smelt so? Pagh!' It marked his recognition of the failure of that Renaissance ideal and a reluctant reversion to the medieval concept *media vita in morte sumus* with a depressing sense that, without the prospect of such lasting fame, life held no attraction. But our own generation has cherished no such contrasting visions, the potential splendour and majesty of the human race in this world and the sense of the infinite faculty of man having long evaporated, leaving only a feeling of emptiness in a dismal and pointless wasteland. For Sylvia Plath, as for most twentieth-century contemporaries who experienced that suicidal urge, the cause was, as she movingly related in *The Bell Jar*, a conviction of lost identity, the painful lack of any meaningful self within, an emptiness that she described mournfully as 'the vacuum of her own ego', a time of 'darkness, despair, disillusion – so black only as the inferno of the human mind can be . . .'[3]

The attribution of this twentieth-century malaise to a general sense of its contrast to the past, to being born into an age so fundamentally different from previous generations as to create an entity to which the individual was unable to adjust, has been accepted by many as defining its distinctive quality. Malcolm Bradbury, in a lively study of twentieth-century literature, has suggested that throughout the thought and art of the period there runs 'a strong sense of the uniqueness of modern times,' an awareness of new processes of production, new types of relationships between people, new social practices.[4] But does such attribution withstand close scrutiny? The ancient Greeks, it has been wryly remarked, suffered from a strange misapprehension, an inability to recognise that they were ancient. Every age sees itself as modern, and almost every age has regarded itself as in some way rebelling against, alienated from, or improving upon its predecessors. Pericles proudly proclaimed (with considerable justice) that fifth-century Athens had achieved in education, in refinement of the arts, in warfare and in its principles of democracy, standards to which history could offer no equal, values that would make it the envy of subsequent generations.[5] A similar sense of uniqueness characterised the emergence of the High Renaissance 'self-fashioner', while the late seventeenth century experienced a sense of gratification very similar to our own at having made a substantial leap forward in human development, marking a salutary break with the deeply flawed, dogma-bound past. In 1667, Thomas Sprat, summarising the aims of the newly founded Royal Society, proclaimed his generation's conviction that its rejection of the religious superstitions, the sectarian conflicts, and the messianic enthusiasms of the past represented the beginning of an essentially new epoch in the history of mankind, reliant henceforth upon universally accepted reason and common sense:

> But now ... the blindness of former *Ages*, and the miseries of this last are vanish'd away; now men are generally weary of the *Relicks* of *Antiquity* and satiated with *Religious Disputes*; now not only the *eyes* of men but their *hands* are open, and prepar'd to *labour*. Now there is a universal *desire* and *appetite* after *Knowledge* and not after that of ancient Sects which only yielded hard indigestible *arguments* or sharp *contentions* instead of food.[6]

Even the technological achievements of the twentieth century upon which the mid-century so often prided itself were not significantly different in their cultural impact from the revolutionary changes experienced in the Victorian era, when the introduction of railways criss-crossing the country, of steamships ploughing their way across the oceans, and of instantaneous telegraphic communication swept away the old world, breaking down the isolation of villages, fostering urbanisation and enormously speeding up the pace of living – a break with the past no less momentous than that of the twentieth century. As Thackeray remarked in 1860, 'We who have lived before railways were made belong to another world ... It was only yesterday, but what a gulf between now and then!'[7] One may suspect, therefore, that the causes of the modernist malaise and of the uniqueness of that era are to be found elsewhere.

The sense of collapsed values and the awareness of the futility of existence, if not yet acknowledged by the wider public, had, by the early decades of this century, come to be profoundly felt in intellectual circles. George Orwell recorded the depressing mood dominant among his peers in the England of that time:

> The trouble was that by about 1930 there was no activity, except perhaps scientific research, the arts and left-wing politics, that a thinking person could believe in. The debunking of Western civilisation had reached its climax and 'disillusionment' was immensely widespread. Who now could take it for granted to go through life in the ordinary middle-class way, as a soldier, a clergyman, a stockbroker, an Indian Civil Servant, or what-not? And how many of the values by which our grandfathers lived could now be taken seriously? Patriotism, religion, the Empire, the family, the sanctity of marriage, the Old School Tie, birth, breeding, honour, discipline ... ?[8]

Like most such commentaries, however, his summary offers no analysis, nor even an indication of the changes that had produced that despondency or 'disillusionment'; and when causes are attributed by historians they tend to be either vague or peripheral. Roy Baumeister has traced the sense of alienation to primarily economic factors, the movement from farms to corporate institutions and the economic depression of the twenties, neither of which would seem very relevant to the sense of cosmic vacuity that dominated the literature of the time.[9] Some have rightly referred to more basic transformations, including the fragmentation of self resulting from Freudian psychology. But it is, I believe, essential for a full understanding of the literary changes that resulted from such factors to focus with much greater precision on the sources of the disparity, on the specific aspects within those sources that produced the various shifts in perspective within literature.[10] We are informed somewhat nebulously by Frederick Karl (and without further elucidation) that the modern novel 'looks out on ultimate chaos, on a world that is no longer seeking instruction but destruction, a world possibly heading nowhere';[11] and although Colin Wilson's *The Outsider: an enquiry into the sickness of mankind in the twentieth century* created a flurry of interest on its first appearance in 1956, respect for it soon waned when it was realised how misty his analysis really was. The sense of alienation he vaguely attributed, again with no further explication, to the 'revolutions in thought brought about by the Victorian sages, J.S. Mill, Huxley, Darwin, Emerson, Spencer, Carlyle, Ruskin …'[12] And that same evasiveness concerning the determinants of the modern situation characterises the work of most other historians, with the added factor that, when sources are suggested, they frequently do not withstand close examination.

It has, for example, become customary to cite two factors as major causes of the twentieth-century loss of identity. Paul Fussell's widely admired study, *The Great War and Modern Memory*, stated categorically that the impact of the First World War, with its appalling destruction of human life, not only marked but *created* the sharp division between the traditional world and the modern. It occurred, he argues, 'in what was, compared with ours, a static world, where the values appeared stable', the slaughter it produced bringing to an end the prevailing meliorist myth of progress that had dominated the public consciousness for a century.[13] A second factor often seen as marking the change is the devastation produced by the atomic bomb in 1945 with the horrific warning that mankind was now capable of annihilating itself. In theory, both events might appear distinctly relevant. But the dates are incompatible with the emergent awareness in literature of the sterility of human existence and the disintegration of traditional values. Conrad's *Heart of Darkness*, providing a devastating challenge to twentieth-century faith in the progress of civilisation by revealing the callousness and self-interest motivating what had been thought of as an enlightened modern culture, was published in 1902; and T.S. Eliot's 'The Lovesong of J. Alfred Prufrock', that major poetic statement of disillusionment with twentieth-century values, depicting the emotional and ideological paralysis of the intellectual in the modern era, was composed in its final form in 1911, both works completed well before any augury of a world war, before any awareness of the altered nature of armed combat and, of course, long before the detonation of the first atomic bomb.[14]

Those developments in mass destruction should be seen, I would suggest, not as causes of the disillusionment but as symbols that were adopted retrospectively because of their aptness in representing the new anxieties. The introduction of the machine-gun in the battles of the

Somme, mowing down hundreds of men in a single murderous sweep, did seem, to the poets and writers personally involved in those battles, to exemplify the individual's loss of identity, reducing humans to the level of animals herded indiscriminately to the slaughter:

> What passing-bells for these who die as cattle?
>   Only the monstrous anger of the guns.
>   Only the stuttering rifles' rapid rattle.[15]

And the detonation of the atom bomb over Hiroshima some three decades later took that image a stage further. In 1917, there had still been some comfort, even after the introduction of the machine-gun, in the belief that each soldier need only fear death if – in the phrase popular at that time – the bullet 'had his name on it'. But that concept was patently inapplicable to an atomic bomb, randomly obliterating over 75,000 people in a single moment. By 1945, therefore, at a time when the wider public was beginning to absorb the new concept, the atom bomb was endorsed as a remarkably appropriate emblem for that contemporary loss of individuality which artists and writers had sensed so much earlier. Neither of those events, therefore, although they may have intensified the general despair and offered appropriate images for it, was itself a causative or determining factor.

A third element often cited as of major importance in producing this loss of identity was the socio-economic upheaval, the introduction of labour-saving devices creating widespread unemployment and encouraging the movement of large sections of the population to the cities in a manner destroying the more comfortable awareness of belonging to a village or small community and depriving the individual of the pride in craftsmanship that had previously provided even the simplest agricultural worker with a feeling of personal value and significance. That aspect cannot be ignored as a contributory element; but any consideration of it as a direct cause of the specifically twentieth-century crisis is weakened by the fact that urbanisation had manifested itself in its most cruel form some hundred years earlier, in the 1820s. The appalling results of that change were movingly recorded in such protest novels as Elizabeth Gaskell's *Mary Barton* of 1848, as well as in Joseph Adshead's documentary study, *Distress in Manchester*, of 1842, testifying to the two thousand fetid cellars in that city in which families were compelled to live in their enforced migration from the country in search of work.[16] In 1854, Dickens had highlighted the loss of individuality resulting from nineteenth-century urbanisation, mordantly commenting on the anonymity and uniformity of the inhabitants of the new industrial cities which

> contained several large streets all very like one another, and many small streets still more like one another, inhabited by people equally like one another, who all went in and out at the same hours, with the same sound upon the same pavements, to do the same work, and to whom every day was the same as yesterday and tomorrow, and every year the counterpart of the last and the next.[17]

Not only did that aspect emerge so much earlier but it was, in addition, intrinsically different from the twentieth-century version. For Gaskell, Dickens and their peers the unemployment, the poverty, even the sameness of urban existence were elements confined to the working classes, social ills which they believed could and should be remedied by enlightened legislation. Dickens attacked the abuses in the administration of contemporary orphanages not as indications of man's innate or incorrigible iniquity but as the result of deplorable governmental supervision, claiming that they were 'brutally conducted, vilely kept, preposterously inspected, dishonestly defended, a disgrace to a Christian community, and a stain upon a civilised land.'[18] They represented grave instances of mismanagement which appropriate judiciary action could rectify and which, largely as a result of Dickens' novels, were indeed significantly corrected. They were not evils inherent in the human lot, grounds for universal pessimism or cosmic despair.

I should like to investigate in some detail the factors primarily responsible for undermining traditional values, and for inaugurating in this century so fundamental a reassessment of the human situation. My purpose in this opening chapter, it should be stressed, is not to innovate but to provide a more precisely defined basis for the examination of leading literary works in the discussion that is to follow, the exploration of ways writers responded to the problems and challenges specific to their time. But two further reservations may be requisite. In presenting in two stages the reaction of intellectuals to the major elements producing such change – a transition from initial optimism, when the new theories seemed to open up immense possibilities for the advancement of mankind, to eventual despondency as their deeper implications were gradually perceived – I am aware that those stages were not clearly demarcated in time, some writers and artists experiencing the transition earlier than others. But the overall picture that emerges is essentially of a twofold, sequential response. Moreover, in examining that response my concern will not be with the establishment, with such conservative elements as the church or traditionalists in other spheres resistant to innovation, whether for religious, personal or ideological reasons. The focus will be instead on the rising generation of intellectuals who espoused the challenging ideas, seeing them as opening up new vistas for the future of civilisation and, subsequently, as bringing with them grave threats to mankind itself. As Carl Jung remarked,

> The man whom we can with justice call 'modern' is solitary ... Indeed, he is completely modern only when he has come to the very edge of the world, leaving behind him all that has been discarded and outgrown, and acknowledging that he stands before a void out of which all things may grow.[19]

It is that intellectual avant garde, the inaugurators and pathfinders of Modernism, upon whom I wish to concentrate.

* * * * *

While at the more popular level the debate on Darwin's *The Origin of Species* focused on man's supposed descent from a hairy, ape-like anthropoid, its most serious challenge was, as its author recognised, its discrediting of the long-held concept of the Great Chain of Being, the notion of an established hierarchy reaching from the Supreme Creator down to the lowest forms of life, which had dominated Western thought for centuries, losing its hold only during the nineteenth century. Included as axiomatic in that paradigmatic system was the principle of 'plenitude', based on the assumption, derived from the biblical text, that in a universe designed by an omniscient and hence prescient Deity everything requisite for the earth's future, including all forms of life, had been generated during the first six days in a perfect and final form. With the possible exception of barren crags, deserts and oceans considered by certain theologians, such as Thomas Burnet, to have been installed at the time of the Deluge as a punishment for the corruption of Noah's generation, each element in nature was believed, after its initial formation, to be fixed for perpetuity. 'The earth is the Lord's and the fulness thereof,' the Psalmist had declared; and that scriptural description of terrestrial 'fulness' was seen as affirming the existence of a universe in which all possibilities of generative action had already been fulfilled.[20] Such belief precluded the possibility of dynamic adaptation, of species modifying their forms in later generations to suit altered environments.

Accordingly Darwin, a man of retiring disposition disliking controversy, attempted in his concluding summary to gloss over the differences and to soothe the theologians. While authors of the highest eminence, he noted, believed that each species had been independently created at the beginning of the world, biological evidence of changes due to the 'indirect and direct action of the external conditions of life' need not be seen as contradicting that view, since this potential for later adaptation to environmental needs had no doubt formed part of 'the laws impressed on matter by the Creator'. That potential for change had thus been divinely built in to the original plan. Darwin hoped thereby to absolve God from scientific disqualification:

> I see no good reason why the views given in this volume should shock the religious feelings of any one … A celebrated author and divine has written to me that 'he has gradually learnt to see that it is just as noble a conception of the Deity to believe that He created a few original forms capable of self-development into other and needful forms, as to believe that He required a fresh act of creation to supply the voids caused by the action of His laws'.[21]

On the other hand, that desire to tone down the impact of the new theory and to conciliate the opposition did not characterise his self-appointed 'bulldog', Thomas Huxley, who, in disseminating it among the wider public deliberately adopted a more aggressive stance. Evolutionist theory he saw not only as a major scientific advance but also as a wonderfully opportune instrument for disburdening his generation of the onerous restrictions and oppressive moral directives intrinsic to Christianity and fettering the society of his time. If, with the caution of an empiricist, he coined the term 'agnostic' to describe his own suspension of Christian belief until verifiable disproof of God's existence should be forthcoming, his public pronouncements were more forthright, assuming as self-evident the necessity of discarding Christianity as an outmoded superstition, now to be replaced by a far healthier rationalist system. Man's shared ancestry with the ape he regarded as in no way derogatory, seeing in the light of the splendid achievements of the human race since its divergence from that species and in its impressive outdistancing of its quondam relatives a human potential for even greater advances in the future. The magnificence of Alpine mountains, he argued analogously in his *Evidence of Man's Place in Nature* (1863), their snowy peaks soaring into the heavens, is not lessened by the knowledge that they originated in primeval mud, nor does that derivation detract from their proud and seemingly inaccessible glory.[22]

In an image vividly expressing his sanguine vision of the world that could and should result from such disburdenment, Huxley, compared the

New Science, of which evolutionary theory constituted a vital part, to the legendary Cinderella. Scorned and exploited by her ugly sisters, Philosophy and Theology, she dreams in her lonely garret of a world incomparably superior to that which had existed under their antiquated auspices. At a time when the natural sciences were regarded with some degree of disdain at the universities and (in marked contrast to our own day) received meagre budgets while the main resources were devoted to the humanities, he declared:

> Men go about proclaiming, 'Woe to this wicked city', and denouncing physical science as the evil genius of modern days – mother of materialism, and fatalism, and all sorts of other condemnableisms. I venture to beg them to lay the blame on the right shoulders; or at least to put in the dock, along with science, those sinful sisters of hers, Philosophy and Theology, who being so much older, should have known better than the poor Cinderella of the schools and universities over which they have so long dominated ...
>
> Cinderella ... lights the fire, sweeps the house, and provides the dinner; and is rewarded by being told that she is a base creature devoted to low and material interests. But in her garret, she has fairy visions out of the ken of that pair of shrews who are quarrelling downstairs. She sees the order which pervades the seeming disorder of the world; the great drama of evolution, with its full share of pity and terror, but also with abundant goodness and beauty, unrolls itself before her eyes; and she learns in her heart of hearts the lesson that the foundation of morality is to have done once and for all with lying; to give up pretending to believe that for which there is no evidence, and repeating unintelligible propositions about things beyond the possibility of knowledge.[23]

Among those 'fairy visions' of the future stimulated by evolutionism was Huxley's conviction that, once those quarrelling shrews downstairs had been banished, men and women would no longer depend for their moral precepts upon obsolete dictates issued by some bearded elder on Mount Sinai, but could henceforth construct their ethical codes upon reasoned dialogue, upon logically designed principles of social equity and justice derived from study of the natural world. Rules of human conduct, he assured his readers in 1877, 'are discoverable – like the other so-called laws of Nature – by observation and experiment.'[24] The dark threats of a Day of Judgement and the fires of Hell that had haunted the Victorians from their childhood onward[25] seemed now to dissolve in the clear light of a rationally based science, positing a universe developing by a process of Natural Selection in which divine participation appeared entirely redundant.

The meliorist concept of Darwinism that characterised this earlier, optimistic phase, the assumption that evolution constituted an upwardly progressive movement from primitive origins to more nobly sophisticated forms had, despite its author's reluctance to venture into the non-scientific implications of his theory, in fact been fostered initially by himself. Mankind, he declared,

> may be excused for feeling some pride at having risen, though not through his own exertions, to the very summit of the organic scale; and the fact of his having thus risen may give him hope for a still higher destiny in the distant future.

And he concluded his thesis with the heartening words:

> Thus, from the war of nature, from famine and death, the most exalted object which we are capable of conceiving, namely, the production of the higher animals, directly follows. There is grandeur in this view of life, with its several powers, having been originally breathed by the Creator into a few forms or into one; and that whilst this planet has gone cycling on according to the fixed law of gravity, from so simple a beginning endless forms most beautiful and most wonderful have been, and are being evolved.

That conception of evolution as consistently progressive, moving to ever higher forms of life, permeated almost all areas of scholarship at this time. In art history, Gottfried Semper's authoritative *Der Stil in den technischen und taktonischen Kuensten* of 1861 and Alfred Haddon's significantly entitled *Evolution in Art* characterised almost all contemporary studies in attributing the lack of realism in the sculpture of ancient tribal craftsmen to their crude inability to achieve accurate representation, failing to appreciate, as Paul Gauguin did some decades later, that it resulted from a deliberate stylising of reality, a desire to move beyond the factual – a concept which, largely through Gauguin's influence, came to serve as a primary element in twentieth-century art. In literary studies, E.K. Chambers's monumental study of *The Medieval Stage* similarly assumed that the simpler plays within the surviving mystery cycles had preceded the more sophisticated versions, an assumption later revealed to be unfounded. And anthropologists seized upon the new theory to justify their sense of the European's superiority to the savage. [26] It was that same meliorist view of continual advancement that animated Huxley's vision of his generation as on the threshold of a new era, freed from the inhibitions of the past and, once it had thrown off the trammels of religious belief, empowered to design a far more attractive world based upon reason and common sense.

In previous debates between atheists and believers in a deity – debates dating back at least to the times of Epicurus and Lucretius[27] – the believers had possessed an almost invincible argument, the universal suitability of each species to its environment, the anteater endowed with a nasal protuberance ideal for ferreting out its prey, the polar bear's white fur camouflaging it against the snow. God, Browning remarked, in creating each insect, animal, and bird, had granted

> ... to each a sphere to be his world,
> Appointed with the various objects needed
> To satisfy his own peculiar wants ... [28]

such universal compatibility being scarcely attributable to fortuitous development from a chance collision of atoms, as outlined in Lucretius's *De Rerum Natura*. In contrast, Darwin's principle of Natural Selection posited a process of adaptability no longer reliant upon fortuity. He explained how, in a herd of cattle suffering from the effects of drought, when all available grass and foliage had been consumed, only those members of the herd possessing slightly longer necks would be capable of reaching higher foliage. As the sole survivors of the herd, they would transmit that genetic tendency of lengthened necks to their offspring, and repetitions of that process of selection during subsequent periods of drought would, over the centuries, result eventually in the giraffe.[29]

Such persuasive, logically based argument, augmenting Lyell's geological explanation of the origin of the earth's crust as predating by aeons the scriptural version, might have been sufficient in itself to shake the foundations of religious belief, but was intensified by emergent reassessments within the church itself, where such new readings of the Gospels as David Strauss's *Leben Jesu* of 1835, portraying Christ as a nobly dedicated but in no way divine figure, joined with Bishop Colenso's *The Pentateuch and Book of Joshua Critically Examined* of 1862 and *The Essays and Reviews* to cast rational doubt on many of the church's basic teachings. For some, these challenges were the source of spiritual anguish – witness Ruskin's cry, 'If only the Geologists would let me alone, I could do very well, but those dreadful Hammers. I hear the clink of them at the end of every cadence of the Bible verses.'[30] But from others they evoked a jubilant sense of liberation from the wearisome dogmas of Christianity, Harriet Martineau repudiating with scorn in 1857 her allegiance to a discredited creed:

> When I experienced the still new joy of feeling myself to be a portion of the universe, resting on the security of its everlasting laws, certain that its Cause was wholly out of the sphere of human attributes ... how could it matter to me that the adherents of a decaying mythology ... were fiercely clinging to their Man-God, their scheme of salvation, their reward and punishment, their arrogance, their selfishness, their essential pay-system, as ordered by their mythology?[31]

The mental adjustment involved in deserting a faith inculcated from childhood was not always easy; Somerset Maugham, in his semi-autobiographical novel *Of Human Bondage*, recorded his own experience in the 1890s, presenting with humour Phillip Callow's moment of recognition that he is at last emancipated from the intolerable dread of hell-fire – 'Freedom! He was his own master at last. From old habit, unconsciously he thanked God that he no longer believed in Him.'[32]

It has often been assumed that the negative impact on religious belief created by these challenges to Christianity was unavoidable, the general exodus of intellectuals from the church and the dwindling in membership during the following decades being an ineluctable consequence. But the assumption that such attacks upon Christian belief would result in a general abandonment of the faith was by no means self-evident. An essentially similar challenge in an earlier generation, potentially no less threatening, had produced a contrary outcome, strengthening and not debilitating religious adherence, eventually reinstating ecclesiastical authority not only with undiminished force but with augmented grandeur. In 1610, Galileo's sighting of satellites had provided equally incontrovertible scientific evidence conflicting with the biblical account of creation, his telescopic sightings confirming Copernicus's heliocentric theory and dismissing for ever the concept of a four-cornered earth situated at the centre of a subservient cosmos. The shock seemed at the time to 'place all in doubt', undercutting the concept of an ordered hierarchy with God at its head. Yet the twofold counter-movement that came to dominate both art and literature during the seventeenth century in the form of Mannerism and Baroque not only offered the Christian believer a comforting haven from disbelief but served to shore up and reinvigorate religious faith. The poetry of John Donne and the paintings of Tintoretto and El Greco confronted that contemporary scientific challenge not by denying the validity of the new evidence, but by transcending its implications. Donne, while granting that the biblical concept of a four-cornered earth was no longer acceptable in its literal form, in his sonnet beginning 'At the round earth's *imagined* corners ...' minimised the implications of the new scientific theories by discounting them as applicable merely to the physical world, while he focused instead upon the inner, spiritual experience of the true believer, circumventing the factual discoveries of the scientists to reach out to a more gratifying, paradoxical, spiritual reality beyond. The powerful run-on line that follows that phrase

> At the round earth's imagined corners, blow
> Your trumpets, Angels, and arise, arise
> From death you numberless infinities of souls ...

reduced the Copernican world to a mere technicality beside the exciting vision of the Day of Judgement. And such baroque artists as Rubens and Milton, again accepting as valid the vastness and materiality of the new scientifically revealed cosmos, saw that discovery not as disqualifying the existence of the divine but as offering added testimony to the magnificence of its Supreme Creator, the Baroque adopting as its motto, *Ad majorem gloriam Dei.*[33]

Theoretically, the challenges posed to faith in the nineteenth century could have elicited a similarly invigorating response from the church and from its intellectual adherents. The contemporary questioning of the authenticity of the Bible had indeed intensified the weakening of religious faith, textual revaluation aimed initially at the Old Testament, yet both by implication and by parallel investigation soon applied to the New. The claim, both in Bishop Colenso's book and in Julius Wellhausen's *Prolegomena to the History of Ancient Israel* (1878), that the Pentateuch incorporated elements written in periods much later than the time of Moses seemed to transform the Bible from a set of divinely ordained ethical precepts into a work of merely human composition.[34] But there is evidence that an adjustment to these charges and to those emanating from the sciences, an adjustment somewhat similar to that of the seventeenth century, might well have taken place. Mrs Humphry Ward's widely discussed novel *Robert Elsmere*, of 1888, recounted with sympathy the spiritual struggle of a young, idealistic clergyman confronted by the doubts cast upon religion concerning the authenticity of the scriptural text, and by the historically based reinterpretation of the mission of Jesus.

Eventually compelled to reject as mere accretions the miraculous elements recorded in the Gospels, Elsmere adopts a more humanistic form of Christianity based upon 'that continuous and only revelation of God in nature', dedicating his own life to imitating the altruism of the humble carpenter Jesus. Yet with all the agony involved in that change, Elsmere remains, one notes, a devout believer in the Deity, consecrating the rest of his life to the fulfilment and dissemination of this modified creed. Mrs Ward's uncle, Matthew Arnold, whom she greatly admired and from whom she may have imbibed that concept, had also argued that religion needed, as a result of the new criticism, to be recast but not to be abandoned: 'At the present moment two things about the Christian religion must surely be clear to anybody with eyes in his head. One is that men cannot do without it; the other, that they cannot do with it as it is.'[35]

There was, therefore, a clear alternative open to thinking Christians. By modifying certain dogmas of the church, in the same way as an earlier age had modified the concept of a four-cornered earth, they could yet retain their faith and avoid jettisoning their religion in its entirety. But there was an aspect of the new theories being advanced by science that made it far more difficult for the nineteenth-century Christian to preserve belief, radically eroding the influence of the church during the early decades of the following century. It was a potential discreditation of Christianity coming from an entirely different direction, casting doubt not, as in the work of Wellhausen and others, on the reliability of the biblical text nor, as in evolutionist theory, on the authenticity of the scriptural account of man's creation, but aimed more damagingly at the most central events of Christianity itself, offering historical evidence for the origins of the faith that no serious Christian could henceforth ignore.

In its initial purpose, James G. Frazer's study of the myths of Adonis, Attis and Osiris, a scholarly investigation by a Cambridge classics professor, seemed comparatively innocuous, remote from the immediate problems of his generation; yet the results of the research were to prove potentially devastating. Marking in many respects the beginnings of cultural anthropology as we know it today,[36] *The Golden Bough* located the narrative of the Christian Gospels in an entirely new context by revealing that the legends woven around those pagan gods and the methods of worshipping them were in fact widespread variations of it, for the most part reaching back to eras long before the advent of Christianity.[37] Carefully annotated, like Darwin's treatise, in a manner making the evidence well-nigh unassailable, his research recorded how, in numerous ancient communities outside the confines of Egypt and Greece and in even the most primitive tribes of darkest Africa, there had existed a fertility rite marking the end of winter and the hope of a bountiful spring. The tribal king (in some instances, a victim was substituted) would be killed or alternatively the tribal god ceremonially removed from his pedestal and buried to symbolise the end of winter, the ceremony to be followed a few days later by the celebration of the king/god's replacement or resurrection, the latter event representing the longed-for advent of a congenial spring as well as, in some instances, the promise of life beyond death. Such rituals were, Frazer explained, the expression of uncivilised peoples fearful of the elements and resorting to superstitious or magical practices in the hope of averting disaster. Among such examples, he recorded the Syrian worship of Cybele, long preceding Christianity, where, at a ceremony held during the springtime, an effigy of the god Attis was buried amidst deep mourning:

> But when night had fallen, the sorrow of the worshippers was turned to joy. For suddenly a light shone in the darkness: the tomb was opened: the god had risen from the dead; and as the priest touched the lips of the weeping mourners with balm, he softly whispered in their ears the glad tidings of salvation. The resurrection of the god was hailed by his disciples as a promise that they too would issue triumphant from the corruption of the grave.[38]

The existence of such widespread rituals in ancient times was in itself damaging enough to Christian belief, with the implication that the central stories of the Crucifixion and Resurrection, revered for so long as events unique in history and inaugurating the one and only true faith, arose from a primitive fertility rite ignorantly sanctified by later generations. But no less subversive in the effect of the work upon his contemporaries was the scorn with which Frazer, writing with the authority of a distinguished scholar, presented his evidence, his phraseology carefully designed to protect him from a charge of blasphemy yet suggesting his contempt for any thinking person failing to draw the obvious conclusions.

He recorded, for example, a ceremony prominent in the Mithraic religion that had originated some fourteen centuries before Christ, had spread through the Hellenic world from Persia at the time of Alexander the Great, and had become the main rival to Christianity during the third and fourth centuries. On the twenty-fifth of December, the winter solstice when the day begins to lengthen and the power of the sun to increase,[39] the Nativity of the Sun was annually celebrated by its adherents. Worshippers retired into certain inner shrines, from which at midnight they issued with a loud cry, 'The Virgin has brought forth!', the newborn sun being represented there by the image of an infant. In addition to the exact correspondence of the dating of this solar nativity with that of the Christian Nativity at Christmas, the fact that the Crucifixion and Resurrection were also seasonally identical, being celebrated in the springtime at the same time as the killing and resurrection of the tribal god in primitive vegetation ceremonies, led Frazer to comment with heavy sarcasm:

> It appears from the testimony of an anonymous Christian, who wrote in the fourth century of our era, that Christians and pagans alike were struck by the remarkable coincidence between the death and resurrection of their respective deities, and that the coincidence formed a theme of bitter controversy between the adherents of the rival religions, the pagans contending that the resurrection of Christ was a spurious imitation of the resurrection of Attis, and the Christians asserting with equal warmth that the resurrection of Attis was a diabolical counterfeit of the resurrection of Christ. In these unseemly bickerings, the heathen took what to a superficial observer might seem strong ground by arguing that their god was the older and therefore presumably the original, not the counterfeit, since as a general rule an original is older than its copy. This feeble argument the Christians easily rebutted. They admitted, indeed, that in point of time Christ was the junior deity, but they triumphantly demonstrated his real seniority by falling back on the subtlety of Satan, who on so important an occasion had surpassed himself by inverting the usual order of nature.[40]

The impact of Frazer's work on the intellectual community at large was both immediate and extensive, undermining faith where the Christian could find no method of coping with the implications or, at the very least, demanding from the believer some radical adjustment to the new concepts. T.S. Eliot was one of the very few attempting to mitigate the effects of the challenge, providing a prototype for the principle of adjustment. He openly acknowledged in his notes to *The Waste Land* his indebtedness to Frazer, whose work 'has influenced our generation profoundly; I mean *The Golden Bough*; I have used especially the two volumes, *Adonis, Attis, Osiris*. Anyone acquainted with those works will immediately recognise in them certain references to vegetation ceremonies.' But Eliot's poem subtly inverted the implications of the vegetational affinities and the tracing of Christian rituals to pagan practices. He was among the first to employ Jung's newly emergent theory of the 'collective unconscious', the idea that there exists throughout the world and throughout history an amalgam of legendary or mythic configurations fundamental to all human experience, underlying all cultures, and hence producing patterns common to the variegated forms of human behaviour, those forms including seasonal celebrations, social customs and religious beliefs. Eliot now suggested in direct contrast to Frazer that the affinities to primitive rites discernible in the traditions of the church, so far from detracting from their value, were evidence of the inherent relevance of Christian concepts and practices to the universal human condition, the rituals and symbols of the church answering to those instinctive spiritual needs whose neglect in the Western world had produced the sterility of twentieth-century experience. The similarity of Christian ceremonies to pagan rites, therefore, was to be seen as authenticating Christianity on new grounds. Hence, the parallel he draws throughout his poem between the Crucified Jesus and the Hanged Man of the ancient Tarot Pack, between the concluding phrase of the Hindu *Upanishad*, 'Shantih, Shantih, Shantih' and, as he comments in a note, one of the central ideas of his own faith, the 'Peace that passeth all understanding.'

For Eliot's contemporary D.H. Lawrence, Frazer's work offered an ideal opportunity for dissociating himself from the ascetic element in Christianity, especially its encouragement of celibacy and sexual continence. His impressive story, *The Man Who Died*, published in the same year as *The Waste Land*, daringly merged the resurrected Christ with the resurrected Osiris, the latter, according to Egyptian legend, having been found, on the reassembling of his dismembered body, to lack the male organ. In Lawrence's fictional sequel to the Christian account, the resurrected Jesus (who is with delicacy never named in the story), having returned to earth, learns, through his meeting with the priestess of Isis and through the gentle stimulus of her touch, the error of having advocated celibacy during his previous life:

It was Isis; but not Isis, Mother of Horus. It was Isis Bereaved, Isis in Search ... She was looking for the fragments of the dead Osiris, dead and scattered asunder, dead, torn apart, and thrown in fragments over the wide world. And she must find his hands and his feet, his heart, his thighs, his head, his belly, she must gather him together and fold her arms round the re-assembled body till it became warm again, and roused to life, and could embrace her, and could fecundate her womb ...

Suddenly it dawned on him: 'I asked them all to serve me with the corpse of their love. And in the end I offered them only the corpse of my love. This is my body – take and eat – my corpse –'[41]

On the other hand, for most intellectuals at this time such anthropological research, by its exposure of the primitive substratum of Christianity, appeared to leave no room for further allegiance to the church while, for those already inclined to doubt, it offered welcome support for their rebellion against the onerous restrictions of a society reliant upon the prohibitions and moral dictates of the faith.

Frazer's findings supplied Freud with an anthropological basis for his *Totem and Taboo, The Golden Bough* being repeatedly cited in the notes. But, in the process of adopting its findings, Freud added a new aspect that lent significant impetus to this sense of liberation. Guilt itself, the mental state encouraged by Victorian educators from childhood as a means of ensuring adherence to the path of virtue, he attributed to outdated taboos existent in primitive societies and preserved residually in Western culture. Moral conscience was in no sense, he implied, of divine origin. Among aborigines, Polynesians and others, objects or actions considered taboo, whether originating from the community's desire to protect the ruler, to discourage incest, or for entirely arbitrary reasons, carried with them severe punishment for offenders, often the penalty of death meted out by the priests or the tribe. But even those whose offence remained undiscovered by the community, he pointed out, experienced a personal sense of contamination, as though they had absorbed the untouchable qualities of the forbidden object and were therefore themselves taboo. That primitive phenomenon, passed on through later generations, resulted in later Western society in feelings of culpability, in anxiety neuroses or, as Freud now termed them, in 'conscience phobias'. Once such hidden phobias had been identified, brought to the surface, and acknowledged as such by the patient, those feelings of personal blame or iniquity could be effectively removed. From the more extreme forms that resulted in mental illness, it was possible, Freud assured his readers, to discover methods of treatment applicable to less severe instances, including those guilt formations induced by cultural or racial pressures:

> the character of compulsion neurotics shows a predominant trait of painful conscientiousness ... which develops into the highest degrees of guilty conscience as their illness grows worse. Indeed, one may venture the assertion that if the origin of guilty conscience could not be discovered through compulsion neurotic patients, there would be no prospect of ever discovering it. This task is successfully solved in the case of the individual neurotic, and we are confident of finding a similar solution in the case of races.[42]

It was a redefinition of guilt anticipated to some extent by Nietzsche who, in his *Genealogy of Morals* published in 1887, had argued that man's natural cruelty, intended by Nature in primitive times to be directed against his prey, had, as urban centres began to be established, created an inner frustration gradually transformed into a guilty conscience. 'Man', he explained, 'invented bad conscience in order to hurt himself, after the blocking of the more natural outlet of his cruelty,' seizing upon religion in order to exacerbate his self-torment to the utmost by inventing a god who sacrificed himself on his behalf. The thought of being in God's debt, he argued, became the city-dweller's new instrument of self-torture.[43] But what had, in Nietzsche, been merely the theorising of a philosopher now took on the quality of scientifically based fact.

This new categorisation of guilt immensely strengthened the conviction, previously expressed by Huxley, that the time had come to develop for society a new form of ethics free from the prohibitions and superstitions that Christianity had imposed for so long, such as the demand for Sabbath observance or sexual continence. And with religion in its Western form defined in the new terminology as resulting from a repressed need for a father-figure, a need nurtured and sustained by biblical instruction, maturity itself could now be defined in that regard as the ability to cast off such dependence and to achieve a new and admirable self-reliance.

Nowhere was that view expressed more forthrightly than in Freud's own treatise, *The Future of an Illusion* (1927), the 'illusion' of the title provocatively redefining religion. While he admitted that the process of breaking away from Christianity or any other religious belief would no doubt prove painful as the comforting trust in a benevolent deity was discarded, that secession was, he argued, a necessary process in the development of the human species from the stage of 'childishness' to that of mature adulthood:

> And so I disagree with you when you go on to argue that man cannot in general do without the consolation of the religious illusion, that without it he would not endure the troubles of life, the cruelty of reality. Certainly this is true of the man into whom you have instilled the sweet – or bitter-sweet – poison from childhood on. But what of the other, who has been brought up soberly? Perhaps he, not suffering from neurosis, will need no intoxicant to deaden it. True, man will then find himself in a difficult situation. He will have to confess his utter helplessness and his insignificant part in the working of the universe; he will have to confess that he is no longer the centre of

creation, no longer the object of the tender care of a benevolent providence. He will be in the same position as the child who has left the home where he was so warm and comfortable. But, after all, is it not the destiny of childishness to be overcome? Man cannot remain a child for ever; he must venture at last into the hostile world. This may be called 'education to reality'; need I tell you that it is the sole aim of this book to draw attention to the necessity for this advance?[44]

Even without the revelation of the primitive origins of guilt in ancient taboos, it now appeared on other grounds that feelings of culpability were baseless. With psychology having demonstrated that human beings are the product of two primary factors – of the genes transmitted to them at birth and of experiences during childhood modifying those hereditary characteristics and often creating the traumas or suppressions that are to direct later behaviour – there seemed no reason to condemn oneself for supposedly wrongful acts committed in adult years. Such acts were now attributable to elements entirely beyond the control of the individual, the blame, if any, to be transferred to parents or other figures from the past who had blighted or damaged their upbringing. For many, therefore, the findings of psychology seemed to provide added support for the belief that the nightmare of the past could be shaken off as they crossed the threshold into a healthier and more deeply satisfying era.

The rise of socialism and communism, with their vision of a more egalitarian era for mankind, to be achieved on political and economic grounds, was not unconnected with the weakening of faith in the Christian religion. For those political systems drew part of their attraction from the exclusively material basis to the ideals they offered, the concept that the amelioration, if not the eventual elimination, of the misery and suffering of the working classes could be attained not by prayer and trust in heaven but through rational and, as Karl Marx now termed it, scientific means, thereby disproving the scriptural doctrine that the poor will not disappear from the earth. Today, in the wake of the ruthless Stalinist repressions in the Soviet Union and the consequent growth in the West of an often feverish anti-communist sentiment, it is somewhat difficult to recapture the mood of almost messianic hope that socialism aroused in the earlier decades of this century, when the term 'socialism' was much broader in usage, including within its definition the non-revolutionary improvement of workers' rights, such as was advocated by the Fabian Society in England, as well as the revolutionary version proposed by communism and carried through by the Bolsheviks under the leadership of Lenin.[45]

M.H. Abrams some years ago noted how innovative movements tend unconsciously to adopt into their altered context some of the central ideas that they have supposedly rejected. He revealed how extensively the seemingly secular ideology of the Romantic poets had retained the forms and even the vocabulary of traditional religion, instinctively transposing the archetypal patterns of scriptural tradition into contemporary equivalents, as in their clothing of the poet in the mantle of the biblical prophet, or their cultivation of the 'sublime' in Nature in terms echoing the religious awe and ecstasy of the Psalmist.[46] Among many of the younger intellectuals in the twentieth century that same process of transference was at work. The impetus that Karl Marx's *Das Kapital* had given to the burgeoning socialist movement and the more vigorous communist doctrines emanating from the USSR, took on a millennial or messianic quality, an attraction intimately related to the factors under present examination.[47] If Frazer's anthropological researches, together with Freudian theory, had seemed to confirm Nietzsche's conviction that God is dead, the absence of a deity had created a spiritual vacuum difficult to fill. As Nietzsche himself admitted, when the Christian myth is rejected, chaos ensues: 'Are we not perpetually falling? Backward, sideward, forward, in all directions? Is there any up and down left? Are we not straying through an infinite nothing?'[48] In a letter to the critic George Jean Nathan, Eugene O'Neill described, as the primary function of the twentieth-century dramatist, a need to respond to the sickness of his time resulting from 'the death of the old god and the incapacity of science and materialism to give a new god to the still-living religious instinct.'[49] However relieved the avant garde might have been in its deliverance from the dogmas of the past, there remained a basic human need for some form of faith to replace those dogmas, but it needed to be a faith which, for the new rationalists, should no longer demand a belief in miracle or the supernatural. That substitute faith socialism was, for many, able to provide, offering a messianic vision based upon logical argument, upon verifiable statistics, and upon a sober knowledge of history.

The collection of essays by past-members of the Communist Party who had been deeply committed to its ideals in the thirties but who had become disillusioned and had eventually withdrawn from the party – the collection edited by Richard Crossman and significantly entitled *The God That Failed* – contained Arthur Koestler's description of his own 'conversion' to the new creed represented by the Bolshevik revolutionists, a description employing the terminology of the church that had been supposedly discarded by so many of his generation:

> I was ripe to be converted, as a result of my personal case-history; thousands of other members of the intellegentsia and the middle classes of my generation were ripe for it, by virtue of other personal case-histories; but, however much these differed from case to case, they had a common denominator: the rapid disintegration of moral values, of the pre-1914 pattern of life in postwar Europe, and the simultaneous lure of the new revelation ... The new star of Bethlehem had risen in the East.[50]

He recalls that, even though not all of the writers he lists were formal members of the Communist Party, the 'period of optimism' and of spiritual renaissance dominant at the time of his conversion had included, as its socialist-oriented models, numerous leading authors, such as Gide, Malraux, Brecht, Auden, Isherwood, Spender, Dos Passos, Upton Sinclair and Steinbeck. Absent from the list because he had represented the non-communist version of socialism was Bernard Shaw, who marked the epitome of the optimistic faith inspired by the new ideology, the sense of maturity reached after the discarding of obfuscating beliefs. His plays, essays and prefaces, however serious or amusing their theme, were animated by a reassuring conviction that, if only humankind would learn to behave rationally and rid itself of the absurd prejudices of the past, society could be happily reorganised to the satisfaction of all. In the preface to *Major Barbara*, he blamed Christianity for having taught that the poor will not disappear from the earth and that the meek will inherit, society having accordingly left the situation of the needy unimproved:

> Now what does this Let Him Be Poor mean? It means let him be weak. Let him be ignorant. Let him become a nucleus of disease. Let him be a standing exhibition and example of ugliness and dirt ... Surely the sensible course would be to give every man enough to live well on ...[51]

the implication being that a small logical adjustment, stupidly ignored for centuries, would solve the problem for ever.

Perhaps a further comment would not be amiss before we leave this initial stage of optimism, to recall that many of the discoveries during those earlier decades, accepted as incontestable, have had, since then, at least some degree of doubt cast upon them. Freudian theory is now suspected of being based to some extent upon Freud's own neuroses and hence as being less universally applicable than had been thought; and if Darwin's hypothesis functions well as an explanation of the lengthening of the giraffe's neck, the idea that chance variation could produce so complex an organ as the eye (which, apart from other intricate elements, demands the simultaneous development of a hole in the skull and of an optic nerve, neither of which could function independently) is considerably less persuasive. One notes how frequently biologists are compelled to talk of 'Nature' directing certain developments when, according to Darwinian theory, there is no such direction from above, only random changes that, when beneficial, permit the survival of those fortunate enough to inherit them. As Samuel Butler noted, Darwin himself, in accounting for the development of the eye, had inserted the passage:

> we must suppose that there is a power always intently watching each slight accidental alteration in the transparent layers, and carefully selecting each alteration which, under varied circumstances, may in any way, or in any degree, tend to produce a distincter image

– a description which, Butler commented, places Nature in a role remarkably similar to that of a Supreme Creator.[52] At the time of writing the *Origin*, Darwin did indeed still consider himself a Christian, concluding his study with praise for the grandeur of the idea that the potential for evolution had 'been originally breathed by the Creator' into the various forms of life.[53] Butler saw in that belief a basic contradiction since, if the theory relied upon essentially chance development, it could not at the same time assume the existence of a directing power, while without such direction chance could not achieve the results claimed:

> if the variations are matters of chance or hazard unconnected with any principle of constant application, they will not occur steadily enough, throughout a sufficient number of successive generations, nor to a sufficient number of individuals ... to admit of the fixing and permanency of modification.

However, at the turn of the century such theories deduced from detailed scientific evidence were by most people regarded as well-nigh unquestionable, the phrase 'Science has proved ' tending to silence all objections. If Samuel Butler was one of the few who dared to query evolutionist theory, he was confronting very solid ranks. As he recorded in his *Notebooks*: 'I attacked the foundations of morality in *Erewhon*, and nobody cared two straws. I tore open the wounds of my Redeemer as he hung upon the Cross in *The Fair Haven*, and people rather liked it. But when I attacked Mr. Darwin they were up in arms in a moment.'[54] Although Freud had been ridiculed by the medical establishment when he first argued that aspects of childhood behaviour are to be attributed to early sexual drives, it took only a few years for his revolutionary ideas not only to be absorbed by the new generation but also to be endorsed as factually incontrovertible, constituting a threshold for a new type of knowledge that would lead eventually, it was thought, to a total understanding of the processes of human thought and behaviour. It is in the light of the unquestionability of science predominant at that time that the effects upon the thinking individual need to be examined.

* * * * *

In the most authoritative account yet of the impact of Darwin upon contemporary thought, Gertrude Himmelfarb has recorded in lively detail the conflict that arose between the pro-Darwinians and those opposed to the theory, most notably the theologians who saw in it a rejection of the biblical world-view.[55] But I would argue that the conflict with the establishment was of far less importance than the gradual change of attitude discernible among the proponents of the theory, among the scientists themselves, as they began to re-evaluate the ideas which they themselves had been promulgating. For their initial confidence in a future cleansed of superstition and prejudice as mankind advanced into the next stage of evolutionary development was progressively replaced by a profound disenchantment, a disenchantment not with the validity of the theory but with the corollaries to be derived from it as well as with certain implications that they had ignored during the process of formulation. Georges Romanes, soon to be appointed professor of physiology at Edinburgh, a scientist who had followed Huxley both in his confident endorsement of Darwin and in publicly declaring himself an agnostic, began to perceive that their shared vision of the 'great drama of evolution' unfolding itself as an advance from primitive forms to increasingly improved and more sophisticated forms failed to be borne out by the facts. By 1892, he reluctantly admitted that their hopes had been based upon their own serious misunderstanding of the phrase 'survival of the fittest'. For the concept of evolution as a process of ameliorative advancement, with civilised man representing the climax of that development, was, he now realised, vitiated by the realisation that the 'fittest' creatures surviving in the struggle for existence are generally not the best in any human conception of that term. The victors in that contest are those most swiftly adapting to the physical demands of their environment, generally by means that scarcely encourage the 'fairy visions' of a benevolent Nature:

We find that more than half of the species which have survived the ceaseless struggle are parasitic in their habits; lower and insentient forms of life feasting on higher and sentient forms; we find teeth and talons whetted for slaughter, hooks and suckers moulded for torment – everywhere a reign of terror, hunger, and sickness with oozing blood and quivering limbs, with gasping breath and eyes of innocence that dimly close in deaths of brutal torture.[56]

So profound was Romanes's disillusionment that, after a lengthy inner struggle, he abandoned agnosticism and reverted to orthodox Christianity.[57]

Thomas Huxley underwent a similar if less radical change as further research compelled him to admit that the noble principles he had fondly imagined to be discoverable within the natural world, waiting there to be catalogued by the impartial researcher, were in fact woefully missing. In 1893, he acknowledged, as had Romanes, that the survivor species in the process of evolution 'may be, and often is, the ethically worst.' But that discovery meant for him, in addition, the discarding of his initial confidence that human ethics could be derived from such supposedly admirable patterns, leading him to the melancholy conclusion: 'Of moral purpose I can see no trace in Nature. That is an article of exclusively human manufacture ...' The advice he now offered, in contrast to his earlier assurances, was that the ethical progress of society depends, 'not on imitating the cosmic process, still less in running away from it, but in combating it.'[58]

Moreover, if, as archaeologists had recently discovered from surviving fossils, the creature most fitted to survive in the fierce competition from generation to generation had proved to be the lowly cockroach – a creature which, it now appeared, had undergone almost no physical development from earliest prehistoric times because of its extraordinary suitability to a wide range of environments, including an ability to crawl, swim, fly and even to feed on sewage – what lesson did that provide for man's pride in his superiority over the spawning creatures of this world? Were the intellectual qualities of man and woman, their spiritual yearnings, their poetic aspirations, and even their scientific investigations in any way relevant within the evolutionist configuration when an unthinking insect had proved so eminently successful without those attributes? Did those endowments place mankind higher on the evolutionary scale? In this instance, a humanist had anticipated the scientists in reaching that conclusion. Charles Kingsley, as early as 1866, had remarked that science, despite its considerable contribution to human comfort, had, in positing an evolutionary system, envisaged a world in which almost everything humankind had prided itself upon turned out to be both useless and immaterial:

> Am I – a man is driven to ask – am I, and all I love, the victims of an organised tyranny, from which there can be no escape – for there is not even a tyrant from whom I may perhaps beg mercy? Are we only helpless particles, at best separate parts of the wheels of a vast machine, which will use us till it has worn us away, and ground us to powder? Are our bodies – and if so, why not our souls? – the puppets, yea, the creatures of necessary circumstances, and all our strivings and sorrows only vain beatings against the wires of our cage?

Virginia Woolf's father, Sir Leslie Stephen, in an article entitled 'An Agnostic's Apology' commented in 1876 in a similar mood of disillusionment: 'Turn and twist the thought as you may, there is no escape. Optimism would be soothing if it were possible; in fact, it is impossible, and therefore a constant mockery.'[59] If men like Ruskin were with difficulty struggling to hold on to their Christian faith despite the theories of Lyell and others, the scientists themselves who had triumphantly accepted the results of their research were, it appeared, no less perturbed at the outcome of their studies.

Did the human race, then, possess no ultimate superiority; was its purpose solely to struggle for survival against the myriad species teeming over the surface of the globe, its only justification for existence being to procreate in constant competition with them? And what purpose was there in such procreation but the begetting of offspring destined in their turn to struggle for survival in order to further procreate, all this in an endless and meaningless cycle from generation to generation? Kafka's short story *Metamorphosis* published in 1916 was not, one may suspect, merely a fictional fantasy, as Philip Rahv and others have argued, a casual flight of the imagination, but deserves to be seen as a disturbing allegory of man's awakening to the dreadful realisation that he was, in the final analysis, merely another version of the rival cockroach or beetle:

> As Gregor Samsa awoke one morning from uneasy dreams he found himself transformed in his bed into a gigantic insect. He was lying on his hard, as it were armour-plated, back and when he lifted his head a little he could see his dome-like brown belly divided into stiff arched segments on top of which the bed quilt could hardly keep in position and was about to slide off completely. His numerous legs, which were

pitifully thin compared to the rest of his bulk, waved helplessly before his eyes.[60]

As we know from the society that emerged from this crisis, the struggle for survival could itself, despite these drawbacks, provide for many people not only an incentive for living but also considerable satisfaction, whether the challenge of playing the stock market or developing industries in a competitive world. But for the creative artist or writer dedicated to aesthetic pursuits – the person who concerns us most closely in this present study – such forebodings led to a sense of utter redundancy in the new dispensation, where the sole criterion was the propagation of the race. Hence Yeats's weary acknowledgement in 'Sailing to Byzantium' (1927) that, unless the human soul could in some way be revalidated, he as artist could find no justification for existence among the spawning salmon, the mackerel-crowded seas, the fish, flesh, or fowl commending the endless process of conception, proliferation, and death:

> That is no country for old men. The young
> In one another's arms, birds in the trees
> – Those dying generations – at their song,
> The salmon-falls, the mackerel-crowded seas,
> Fish, flesh, or fowl, commend all summer long
> Whatever is begotten, born, and dies.
> Caught in that sensual music all neglect
> Monuments of unageing intellect.

Within that poem there are audible echoes of Keats's 'Ode to a Nightingale', echoes very relevant to our present concerns. For where Keats, envying the nightingale living in harmony within the beauty of nature, had selected its immortal song as the symbol of his own poetic impulse, identifying himself with the bird 'pouring forth thy soul abroad/ In such an ecstasy', it now appeared that Tennyson's response to the evolutionary tendencies of his day had been depressingly closer to the mark in viewing nature as 'red in tooth and claw'.[61] A generation later, Yeats could only conclude that, in a world based upon a dehumanised process of combative survival where beauty held neither place nor value, the song of a bird in nature could no longer be representative of his art. Accordingly, withdrawing in disgust from the pointless cycle of animal procreation, he selects his new symbol for poetry not from the natural world but from the realm of the unchanging jewelled artefact, the bird of hammered gold:

> Once out of nature I shall never take
> My bodily form from any natural thing,
> But such a form as Grecian goldsmiths make
> Of hammered gold and gold enamelling
> To keep a drowsy Emperor awake;
> Or set upon a golden bough to sing
> To lords and ladies of Byzantium
> Of what is past, or passing, or to come.[62]

The gradual realisation by Romanes and Huxley that the fittest to survive were not necessarily the best but, far oftener, the most ruthless and parasitic began now to be perceived not as a minor or chance factor but as integral to the principle of natural selection, where the most aggressive creatures and those most exploitive of others had the greatest likelihood of avoiding extinction. From that new perception, the implications for new standards of human behaviour – the ethical principles supposedly deducible from nature on which Huxley had based his hopes – were only too plain and only too appalling. According to the new doctrine, the Christian principles of humility, selflessness and the turning of the other cheek that had for centuries formed the ideological basis of Western ethics, were, it now appeared, merely a prescription for the demise of the human species in a world where those possessing gentler characteristics would in due course be crushed and consumed by others more suited to resist environmental pressures. Nietzsche, deeply influenced by Darwin's theories, not only castigated Christianity for creating the guilt complex but charged also that it had been invented as a defence mechanism by the more feeble and inadequate members of human society:

> Read in cold blood, it means nothing more than 'We weak ones are, in fact, weak. It is a good thing that we do nothing for which we are not strong enough.' But this plain fact, this basic prudence, which even the insects have (who, in circumstances of great danger, sham death in order not to have to 'do' too much) has tricked itself out in the garb of quiet, virtuous resignation thanks to the duplicity of impotence – as though the weakness of the weak, which is after all his essence, his natural way of being, his sole and inevitable reality, were a spontaneous act, a meritorious deed.[63]

Within Nature, as evolutionary theory views it, compassion, benevolence and altruism have no justification. The only instances of selflessness discernible within the animal world are those related to the procreation of the species – a parent's fierce defence of its young who, once they are able to care for themselves, become transformed into territorial rivals to whom no quarter is given. If we extend that precept to human affairs, two friends, attacked in a forest by a pack of wolves, would, under the new dispensation, no longer be morally bound to assist each other. The principle of survival would now dictate that the stronger of the two should fling his friend to the wolves and, while they are occupied in tearing the corpse apart, climb the nearest tree to safety. He would thus, by preserving his life, have retrospectively proved himself to have been the most fitted to survive and, no less important, would thereby be qualified to pass on to the next generation the eminently serviceable traits of quick thinking and self-preservation.

Exaggerated as that instance may appear when so baldly stated, we should recall the heinous fact that it was on this same principle of the survival of the fittest that, a few decades later (whether following Nietzsche's doctrines of the superman or through misunderstanding him remains a matter for dispute) the Nazis calculatedly murdered the weaker members of society – gypsies, Jews, the handicapped, and other 'inferior' categories – in order to ensure that their own 'pure' Aryan stock would survive and conquer.[64] Even enlightened intellectuals in the rest of Europe were, in those decades, frequently attracted to the new-found principle. There arose the cult of ruthlessness in Wyndham Lewis's novel *Tarr*, the gradual drift towards fascism of Ezra Pound, the Futurist Marinetti's enthusiastic support of Mussolini and the foundation of the British Union of Fascists in 1932 by a member of the aristocracy, a distinguished parliamentarian and past cabinet minister, Sir Oswald Mosley.

There was, however, even for those temporarily attracted to the new principle, a disturbing recognition that, if the old morality had been invalidated, the behavioural code of callous self-interest now replacing it offered little solace either to the scientist or to the humanist. Kindness and generosity still appealed as principles of human conduct; but there remained, for the thinking individual, the puzzling perception that, according to the new theories espoused, such virtues were no more than illogical, emotional impulses irrelevant to the evolutionary process at large. Charitable acts were rationally defensible only on the grounds that they might evoke reciprocal acts of kindness or generosity from others – a motive arising, it was realised, not from altruism but from self-interest. Communism alone could adopt the new principle wholeheartedly in urging all members of society to work selflessly, as in a beehive, for the good of the community or of the species at large, developing a political system of especial appeal to intellectuals at this time and attracting many of them to its ranks in their search for a morality that could be rationally validated. That new communist ethic, however, contained a serious flaw in logic, not easily distinguishable at first, a flaw that I would prefer to discuss in a later chapter. In brief, while atheists and agnostics might continue to be no less moral in their behaviour than their Christian counterparts, the rational basis for their moral acts was no longer easily justifiable according to the terms of the newly revealed universal system that had prompted them to discard traditional ethical imperatives. They could authenticate their benevolent acts as helpful to the advancement of mankind or of their immediate society, but those aware of the full implications of the system did so with the uneasy feeling that their supposedly virtuous acts constituted no more than those of an ant contributing its services to the anthill as part of an ultimately pointless cycle of competitive survival.

There was, moreover, an even more disturbing factor intrinsic to Darwinian theory that had tended to be overlooked during the initial stage as the more positive effects of Natural Selection were examined, and as researchers and readers focused on the fascinating process of adaptation to changing environmental needs. It was the fate of those creatures discarded in the evolutionary process – the realisation that, in the gradual development of the giraffe over the years, hundreds, perhaps thousands of animals lacking a tendency to develop longer necks would be casually sacrificed by the system in order to improve the prospects of survival for the more fortunate few. In fact, as the economy of nature began to be studied more closely, that principle of wholesale rejection, the abandonment of the multitude for the sake of a minuscule surviving number, was seen to form an essential ingredient of its carefully balanced pattern. The female house-fly, we are told, lays approximately a thousand eggs during its lifetime. Of those, a certain proportion will be consumed by other insects before being hatched, while of the flies emerging into adulthood a further large percentage is designated, in the economy of nature, as food for the birds, spiders, and other creatures in that vicinity in need of nourishment. If only two or three flies out of the thousand eggs survive to produce their own offspring, nature will have succeeded in preserving the species, as well as having ensured adequate sustenance for other creatures in the area. But what of the nine hundred or so sacrificed in that process? Have they no intrinsic value apart from serving as food for other creatures?

The question may be of little interest in terms of the house-fly; but once humankind was seen to be not the lord of creation fundamentally differentiated from other species but an intrinsic and inseparable part of that economy functioning on the same statistical and biological principles, the value of the individual seemed nullified in a manner unparalleled in previous generations. The biblical tradition had never doubted the innate worth of every human being, however lowly. 'What is man that Thou shouldst know him?' the Psalmist had asked in wonder, amazed that a supreme and omnipotent God should be concerned with a mere mortal. Yet his rhetorical question arose from a profound conviction that each mortal *was* intimately known to his or her Maker. The belief in the ultimate significance of every human being, that good and bad deeds performed in this world by that individual would be carefully weighed on the Day of Judgement did, intimidating as that final prospect may have been, include as its corollary the comforting assurance that, however dispensable in the eyes of others, each living person was of concern to the deity. The statement that God created Adam in the divine image meant that even the lowliest individual carried within a divine element ensuring his or her inviolable sacrosanctity. And Christianity's claim that the meek would inherit the earth had endowed even the humblest member of the community with a sense of ultimate significance.

The new configuration offered no such comfort. And its absence was to serve as a major factor in initiating that search for meaningful identity, the quest for selfhood, that was to form so central a concern of twentieth-century writing. As Bernard Shaw (who sided with Samuel Butler in criticising Darwin's theories) remarked with disgust in the preface to his *Back to Methuselah* (1922), if Darwin is correct, then the beauty of nature, the splendour of the heavenly stars, the loveliness of mountain and hill are grossly deceptive, the process of Natural Selection serving only 'to modify all things by blindly starving and murdering everything that is not lucky enough to survive in the universal struggle for hogwash.'

If Darwinism began to be seen in this less positive light, the negative reaction to Freudian psychology was no less disquieting, once its further implications had been grasped. The sense of liberation many experienced on first encountering the theories it offered, a freedom from guilt where fears and anxieties were now defined as treatable symptoms of childhood traumas, began to be replaced by a bewildering doubt concerning the nature or identity of the individual undergoing those experiences – a doubt different from that implicit in evolutionary theory but equally disturbing in its effect, posing once again a problem never faced in earlier generations and hence specific to this century. If, as psychology had shown, the personality of each individual was a blending of factors inherited at birth with the effects of childhood experience and, at the same time, constituted a constant inner struggle between the ego, the id, the libido and the superego, over none of which the individual could exert control, were the decisions and choices made by an individual really one's own? Pavlov's widely publicised experiment in 1910, demonstrating that dogs, trained to expect food on the ringing of a bell, would subsequently salivate at that sound even when no food was provided, now raised the question whether the human being too was merely a bundle of preconditioned reflexes, with all actions unknowingly directed either by the conflicting components of the psyche or by some forgotten event in the past that predetermined the reaction. Such experiments raised the dismaying spectre of a future time when psychology might be sufficiently developed to predict with precision the actions of any individual on the basis of detailed investigation of past experiences, a vision grimly undermining confidence in the individual's sovereignty over his or her decision-making powers.

How deeply this anxiety affected that generation is indicated by the flurry of interest aroused among theologians, philosophers, and more general intellectual circles by an apparently abstruse scientific discovery that seemed, for a brief time, to offer a refuge from such fears. The so-called indeterminacy principle formulated by Werner Heisenberg in 1927, which demonstrated that it is impossible to identify simultaneously both the position and velocity of a particle, provided evidence that measurements established empirically, especially in the area of quantum mechanics, were ultimately unreliable and hence that projections based upon such measurement were liable to be faulty. That new concept, with its suggestion that the laws according to which the universe functioned were less deterministic than had been thought, was eagerly seized upon by educated laymen disturbed at the direction science had taken. Some (usually the religious) regarded the principle of 'uncertainty' as providing a loophole for continued belief in the freedom of the will, since the mind now had room to avoid total submission to the dictates of determinism, including preconditioned reflexes, while others (among them the atheists) saw in it confirmation of the view that chance alone directed the universe. But after that initial spurt of interest, it came to be acknowledged, especially after the appearance of P.W. Bridgman's widely read article of 1929, that, since the new principle could provide evidence for either side of the debate, its relevance to the urgent problem of freewill was ultimately nugatory.[65] In fact, the fear that psychology would eventually be able to predict the responses of individuals has fortunately failed to materialise, as it has proved to be the least exact of the sciences.[66] But that was not known during those earlier decades, and the nightmare arose that, if such a situation were to eventuate, psychoanalysis could provide a form of predestination more intimidating than the most extreme versions of Calvinism.

Here too, the profession of writer or artist was especially vulnerable. After the completion of some major work of music, literature or painting demanding agonising decisions, intense concentration and the input of unbounded creative energy, could that work justifiably be claimed as the artist's? Was it merely the unconscious sublimation of a repressed experience from the past, the unintentional revelation of some unhealthy element in the psyche? That growing suspicion was soon to be impressively fortified. In 1910, Freud published a monograph on Leonardo da Vinci that was to set the pattern for the flood of psychoanalytic studies of artists and writers produced by his successors. In it he maintained that the essentially new depiction of the Madonna and Child in Leonardo's paintings, a depiction so influential for subsequent High Renaissance art, arose not, as had been believed, from the artist's sensitive response to the changing concepts of that era – the transformation of the medieval Madonna, sadly speculating on the future suffering of her Child, into a representative of the Beautiful-and-Good marking the pinnacle of Neoplatonic harmony. It arose instead, his readers were informed, from a personal handicap, from Leonardo's repressed longing for his natural mother, a peasant woman from whom, as an illegitimate child, he had been separated at an early age, to be raised in his father's house by a stepmother. Subconsciously needing to compensate for the traumatic inadequacies of his childhood experience, Leonardo had represented the Madonna as an idealised symbol of maternal peace and tranquillity and led, again subconsciously, by that repressed impulse, had introduced into one of his Madonna paintings a second representative of benevolent maternity, the Madonna's mother, St Anne, thereby imaginatively merging there his natural and his substitute mother. Moreover, to that childhood crisis Freud attributed the origins of what he claimed were covert homosexual leanings on the part of the artist. This treatise was, it should be stressed (as one would expect from Freud), an extraordinarily impressive study, not easily to be dismissed even if one remains finally unconvinced. In the same way his disciple Ernest Jones's study, *Hamlet and Oedipus*, originally presented in the form of an article in 1910 and later expanded to book-form, offered a highly original interpretation of the play based on the idea that Shakespeare, who had lost his own father in the year he wrote the drama, was, in the process of creating the character of Hamlet, unconsciously expressing through him his own oedipal guilt feelings.

Clearly, such analysis was to prove severely damaging to the status of the artist, seeming to leave little to admire in the accomplishments of aesthetic genius. Apart from the example provided by his study of Leonardo, Freud had classified artists in general as being either neurotic or on the verge of neurosis, a categorisation that proved profoundly disparaging to those professionally concerned with aesthetic creativity. Such creativity he described in his *Introductory Lectures on Psychoanalysis* (1917) as occurring in persons who long to attain to honour, power, riches, fame, and the love of women but who lack the means of achieving these gratifications in the real world. Accordingly, they transpose those desires, together with the promptings of their libido, to the world of fantasy in a form of sublimation – art by that definition arising not from genius but from a flaw or blemish in character.[67] Similarly, his statement that incestuous or narcissistic impulses experienced by children, if not directed into suitable channels during puberty, are liable to transform them 'into neurotics, perverts, artists or madmen' proffered a category in which, to say the least, it was uncongenial for artists to find themselves placed. Such severely reductive assessments – especially by one who was clearly well-read in both art and literature, frequently quoting Shakespeare, Goethe and others in the course of his writings – evoked in 1924 a stern rejoinder from the noted Bloomsbury art historian, Roger Fry, in which, addressing a meeting of psychiatrists, he objected strongly to the theory that art originates in the sexual feelings of man. Shortly thereafter, the dispute entered the public domain in the form of a blistering attack on Freud in *The Nation and Athenaeum* by Fry's colleague, Clive Bell, who, vehemently objecting to artists being called 'introverted and on the brink of being neurotic', commented sarcastically:

> Art is, to stick to the Freudian jargon, 'wish fulfilment'; the artist 'realises' his own dreams of being a great man and having a good time, and in so doing gratifies a public which vaguely and feebly dreams the same dreams, but cannot dream them efficiently.
>
> Now this, I dare say, is a pretty good account of what housemaids, and Dr. Freud presumably, take for art. Indeed, the novelette is the perfect example of 'wish fulfilment in the world of phantasy.' The housemaid dreams of becoming a great actress and being loved by a handsome earl; Dr. Freud dreams of having been born a handsome earl and loving a great actress. And for fifteen delirious minutes, while the story lasts, the dream comes true. But this has nothing to do with art ... The artist is not one who dreams more vividly, but who is a good deal wider awake than most people. His grand and absorbing problem is to

create a form that shall match a conception, whatever that conception may be. He is a creator, not a dreamer ... [68]

Dr. Freud had, he argued, made himself ridiculous by talking about things of which he knew nothing and, being ignorant, Bell concluded, he ought to have held his tongue.

Bell's rejoinder was clearly a travesty or, at the very least, an exaggeration of Freud's theories; but it does indicate the anger that psychoanalytical writings aroused in artistic circles. Forceful as the article was and respected as he and Fry were as art critics, they could do little to alleviate the damage to the status of writer, painter and sculptor by concepts promulgated with all the authority of a new science. And the process of disparagement continued, exemplified by Albert Modell's *The Erotic Motive in Literature*, which, assuming that creative genius in authors is generally traceable to elements in their 'infantile love life', classified Byron as 'an example of hysteria in literature', and identified the genre of satire at large as being attributable to sadistic instincts suppressed during the writer's childhood.[69] The novelist was no longer the talented artist commenting profoundly on the ideas or social manners of the day, responsive to subtle changes not yet perceptible to the public at large, but had come to be seen as merely relieving childhood frustrations by means of escapist fantasy, or experiencing exhibitionist cravings to obtain social approval. The response of the Dadaists, who, although themselves dedicated professional artists, ridiculed the very principles of art, may be seen in this context as arising from their frustration not only at the reductive attitude to aesthetics presented by the conclusions of the new science but at their own reluctant admission of its justification. It is a point especially significant as André Breton, a leader of that movement, had worked as a medical assistant in a psychiatric hospital in his younger days and was accordingly familiar with the implications of the new theories, acting as a conduit for them to the group of artists he had joined.[70] Their vehement burlesquing of art in such lunatic performances as the one held at the Cabaret Voltaire in Munich in 1916, when Richard Huelsenbeck and Tristan Tzara simultaneously recited poems in different languages, while Marcel Janco crooned a popular American song alongside to ensure the performance's total intelligibility for the audience, revealed their predicament – a longing to continue to perform as artists coupled with the debilitating recognition that art was no longer viable or defensible.

A further source of consternation to the wider public was the revelation that even the sanest and seemingly most normal individuals had, in the development of their personalities from infancy to adulthood, passed through stages identified by Freud by such unsavoury terms as 'anal', 'urethral', 'oral', 'oedipal' and 'genital'. The only distinction, it now appeared, between neurosis and mental well-being was one of degree. What had been previously regarded as reprehensible sexual or moral perversions were, if the new theories were correct, psychological conditions intrinsic to the human personality. If ethical principles had been undermined by the new definition of social standards as mere residual taboos, the process was intensified since sadism, masochism and other such supposed perversions could now with difficulty be censured by society's moralists when those impulses were, as they now learned, inherent in their own characters. And if they could to some extent pride themselves on having overcome such impulses, they were now compelled to acknowledge that those who did succumb did so not through wilfulness but through some fault in the process of maturing from infancy, a fault for which they could not be held responsible. The distinction between good and evil as moral factors no longer seemed valid.

An even more dismaying aspect of the new science with direct implications for current principles of ethics and morality was the psychologist's ability to reverse normal interpretations of human behaviour. Here it was Adler who provided the new approach, a concept once again very familiar to our generation but astonishing during those earlier decades, his revelation that a person constantly bragging of his successes was not, as had previously been believed, conceited or arrogant but suffering from an inverted inferiority complex. That small word *inverted* became all-powerful, impossible for the layman to argue with, since these behavioural patterns were, it was explained, the result of suppressed impulses of which the victim was unaware. However convinced a person might be of his or her conscious intentions, ideals or beliefs, the psychologist could now pronounce the opposite to be true, insisting that they arose as inadvertent attempts to compensate for hidden deficiencies. It was a principle that affected all values, especially those related to established standards of behaviour. One such value, a virtue unquestioned in previous generations, was that of bravery. A soldier, pinned down together with his friends by enemy fire, leaps from the trench at the risk of his life to pitch a grenade into the machine-gunner's post, thereby rescuing them all from certain death. Such action would, in the past, be awarded the highest medal for valour. But as the psychologist now interpreted the situation, the soldier was impelled by a covert death-wish, a suicidal impulse of which he was unaware and which prompted him to exploit the opportunity in order to fulfil his hidden desire for self-destruction – an interpretation no longer redounding to the hero's credit and placing the entire concept of valour in doubt.

The process of ethical inversion was applicable to all such supposedly meritorious acts. Chastity was now redefined as a symptom of sexual inadequacy, scoutmastering as suppressed pederasty, and even that most firmly established virtue, respect for one's parents – a trait highly regarded throughout the generations and invariably requisite for hero or heroine in the nineteenth-century novel – began to be viewed with scepticism. Instances of affection for a parent now raised, at the very least, the suspicion of an Oedipus or Electra complex – witness the response to D.H.Lawrence's autobiographically based *Sons and Lovers*, written in 1913 before he had come into contact with Freudian theory, which was at once interpreted by critics conversant with Freud's writings as a patent instance of a mother fixation, the maternal bond hampering his relations with other women. Ethical principles at large seemed suddenly to collapse in the light of the new theories, with the attribution of even the noblest actions to repressions unknown to the performer. Saint Francis, revered for centuries as a classic symbol of Christian altruism, devoting his life to caring for the sick and selflessly alleviating their suffering, was now described in all seriousness in a novel of the twenties (by a character whom the reader is meant to admire) as a 'disgusting little pervert' who, unable to maintain healthy relations with women, could 'only get a thrill out of licking lepers' ulcers. Not curing the lepers, mind you. Just licking them. For his own amusement. Not theirs. It's revolting!'[71] It was difficult to see how any moral ideals could now be effectively preserved or defended. That aspect T.S. Eliot identified as a primary cause of the spiritual paralysis of the twentieth century, his Prufrock cringing helplessly before the eyes that 'fix you in a formulated phrase', reducing richly varied individuals into predetermined psychological categories, into inflexible patterns of behaviour, like some beautiful butterfly coldly defined by its scientific name:

> And I have known the eyes already, known them all
> The eyes that fix you in a formulated phrase,
> And when I am formulated, sprawling on a pin,
> When I am pinned and wriggling on the wall,
> Then how should I begin ?

Indeed, the function of the psychiatrist, who was now taking over the task of mentor or confessor for the public at large, had changed fundamentally from that of the traditional counsellor. His purpose was no longer to assist the advisee to attain to a nobler form of life and to repent evil ways. His sole aim in the new dispensation was to assist the patient to attain social functionability irrespective of any moral values. As one writer was to define the situation,

> On the analyst's couch he is made to discover that his crusading zeal was derived from unconscious guilt; he is persuaded to say farewell to arms, and to adopt the ways of down-to-earth reasonableness, opportunism and expediency. In the type of psychotherapy practised … there is no provision made for ethical absolutes; its aim is to make the patient accept reality.[72]

If until now the impact of these various new forces has been examined here under the separate headings of evolution, anthropology and psychology, they did, of course, interact in many areas, both in their positive and negative aspects, one of the most interesting being an area that has become especially characteristic of the twentieth century, namely the altered attitude to love. Steven Marcus has revealed how, even in so seemingly prudish and strait-laced an era as the Victorian, beneath the prim surface there was a vigorous world of sexual promiscuity, brothel-visiting and pornography; and the private diaries of both Samuel Pepys in the seventeenth century and James Boswell in the eighteenth provide evidence that human nature does not change radically from generation to generation in that respect.[73] There is, nevertheless, a fundamental difference in the centrality that sex came to occupy in the early decades of this century.

One section of *The Origin of Species*, devoted to what Darwin termed 'Sexual Selection,' namely the battle between male animals or insects for possession of the female, cast, for those first reading it, an astonishing light upon a central aspect of Western tradition. He describes there the seasonal fights between males of the same species:

> This form of selection depends, not on a struggle for existence in relation to other organic beings or to external conditions, but on a struggle between the individuals of one sex, generally the males, for the possession of the other sex. The result is not death to the unsuccessful competitor, but few or no offspring … Generally, the most vigorous males, those which are best fitted for their places in nature, will leave most progeny. But in many cases victory depends not so much on general vigour, as on having special weapons, confined to the male sex.

Sexual Selection, by always allowing the victor to breed, might surely give indomitable courage, length to the spur, and strength to the wing to strike in the spurred leg, in nearly the same manner as does the brutal cock-fighter by the careful selection of his best cocks. How low in the scale of nature the law of battle descends, I know not; male alligators have been described as fighting, bellowing, and whirling around like Indians in a war-dance, for the possession of the females; male salmon have been observed fighting all day long; male stag-beetles sometimes bear wounds from the huge mandibles of other males; the males of certain hymenopterous insects have been frequently seen … fighting for a particular female, who sits by, an apparently unconcerned beholder of the struggle, and then retires with the conqueror.[74]

Such scenes, Darwin explained, were nature's method for ensuring that the male selected for the purposes of reproduction should be best qualified to transmit to the coming generation the fighting ability and bodily attributes necessary for the preservation of the species. In itself, it was a dry, biologically based observation. But for the more general reader it constituted a crushing negation of the long-established chivalric tradition, with knights in armour nobly fighting for the hand of the fair lady, a chivalric tradition absorbed into Western culture and preserved as a romantic element of the love relationship well into the twentieth century. Love, it now appeared in the light of evolution, was no longer the marriage of true minds that looks on tempests and is never shaken, the adoration of beauty, of charm, of grace, of exemplary thoughts and high ideals, but a prosaic subliminal search on the part of the female for the possessor of the most resilient genes in the battle for survival. Basing himself upon that evolutionary principle, Freud identified the libido as the element in the psyche prompting humans, even in the very earliest stages of infancy, to experience pleasure in erogenic areas in order to prepare them for their primary task of procreation in adulthood, that task now seen as the major function assigned to the human being.

Indeed, the gradual shift in our own century from a concern with 'love' to a more general concern with 'sex' (a word previously used solely to distinguish gender, and never as a substitute for sexual intercourse)[75] reveals the new recognition of such activity not as the consummation of a spiritual relationship but as a physical act arising from a biological urge to preserve the species. The predicament of the young intellectual aware of these new ideas in the nineteen-twenties was in many ways unenviable. Strolling with a charming young lady beneath the moonlight, a young man would experience a passionate desire to take her in his arms and declare his undying love. But at that point, his intellect coldly interrupts, reminding him (unanswerably) that the supposed passion was merely a covert impulse provided by nature to ensure the continuation of the human race, the emotional ardour he experienced being no more than a neurological titillation, an illusory stimulus prompting him to fulfil his procreative role. He is, by that realisation, like Philip Quarles in the novel by Thomas Huxley's grandson Aldous, cerebrally paralysed, his reason freezing his emotion and leaving him unable to proceed with the love scene. At such moments, he is compelled to see his situation in terms of the larger, coldly scientific context of animal procreation. Hence it is that Quarles at a potentially romantic moment, in place of the words of affection his wife craves, offers her a lecture on the biological aspects of sexual attraction, a lecture scarcely congenial to the mood of the moment:

> 'There's nothing human quite analogous to heat in mares or she-dogs. Except,' he added, 'except perhaps in the moral sphere. A bad reputation in a woman allures like the signs of heat in a bitch ... Absence of heat is the animal's equivalent of the chaste woman's habits and principles ... '
>
> Elinor listened with interest and at the same time a kind of horror ... It was amazing, it was unexpected, it was wonderfully interesting; but oh! she almost wanted to scream.

The young lady in the scene beneath the moonlight was thus left frustrated – unless she, as the New Intellectual Woman, had been undergoing a similar analytical paralysis.[76] The incident may sound comic, but it had serious, even tragic implications. One of those was a conscious resistance to the biological impulse, a refusal to succumb to the seductive lures of the procreative system, the new concept now arising in the Flapper Twenties of 'sleeping around'. Thereby, with the assistance of contraceptive devices, one could satisfy the bodily craving while spurning the procreative process, defying nature's prompting to set up a household as a framework for the upbringing of children, marriage now being seen as a form of capitulation to Nature's reproductive plan. 'Love' becomes designated as antiquated, belonging to the romantic fantasies of the past. The new aim is no longer, as in the old sense of the term, a longing to protect, serve, adore the person beloved, but rather to gratify one's personal sexual needs in a manner free from further obligation.

In the light of this breakdown of traditional values on apparently incontrovertible scientific grounds and the fragmentation of the individual into the constituent and constantly warring parts of the psyche, it is not surprising that, within painting, the human, so long the centre of interest, began to disappear from canvases, to be replaced by abstract geometric figures or, when depicted at all, represented by such harsh and jagged forms as Picasso's mid-century portraits.[77] In literature too, the individual had lost the sense of a coherent, binding integrity, a character in one of Virginia Woolf's novels bewildered by that experience, enquiring:

> What am I? I ask. This? No, I am that . . . it becomes clear that I am not one and simple, but complex and many. Bernard, in public, bubbles; in private, is secretive. That is what they do not understand, for they are now undoubtedly discussing me, saying I escape them, am evasive. They do not understand that I have to effect different transitions; have to cover the entrances and exits of several different men who alternately act their parts as Bernard.[78]

Modern man and woman no longer communicate as integrated individuals, but exist as churning complex personalities hiding behind facades and able to make contact only through masks, each needing, as T.S. Eliot phrased it, to 'prepare a face to meet the faces that you meet.'

In 1929, an extraordinarily perceptive work appeared, Joseph Wood Krutch's *The Modern Temper: a study and a confession*. Written by a leading drama critic, it both acknowledged and analysed the mood of despair affecting himself and so many of his contemporaries early in the century. He and his peers had come to realise, he declared, that the scientific optimism of Thomas Huxley's generation had proved illusory:

> We have learned how certain truths – intimate revelations concerning the origin and mechanism of our deepest impulses – can stagger our souls, and how a clear perception of our lonely isolation in the midst of a universe which knows nothing of us and our aspirations paralyses our will. We are aware, too, of the fact that art and ethics have not flowered anew in the light, that we have not won a newer and more joyous acceptance of the universe, and we have come to realise that the more we learn of the laws of that universe in which we constitute a strange incongruity, the less we shall feel at home in it. Each new revelation fascinates us. We would not, even if we dared, remain ignorant of anything which we can learn, but with each new revelation we perceive so much the more clearly that half – perhaps the most important half – of all we are and desire to be can find no comfort or support in such knowledge.

Moreover, far in advance of George Steiner he argued, in defining the impact of the new dispensation upon literature, that tragedy, so long regarded as the noblest of the literary genres in its exploration of the human predicament, could no longer function in the modern world, since it demanded as a prerequisite some conviction, however limited, of the importance of the human being in the universe at large and the existence of some supernal power directing human affairs:

> Like the belief in love and like most of the other mighty illusions by means of which human life has been given a value, the Tragic Fallacy depends ultimately upon the assumption which man so readily makes that something outside his own being, some 'spirit not himself' – be it God, Nature, or that still vaguer thing called a Moral Order – joins him in the emphasis which he places upon this or that and confirms him in his feeling that his passions and his opinions are important.

In those terms, it became apparent that once the human being's instinctive faith in the importance of self had faded, leaving him an insignificant entity standing alone in a universe snubbing him with its indifference, any search, as in tragedy, for some means of reconciling his situation with the forces of fate or the justice of the gods becomes pointless.[79]

With the weakening or disqualification of those moorings that had previously offered a sense of security – the dwindling of religious faith, the revelation of a universe indifferent to the individual, the disintegration both of the social hierarchy and of the family unit that had together provided a feeling of comparative stability – the sense of self-identity was inevitably impaired. Essential to a strong awareness of self is a consciousness of biographical continuity, an enduring concept of the binding relevance to the present of one's own past resolutions and commitments. Without such awareness, as social structures and ethical values move into a state of flux, that assurance of a developing personal narrative is disrupted, creating an impression of dislocation, of life as a series of isolated and hence meaningless snippets or segments, a condition threatening all human relationships, including those within marriage, relationships now subordinated to the immediate needs of the moment, to personal gratification rather than to any lasting commitment.[80] It creates what Alan Wilde has called the 'disjunctive irony' of this century, the break up of continuities.[81] How radical the break was with previous conceptions where commitments represented lasting obligations is evidenced by the advice offered in a recent academic guidebook for the troubled which marks the culmination of the changes we have been following. Janet Rainwater in *Self-Therapy* (1989) states authoritatively:

> People who fear the future attempt to 'secure' themselves – with money, property, health insurance, personal relationships, marriage contracts. Parents attempt to bind their children to them ... Husbands and wives try to guarantee the continuance of the other's life and services. The harsh psychological truth is that there is no permanence in human relationships ...[82]

The reader is accordingly advised to place no reliance on commitments such as marriage, and to learn to live only in the present and for the fulfilment of their own personal needs. The result of that change, which occurred initially in the earlier part of the century, was inevitably a process of instability, of continual self-analysis and self-evaluation in relation to the various roles one is expected to fill, of ceaseless interaction with the environment in an attempt to adjust to a recurrently fluctuating scene in which no permanence or security could be found and no coherent self established.

The mid-century had seen in many areas a remarkable amelioration of the human situation. The introduction, into at least the more advanced societies, of unemployment benefits eliminating starvation among the poor, of laws ensuring improved working conditions, had raised considerably the general standard of living. It is all the more significant, therefore, that the artists and writers of that period, those members of society most sensitive to cultural change, adopted, almost unanimously and in direct contrast to that sense of advancement, a deeply pessimistic view of the human condition. As Eugène Ionesco complained in 1957: 'Cut off from his religious, metaphysical, and transcendental roots, man is lost; all his actions become senseless, absurd, useless.'[83] How these changes affected the literature of the twentieth century will be the subject of the following chapters.

If Krutch was correct concerning the inevitable disappearance of tragedy (at least in the form familiar to us from earlier eras) and in his assessment of the depressed, sombre mood of the twenties, he was less correct in prophesying that art, in the broadest sense of that term, would be unable to flower under such conditions. Within the plastic media, painting, architecture and sculpture proved dazzlingly innovative, reflecting within those art-forms the altered view of humankind, as well as responding impressively to scientific revelations concerning the constituents of the physical universe. The inauguration of molecular research, of quantum mechanics and of relativist theory propounded by Bohr, Planck, Einstein and others, having called into question the solidity and reliability of the visible world, prompted painters to desert the long-established tradition of mimetic representation and to create the new and exciting idioms of Cubism, Expressionism and Kinetic art. In architecture, Functionalism, prompted in part by Sir D'Arcy Wentworth's discovery of nature's 'streamlining', its removal in fish and other creatures of protruding elements blocking the flow of water, discarded the traditional embellishments of classical scrolls and pediments to create instead the sleek profiles of twentieth-century skyscrapers. In sculpture, the naturalism of Rodin was jettisoned in favour of the geometrical abstractions of Jacques Lipchitz and Jean Arp. In line with those changes, the literature produced in the mid-century proved equally invigorating and no less inventive, the one difference being that, in a medium more expansive than the visual arts, unrestricted to a single moment in time, each writer was able to cope more explicitly with the implications of the new view of the cosmos and the place of humankind within it.

In a recent interdisciplinary study examining how the different media reacted to those changes during the earlier part of the century, I dealt in some detail with writers up to the period of the thirties, with the focus of attention on Conrad, T.S. Eliot, Hemingway, Aldous Huxley, Joyce, Virginia Woolf and others. This present book addresses the sequel, the period from the nineteen-forties to the late nineteen-sixties, this time not in relation to the visual arts (tempting as that may be) but in relation to the changes emerging within literature itself. The mid-century produced a rich literary response to the contemporary crisis, including such essentially new forms as the anti-hero, existentialist writing and the Theatre of the Absurd, each marking a strategy for responding to the disturbing problems that the era posed. The advent of postmodernism in the late nineteen-sixties, introducing the radical shifts in literary works that such theory encouraged, provides a useful dividing line at which to close the investigation of a spiritual predicament specific to the period of modernism.

Two criteria were adopted in choosing the works to be examined – their literary merit and their primary focus upon the cultural dilemma of the time, both aspects being requisite for inclusion. Richard Wright's *Native Son* (1940) and Ralph Ellison's *Invisible Man* (1952) meet without question the former criterion but their subject-matter, the plight of the black person in Western society, even when set in the twentieth century with imagery of paint factories and electric lightbulbs, is a problem, sadly enough, of much longer duration, not specific to the crisis that forms the central theme of this study. The novels of Nabokov, John Hawkes, Thomas Pynchon and Donald Barthelme, fascinating as they are, are excluded for a different reason, namely that they represent a withdrawal from reality into a symbolic world, a world marked, indeed, by a violence and horror reflecting the psychological perturbation of their time but placed within an extraterrestrial setting, removed from the actuality of daily experience. As Tony Tanner has remarked, Lewis Carroll, the model whom Nabokov greatly admired, although encouraging excursions into dreams, had framed his account of Alice's adventures by locating the beginning and the end of the story within the tangible world of reality, where she is seated on the grass stroking her kitten, so that we know at all times where the narrative is situated and when we move into the dream world, while such novels as Nabokov's *Pale Fire*, Hawkes's *The Cannibal* and Barthelme's *The Dead Father* exclude actuality completely, creating an imagined entity that replaces it. As Hawkes declared, 'I want to try to create a world, not represent it.'[84] I have concentrated, therefore, on literary works that confront the problems of the twentieth century as experienced in actuality.

Although the works to be examined were selected on the basis of that twofold criterion – literary merit and a predominant focus upon the loss of identity – what emerged constitutes in fact a representative cross-section of mid-century writing, encompassing a range of literary genres as well as a spectrum of religious, political and gender affiliation. Among novelists, Koestler explores the communist response to the problem, Greene provides a specifically Catholic reaction, Roth a Jewish viewpoint, Salinger depicts fictionally that of the adolescent, while Barth ponders the effectiveness of the solution offered by the existentialists. For the theatre, Beckett, Albee, Osborne, Pinter and Stoppard supply, from both sides of the Atlantic, contrasting instances of the innovations requisite for coping with the hollowness and anxieties of twentieth-century existence. And James Baldwin, despite the exclusion of black writers mentioned above, enters this study for certain other reasons, his inclusion enabling investigation of the specifically modernist aspects of racial conflict.

The period under examination was distinguished by the emergence of a new and dynamic movement, the writings of Doris Lessing, Nadine Gordimer, Adrienne Rich, Margaret Drabble Margaret Laurence and others, writers no longer conforming to the traditional patterns of male-dominated literature but exploring the feminine experience as a subject valid in its own right. Theirs has indeed been, as evidenced in the name bestowed by Lessing on her leading character, a 'quest' for identity; but it was a quest fundamentally different from that engaging us here. The discontent of those writers arose not from cosmic disillusionment, not from despair at the transformation of the human into a statistically negligible creature in a vast universe, but from a more positive impulse, a determination to establish for themselves an identity independent of their male counterparts, to create, in Elaine Showalter's term, 'a literature of their own.'[85] Their preoccupation with that urgent cause does not mean, however, that the search for identity in its cosmic setting was a masculine enterprise. Virginia Woolf in the decades immediately prior to their emergence had been motivated primarily by an attempt to cope with that problem, initiating through the technique of stream of consciousness a means of reasserting the authenticity and uniqueness of the individual. In defiance of Freud, whose theories she could not abide, she presented her characters not as disqualified by the psychological patterns into which they could be pigeon-holed but as differentiated and individualised by the specific childhood traumas they had experienced. It is those past events, momentous to each, that distinguish Rhoda from Susan, Bernard from Louis, endowing their lives with the particularity that gives them depth and meaning:

> 'In this hot afternoon,' said Susan, 'here in this garden, here in this field where I walk with my son, I have reached the summit of my desires . . . The violent passions of childhood, my tears in the garden when Jinny kissed Louis, my rage in the schoolroom, which smelt of pine, my loneliness in foreign places, when the mules came clattering in on their pointed hoofs and the Italian women chattered at the fountain, shawled, with carnations twisted in their hair, are rewarded by security, possession, familiarity . . . I have grown trees from the seed.'[86]

In such novels as *A God and His Gifts* (1963), Ivy Compton-Burnett, following her lead, moved through the externals of her scenes into the private inner world of each character, whose past experiences, private preferences and personal ambitions mould the specific quality of their being, lending them their authenticity. But most notable of all in the mid-century was the emergence of a distinguished poetess stirred at the profoundest level by her dismay at the intimidating alienation of the individual. Sylvia Plath, in the brilliant verse that was to transform her into a cult figure, not only forged for her generation a new type of poetry but transmitted through it her own tragic experience of the vacuity and despair of her era, her feminine sense of the appalling cruelty of an indifferent and cruel universe, a cruelty that, ultimately, she herself found unable to bear.

As the list of authors in this book suggests – a design not preimposed but emerging naturally from the criteria for inclusion – the crisis of alienation affected all sectors of society irrespective of class, gender, race, politics or religion. It was a concern, we have seen, especially troublesome to creative artists and writers, not only because of their innate sensitivity to cultural change but because such creative activity is utterly unrewarding unless it is conceived as emanating from the controlling faculty of the individual imagination, not from neuroses or preconditioned reflexes. That universal disquiet prompted writers, no longer at ease in traditional genres reliant on established ethical values, to evolve the innovative literary techniques that form the subject of this present volume, techniques enabling them to communicate to the wider public the tribulation experienced so acutely by the intellectual élite of the time.

2
Commissar and Priest

Those intellectuals resistant to communism in the 1930s were frequently puzzled by the willingness of their peers to surrender their freedom of thought on joining the party and to submit voluntarily to a discipline that demanded unequivocal obedience to the edicts of the Russian Comintern, however illogical or unpalatable those edicts might be. Such novices were conscious that membership involved not only suppression of their independent judgement but also harsh personal discrimination aimed deliberately against them. The movement's identification with the working class, from which the leaders of the communist cells were generally drawn, made the middle-class academic who joined them suspect as a potential informer and therefore prone to distrust and scepticism. He became the victim of frequent acts of humiliation intended to impress the newcomer with his inferiority to the manual labourer, and to remind him of the reversal in status being effected by the revolution. Such disdain constituted at that time official party policy, the academics who had joined their ranks being informed regularly that they were tolerated only because Russia was, until it had trained its own workers, temporarily in need of specialists in such areas as medicine, engineering and journalism, but they were warned expressly of the condition that they were forbidden to use their trained minds to suggest new policies or to deviate in any way from the party line established from above. Unexplained tergiversations, including the Soviet Union's unexpected signing in 1939 of a treaty of non-aggression with its supposed arch-enemy, fascist Germany, were to be accepted unquestioningly.

As Richard Crossman, who had himself taken that path, recalled, the reason prompting them to join formed part of a process mentioned briefly in the previous chapter: the tendency in all eras to form the new patterns of thought and behaviour in the moulds of those traditional in the past, in this instance, the socialist ideal being regarded as a secular substitute for the practices of the Christian religion which it had come to replace. The intellectual's willing surrender to such rigid cerebral discipline was not dissimilar, Crossman remarked, to the desire that had, through the centuries, stimulated leading scholars to join such priestly orders as the Society of Jesus whose members, often famed for their academic brilliance, pledged total obedience to the Pope, readily, even eagerly abjuring liberty of thought in favour of self-abasement:

> The strength of the Catholic Church has always been that it demands the sacrifice of that freedom uncompromisingly, and condemns spiritual pride as a deadly sin. The Communist novice, subjecting his soul to the canon law of the Kremlin, felt something of the release which Catholicism also brings to the intellectual, wearied and worried by the privilege of freedom.
>
> Once the renunciation has been made, the mind, instead of operating freely, becomes the servant of a higher and unquestioned purpose. To deny the truth is an act of service. This, of course, is why it is useless to discuss any particular aspect of politics with a Communist. Any genuine intellectual contact which you have with him involves a challenge to his fundamental faith, a struggle for his soul. For it is very much easier to lay the oblation of spiritual pride on the altar of world revolution than to snatch it back again.[1]

It was not the required subjection of intellect, therefore, that led so many of them to experience eventually a disillusionment with communism and to revoke their membership in the party. The source of that retraction, closely related to the theme of this present study, finds its most penetrating analysis in Arthur Koestler's *Darkness at Noon* (1940), even though the message of that book has often been misinterpreted.

The main surprise in a novel patently dedicated to exposing the fallacies of communism is the sympathetic portrayal of its central character, Rubashov, a figure modelled in large part upon Nikolai Ivanovich Bukharin, who had served as a leading figure in both the Comintern and the Politburo. Bukharin, who had authored major treatises on Soviet economic policy adopted by the party and had served as editor of the official government newspaper, *Izvestia,* was discredited and executed in the last of the Moscow trials, the ruthless Stalinist purges of the 1930s perpetrated shortly before the publication of this novel. In the fictionalised version (as no doubt in the case of Bukharin himself), Rubashov had been, as a senior party member, directly responsible for the execution of a number of perfectly innocent individuals who had found themselves on the wrong side of some unexpected policy reversal on the part of the leadership or who needed to be sacrificed in order to absolve someone of more value to the movement. Were this a political treatise rather than a novel, one would expect Koestler's characterisation of Rubashov to be unequivocally hostile, stressing the callous indifference of party leaders to the lives of those they were supposed to be caring for, and noting the irony that such leaders were also to be discarded in their turn when it served the party's purpose. But from the first, Koestler presents him as a person deserving of the reader's sympathy and, indeed, admiration. His dedication to the cause he has undertaken is absolute, the standards he demands both from himself and from others are uncompromisingly high, accompanied by a recognition that he too must be sacrificed should the needs of the state demand it, a likelihood confronted with unswerving courage. The novel, recounting the final weeks of his life, from his arrest for treason to the moment of his execution, provides an opportunity for the reader to share with him the gradual process of identifying and coming eventually to acknowledge the fallacy that Koestler perceived at the heart of the communist system, the system that Rubashov himself had helped to inaugurate and that Koestler himself had so firmly believed in during the period of his membership of the party.

The nature of that fallacy as Koestler defines it is, I believe, significantly different from that usually ascribed to the novel. John Atkins, acknowledging the book to be a literary masterpiece, complained nonetheless that its message, emerging only in the final section, was simplistic – the view that Russian communism had fallen into the wrong hands, the ideal being invalidated by the wanton cruelty of such leaders as Stalin who had unfortunately taken control. As Atkins puts it, 'it was not the accused who had forsaken the Revolution but the accusers.' George Orwell, in contrast, saw the corruption of the leaders not as a chance factor but as intrinsic to the system, the novel transmitting the message that such barbarity was inevitable when leaders attain to totalitarian power. 'It is not merely that "power corrupts": so also do the ways of attaining power. Therefore, all efforts to regenerate society by violent means lead to the cellars of the OGPU, Lenin leads to Stalin, and would have come to resemble Stalin if he had happened to survive.'[2] The majority, however, have, like Malcolm Cowley, identified the novel's message in the phrase that 'noble ends do not justify ignoble means'; that the apocalyptic vision towards which communism had been working, however admirable in itself, could not condone the brutality of the Stalinist regime.

Common to all such readings is the assumption that Koestler's main purpose in the novel was to justify his own abrogation of communism by impugning the current leaders of the Soviet Union, by arguing that Stalin had betrayed the high ideals inherent in communism by his inhuman slaughter of over two million citizens during the period of these trials, and had thereby perverted the commendable political concepts initiated by Marx, Engels and Lenin. Or to put it differently, that if so callous a leader as Stalin had not arisen, all would have been well. But the text, it seems to me, does not support such a reading. As Rubashov gazes at his coldly efficient interrogator Gletkin, the expressionless, unfeeling representative of the state who has replaced the more congenial Ivanov, he recognises that he has no basis for complaint; for Gletkin constitutes in every sense a *fulfilment* of the ideals that he and his friend Ivanov had worked so hard to effectuate. He and Ivanov had, unlike Gletkin, belonged to the transitional generation, a bridge from the old civilisation to the new, still bearing with them certain traces of the humanist past, while Gletkin, the so-called Neanderthal man 'lacking an umbilical cord', had never known that earlier ethical tradition, and could, as the perfect consummation of their efforts, act unhesitatingly in accordance with the new principles:

> Rubashov repeated to himself for the hundredth time that Gletkin and the new Neanderthalers were merely completing the work of the generation with the numbered heads [the founders of the movement]. That the same doctrine became so inhuman in their mouths, had, as it were, merely climatic reasons. When Ivanov had used the same arguments, there was yet an undertone in his voice left by the past by the remembrance of a world which had vanished ... The Gletkins had nothing to erase.[3]

Indeed, far from arguing that the leaders have departed from the true path or have perverted the original intent, Koestler repeatedly suggests the existence of a fatal defect concealed within the doctrine of communism itself, a defect which Rubashov must confront and gradually come to acknowledge during his final days. The literary strategy whereby the fallacy manifests itself is fascinating to watch.

The sympathetic depiction of Rubashov as a person of high integrity and stern self-discipline, continually rubbing his *pince-nez* as a symbol of his insistence on discerning the facts with absolute clarity and honesty, or deliberately burning his skin with a lighted cigarette in order to prepare himself to withstand the torture in store for him, all these elements form part of the author's constant reminder to a readership generally antagonistic to that political movement that the ideal motivating communism, the inducement that had originally drawn Rubashov and his peers (including Koestler himself) into that movement, had been fundamentally noble and humane. It had arisen from genuine compassion, from the horror of seeing men, women and children dying of cold and starvation in the midst of capitalist plenty. While both Rubashov and Koestler emerged from the security of middle or upper-class settings, for the most part immune to such suffering,[4] their consciences had prompted them to forgo the safeguards of home and career in order, at the risk of their lives (and it was a very palpable risk) to stretch out a helping hand to the poor and hasten the fulfilment of the communist ideal. They were dedicating themselves to the time when capital would be equally distributed and the ultimate purpose of communism, the greatest happiness of the greatest number, would be finally achieved.

Where, then, was the fallacy and how was it related to the broader predicament of the time that forms the subject of this present study? Rubashov's gradual awakening to the error inbuilt in such reckoning begins obliquely, as no more than a hint, momentarily troubling to him, and tantalising to the reader because of its initial inexplicitness. Peering through the spyhole of his cell door, he perceives a nameless prisoner, known only by his prison number 407, holding out his thin, bare hands to receive a meagre bowl of food. The scene prompts in Rubashov a vague feeling of unease, a reminder of something he cannot at the moment identify. Only in the following chapter does he suddenly recall the source, realising that the scene had triggered the memory of a depiction of the *Pietà* glimpsed only out of the corner of his eye, on an occasion that is to prove central for his eventual desertion of the ideal to which his adult life had been dedicated. The incident had occurred many years earlier, when, hounded by the police, he had, for reasons of secrecy, arranged to meet a young man in the local art gallery, a young man named Richard whom he, in effect, condemns there to death, expelling him from the party and thereby assuring his betrayal by his former colleagues for having unintentionally deviated in some minor way from the current political line:

To Richard's left hung a pen drawing by a German master; Rubashov could only see a part of it – the rest was hidden by the plush back of the sofa and by Richard's head: the Madonna's thin hands, curved upwards, hollowed to the shape of a bowl ...

The significance of that incident emerges against the background of Rubashov's interrogation, first by Ivanov and then by Gletkin, an investigation echoing the official line of reasoning to which Rubashov had so long subscribed, with quotations from his own diary repeatedly cited as evidence against him. It thus constitutes a recapitulation of the principles to which he had dedicated his life and which had directed his actions performed in the name of the party. In the course of that summary, the debt of Marxism to evolutionary theory and, in fact, its derivation from it become clear, even though the *Communist Manifesto* was published in 1848, a decade before the appearance of *The Origin of Species*. The concept of evolution, while not yet scientifically proven but already being widely discussed at that time, provided a large part of its impetus, the effect of the theory itself once formulated and published being incorporated more fully as the movement developed in subsequent decades.[5] The concept of an impersonal historical necessity sweeping mankind along, impervious to the individual and concerned only with the advancement of the human species, is patently relevant here, cited as the justification for the communist system itself:

> the movement was without scruples; she rolled towards her goal unconcernedly and deposed the corpses of the drowned in the windings of her course. Her course had many twists and windings; such was the law of her being. And whosoever could not follow her crooked course was washed on to the bank, for such was her law. The motives of the individual did not matter to her. His conscience did not matter to her, neither did she care what went on in his head and his heart. The Party knew only one crime: to swerve from the course laid out; and only one punishment: death. Death was no mystery in the movement; there was nothing exalted about it: it was the logical solution to political divergences. (p. 65)

From within that statement there emerges an element chilling in its implication and marking a basic distinction between the new movement and all previous forms of totalitarian rule. For in the earlier versions, however ruthless the ruling power might be, there had at least been the assumption that loyalty to that power would be regarded by the authority as meritorious. But now, the intentions of the individual, however steadfast, become entirely irrelevant. Not only must he continually swerve in accordance with changes in party policy or his corpse be washed up on the bank, but he is now vulnerable on a further count, despite the blatant illogicality involved. For dutiful acceptance of the party line as it is operative today makes that same member, when the policy changes, retrospectively guilty for having followed it then, his body thrown up on the bank whenever the course of the river changes. As Gletkin quotes from Rubashov's diary written during his adoption of communist principles: 'For us the question of subjective good faith is of no interest. He who is in the wrong must pay: he who is in the right will be absolved.'

As part of this total disregard for the intentions of the individual is the treatment of those genuinely eager to contribute to and advance the communist state but whose actions happen to conflict with the current policy of the ruling power. Such divergence, however technical, is a 'crime' punishable by death. A scientist discovering a form of nitrate manure that can greatly increase agricultural productivity and thereby help prevent starvation, if that policy happens not to suit the prevailing government programme, must not merely be ignored and his discovery suppressed. He and his thirty research assistants must be publicly tried and executed as saboteurs, as, of course, actually occurred when agricultural production was under the control of the controversial Soviet biologist and agronomist, Lysenko. History, we are told, will vindicate the authorities for such acts, 'and the execution of the thirty-one men will be a mere bagatelle.' (p. 82)

The irrelevance of the individual's intentions within the larger scheme of the advance of the masses was thus, both in this novel and in the Russian system itself, neither an aberration nor a perversion of communist doctrine but an integral part of its philosophical stance, fully in accord with the collapse of traditional ethical values implicit in the evolutionary concept where the only ultimate criterion is not good or evil but the survival of the species or nation, however many individuals need to be sacrificed en route. Within communism, that changed concept was reflected linguistically in the introduction of a new terminology. Where in previous generations opponents of a totalitarian regime had been 'executed', 'hanged' or 'murdered', terms indicating the deliberate extinguishing of life, dissidents now were to be 'liquidated', their death constituting a form of evaporation, the end of their political usefulness, a disappearance from a scene in which they had no further contribution to make to the forward movement of the species and were therefore irrelevant, like the drones cast out of the beehive to die when they have no further contribution to make. The individual, in that context, ceases to have any significance, in much the same way as corpses stripped of their skin to make lampshades for Nazis marked a contempt for the human being that even the most vicious tyrannies of the past had not evinced. Such communist 'drones' were casually disposed of in cellars or yards, only deposed leaders or those whose demise could provide a grim lesson for others needing to be publicly tried and made to confess.

The ethical significance of that change is deftly illustrated in this novel in the contrasting interpretations of Dostoyevsky's *Crime and Punishment,* which become central in Rubashov's lengthy interrogation by Ivanov. Raskolnikov was guilty, Ivanov argues, not because he killed an old woman – her death being of no importance whatever to the state – but because he did so in his own interest. Had he done so at the command of the party, 'to increase strike funds or to install an illegal Press, then the equation would stand, and the novel with its misleading problem would never have been written.'

That term 'equation' provides a key for identifying the fallacy that Koestler will eventually reveal as inherent in the communist system. At a crucial moment in Rubashov's meditations on his political allegiance, he echoes that word when he senses: 'There was somewhere an error in the calculation, the equation did not work out.' In discussing this novel many years later, Koestler was more explicit about that fallacy, although the point emerges sufficiently clearly within the literary work itself. In his autobiographical *The Invisible Writing*, Koestler quotes the above sentence from the novel, explaining the reference to the invalid 'equation' in mathematical terms:

> In the social equation, the value of a single life is nil; in the cosmic equation it is infinite. Now every schoolboy knows that if you smuggle either a nought or the infinite into a finite calculation, the equation will be disrupted and you will be able to prove that three equals five, or five hundred. Not only Communism, but any political movement which implicitly relies on purely utilitarian ethics must become a victim to the same fatal error.[6]

To elaborate the nature of that fatal error one needs to trace a subtle change in the meaning of an axiom that was to become so central to the communist system. In its original context in Jeremy Bentham's *Common-place Book*, the phrase 'the greatest happiness of the greatest number' had represented a democratic, humanistic ideal intended to function, in Bentham's words, as 'the foundation of morals and legislation'. John Stuart Mill, in extending that concept, stressed repeatedly that the idea of utilitarianism, aiming at the happiness of members of society, did not conceive of the pursuit of personal pleasure in any epicurean sense. The concept was of a pleasure more cultivated, to be nurtured by education and incorporating as an essential ingredient consideration for others:

> In an improving state of the human mind, the influences are
> constantly on the increase which tend to generate in each individual
> a feeling of unity with all the rest; which, if perfect, would make him
> never think of, or desire, any beneficial condition for himself, in the
> benefits of which they are not included.[7]

The transference of the doctrine to the communist platform, certainly in
its Bolshevik form, had, however, involved a very different form of
calculation. It was now assumed that if, of twenty million people,
nineteen million could be satisfactorily provided for, each contributing
according to ability and receiving recompense according to need, then
(with echoes of Natural Selection) the remaining million could be
dispensed with. Indeed, Ivanov, speaking in the name of the party,
employs that Darwinian principle as the justification for its actions,
arguing that if nature can dispense with myriads of individual creatures to
attain its ends, then mankind is no less entitled to do so:

> Every year several million people are killed quite pointlessly by
> epidemics and other natural catastrophes. And we should shrink from
> sacrificing a few hundred thousand for the most promising experiment
> in history? Nature is generous in her senseless experiments on
> mankind. Why should mankind not have the right to experiment on
> itself? (p. 131)

Koestler's eventual discovery, the reason for his desertion of the party,
lay in his profound perception that in the process of developing the
communist principle, the value of the individual had been utterly
discarded. It was a perception he projected in arithmetical terms. As his
comment concerning the introduction of a nought into a mathematical equation indicated, twenty million has a positive value only if it is
the product of twenty million *times one*. Twenty million *times zero* is
zero. If the individual is a valueless nought in the eyes of the
movement, the entire system is invalid from its inception, and not
because of any subsequent deviation or aberration on the part of the
rulers. Hence Rubashov's response to Ivanov's argument as he himself
now perceives the situation. The old woman whom Raskolnikov
murdered may have been utterly useless to the world while the young
student himself was, in contrast, talented, intelligent and with his
future before him; but 'the equation collapses ... because Raskolnikov
discovers that twice two are not four when mathematical units are
human beings.' (p. 127)

To identify as the book's message the discovery that 'noble ends do not justify evil means,' that the leaders of the movement had perverted the communist ideal by ruthlessly executing dissidents in the interim period before the fulfilment of the ideal, is to assume that Koestler in this book still regarded the final aim of communism as valid, objecting only to the intervening horror of the Stalinist purges. But the conclusion he eventually reached, as expressed through Rubashov's spiritual odyssey, was far more damning, a recognition that the basic idea of communism, which had, by its messianic vision, attracted so many intellectuals to its ranks, was itself fundamentally defective; that not only the means but the beginning, the intervening period, and the end envisaged were all equally reprehensible. Compassion for the woman or child dying of starvation in the midst of capitalist plenty may have served as the initial impetus for Marx as for Rubashov and Koestler, their outrage at the callousness of a society exploiting the proletariat and ignoring the suffering of those unable to compete effectually; but the political system that resulted from that impetus had undertaken, as an integral part of its philosophy, the nullification of the worth of the individual, and hence a disqualification of the compassion itself. As Ivanov declares in the name of the party, the true communist has no room and no justification for a conscience:

'he is cold and unmerciful to mankind, out of a kind of mathematical mercifulness. He is damned always to do that which is most repugnant to him: to become a slaughterer, in order to abolish slaughtering, to sacrifice lambs so that no more lambs may be slaughtered, to whip people with knouts so that they may learn not to let themselves be whipped, to strip himself of every scruple in the name of a higher scrupulousness, and to challenge the hatred of mankind because of his love for it – an abstract and geometric love. *Apage Satanas!* Comrade Rubashov prefers to become a martyr … He has discovered a conscience, and a conscience renders one as unfit for the revolution as a double chin.' (p. 122)

But it is Ivanov that speaks here, a communist still believing in the apocalyptic era when such slaughter and whipping will no longer be necessary, while Rubashov has already begun to perceive that the supposed messianic age is a mere myth, a fantasy never to be realised. It is a chimera not because the revolution will fail but for reasons instrinsic to the movement itself, because the sacrifice of the individual to the state integral to the communist ideal means that at all times, even after the socialist goals have been fully achieved, the slightest divergence from party line, intentional or not, will continue to be punishable by death and the 'drones' of the beehive imperturbably discarded. The innocent woman or child unwanted by society or irrelevant to its progress, instead of dying of starvation under a bridge, would, in that new world, be callously liquidated for the good of the state. Ivanov, because of his residual attachment to the old world of humanism, can at least understand Rubashov's distaste for the slaughter necessary in the 'transitional' period; but Ivanov's swift execution because of that attachment and his replacement by Gletkin, representing the fulfilment of communism, leave no doubt that the problem, in Koestler's view, lies not in any intervening period but in the policy itself.

The critics' misunderstanding of the underlying theme of the novel may have had its origin in a statement about the novel made by Koestler himself some years after its publication. The problem of the revolutionaries in *Darkness at Noon* was indeed, he remarked in 1954, a matter of ends and means. But if one reads his comment closely, it is apparent that he is not referring to the means and the end as usually understood: 'The common denominator of their guilt is *having placed the interests of mankind above the interests of man*, having sacrificed morality to expediency, the Means to the Ends' [my italics].[8] The means, in this view, are not the ruthless purges that, as so many of his critics had argued, corrupted the ultimate noble ideal through the chance fact that Stalin achieved control of the party but the sacrifice inherent in the basic programme of communism, the Darwinian subjection of the interests of *man* in an attempt to serve the interests of *mankind*. It is a distinction that Koestler was to clarify in his definition of the two philosophical types dominating human thought, the Yogi who focuses on the inner self, invalidating the significance of any 'ends', and the Commissar-type for whom the end justifies all means, 'including violence, ruse, treachery, and poison.'[9]

The connection between the theme of this novel and the twentieth-century problem of selfhood is powerfully enhanced here by Koestler's choice of the cultural tradition to be used as the contrast to communism. Throughout this novel, the antithesis adduced to highlight its failings is the biblical world-view, the ethical and religious tradition that had served as the substructure of Western culture throughout the previous generations. It is an antithesis especially interesting in view of Koestler's own distancing from that tradition, his personal rejection of religious belief.[10] Moreover, in that use of the scriptural tradition as the converse of modern concepts he was not alone, the biblical setting being repeatedly invoked in the literature of the twentieth century at large by authors who no longer subscribed to Christianity; and the reason for its inclusion in this novel holds true for the more general usage. Koestler, while he could not subscribe to religious belief, recognised that something of major value had been lost together with the jettisoning of Judeo-Christian rituals. The element that had been surrendered was the sanctity of the individual, for which no substitute could be found in the secular world that had replaced it. It was a quality ensuring, by its claim that mankind was created in the image of God, the inviolability of each human being, an inviolability that no scientific or materialistic philosophy could replace. As Ivanov admits (even though he is at that point arguing in favour of communism):

> There are only two conceptions of human ethics, and they are at opposite poles. One of them is Christian and humane, declares the individual to be sacrosanct, and asserts that the rules of arithmetic are not to be applied to human units. The other starts from the basic principle that a collective aim justifies all means, and not only allows, but demands, that the individual should in every way be subordinated and sacrificed to the community – which may dispose of it as an experimentation rabbit or a sacrificial lamb. (p. 128)

Rubashov, gazing through the window, muses on the results of that newer system, that in the interests of a just distribution of land the authorities had deliberately let some five million farmers and their families die of starvation in one year; that in the liberation of human beings from the shackles of industrial exploitation they had despatched some ten million people to forced labour in the Arctic regions and the jungles of the East, like the galley slaves of antiquity. It was, he acknowledges, a principle established by the sciences that had led them to this quandary. 'We all thought one could treat history like one experiments in physics. The difference is that in physics one can repeat the experiment a thousand times, but in history only once. Danton and Saint-Just can be sent to the scaffold only once.' The single human being, he realises, could be neither replaced nor regenerated.

It was, we may recall, Rubashov's recollection of the drawing of the *Pietà*, with the Madonna's hands held out in suffering, that had first triggered in his mind an association buried deep in his memory, an association that his mind consciously resists but that is to function as the motive force for his growing doubts concerning the communist ideal. The theme of the *Pietà* functions as a haunting refrain, first as a suppressed memory, next as a recalled background setting, and subsequently as a scene to be alluded to and reinforced at various moments in the story. The spyhole in the cell door through which Rubashov catches a glimpse of the prisoner holding out his bowl Koestler calls, significantly, the 'judas-eye'. The step-by-step recollection of the scene in the museum is spread over some twenty-five pages, to culminate in Rubashov's recognition of the contrast between the communist and the scriptural valuations of the individual. As doubts enter his mind concerning his treatment of Richard, he asks himself irritably, 'Was there another measure besides that of reason? What was this? A breath of religious madness?' As long as he had held firmly to his political creed, the people he sent to their deaths, including his mistress Arlova, the faithful Loewy and the newly married Richard, had been to him no more than statistics in the overall calculation to which he was committed, pawns to be justifiably discarded and forgotten. Only when he sees with his own eyes the terror and suffering of one individual, Bogrov, do those statistics become transformed into pitiable human beings, the term *equation* recurring throughout his meditation:

> Now, in the nausea which turned his stomach and drove the wet perspiration from his forehead, his past mode of thought seemed lunacy. The whimpering of Bogrov unbalanced the logical equation. Up till now Arlova had been a factor in this equation, a small factor compared to what was at stake. But the equation no longer stood. The vision of Arlova's legs in their high-heeled shoes trailing along the corridor upset the mathematical equilibrium. The unimportant factor had grown to the immeasurable, the absolute; Bogrov's whining, the inhuman sound of the voice which had called out his name, the hollow beat of the drumming, filled his ears; they smothered the thin voice of reason, covered it as the surf covers the gurgling of the drowning. (p. 117)

His reason, like the calculations of the scientist, the biologist or the chemist seeing the human solely in terms of verifiable, physical facts and deducing from such data theories about the purpose and function of society, had found no place for the human soul or spirit, for that intangible element that differentiates one human being from another. The evolutionist source of communism, like Darwinism itself, excluded moral criteria as irrelevant in the advancement of the species and the preservation of the type at the expense of its individual members. But his confrontation with human suffering arouses in Rubashov an irresistible compassion and, with it, an accompanying misgiving concerning the political system, a misgiving that no logical reasoning can suppress.

It is this burgeoning doubt which constitutes the 'grammatical fiction' that forms the title of the final section of the book, the consummation of a thought troubling him from much earlier in his search for truth – his growing awareness of the existence of a silent partner, his moral conscience, that had been stifled throughout the years, a hidden self that began its meditations where logical thought ended, that now emerges to challenge the 'we' that both he and the party had habitually accepted as the single criterion for action:

> The sole object of revolution was the abolition of senseless suffering. But it had turned out that the removal of this second kind of suffering was only possible at the price of a temporary enormous increase in the sum total of the first. So the question now ran: Was such an operation justified? Obviously it was, if one spoke in the abstract of 'mankind'; but, applied to 'man' in the singular ... the real human being of bone and flesh and blood and skin, the principle led to absurdity. (p. 202)

At this point, Rubashov is still thinking of the flaw in terms of a temporary, interim period in the process of revolution. But the contrast between the two views of humanity as the novel develops leads him to the recognition that the discrepancy is more fundamental.

Towards the end of the novel, after Rubashov's condemnation, the elderly porter Vasily, belonging to a past generation, hears his communist daughter read aloud the official newspaper account of the trial. Although deprived by her of his beloved Bible, he quietly murmurs to himself from memory: '*And the soldiers led him away, into the hall called Praetorium ... And they clothed him with purple and they smote him on the head with a reed and did spit upon him,*' piously adding at the conclusion of the account, 'Thy will be done, Amen.' Sidney Pearson, puzzled by the parallel drawn here between Rubashov and Christ, interprets the scene as indicating the author's disapproval of both systems, that 'Christian principles are no more effective in Koestler's view than those of the commissar ... the result is the same, the death of each without changing the human condition.'[11] But such a reading ignores the emotional response evoked at that stage of the novel – the unloving communist daughter gullibly accepting the official version of Rubashov's disgrace and the more humane Vasily envisioning him with admiration as a suffering Christ-figure in a world where compassion and altruism should remain valid ideals but have been swept away.

I have referred on more than one occasion to Rubashov's eventual recognition that there is a fatal flaw within the communist system. But that is not quite so. An aspect of the book that has proved disquieting both to readers and to critics is Rubashov's final decision to confess his guilt, to submit to the demands of his captors and admit his supposed political sins – a confession that seems a negation of the long spiritual journey he has travelled during the course of his interrogation and trial. In line with Danton's fearless speech before the French Revolutionary tribunal recalled with a touch of envy by Rubashov, one would expect him boldly to renounce communism at the trial, performing a courageous act which, however useless (since it would never be reported in the communist-controlled press), would at least be honest, and consonant with his changed view. Goronwy Rees attributes his submission to weakness, concluding that, although he has rejected communism, he no longer has the strength of mind to withstand Gletkin's arguments, that he is 'intellectually and emotionally exhausted; that he is, in fact, beaten.'[12] Were that correct, it would not only suggest that the novel fails in conveying its primary message but would also contradict the character of Rubashov as consistently depicted throughout the work. From the first, we have been led to admire his fortitude, not only in resisting the physical and emotional pressures of his imprisonment and energetically combating the dialectical entrapments of his inquisitors, but above all in his unremitting search for the truth. For him to hand the concluding victory to Gletkin would seem totally inconsistent with those qualities as well as an affirmation of the communist viewpoint that Koestler wished so firmly to reject. George Orwell, who admired the novel as a literary masterpiece achieving the stature of tragedy, was also disturbed by the conclusion, deciding, like Rees, that Rubashov's confession was actuated by despair, by mental bankruptcy, and by a habit of loyalty to the party that makes him experience a peculiar feeling of honour in capitulating.[13] But that too would appear a feeble ending to the long account of his valorous resistance.

Koestler, I would suggest, has been more subtle than the critics, recognising a factor related to the tragic quality of the novel as perceived by Orwell. In the genre of tragedy, a hero such as Othello or Lear learns the error of his ways only shortly before his death, when it is too late to make use of the lesson; but the audience, who have accompanied him through the agony of learning, are privileged to survive, to carry away from the theatre the lesson they have learnt vicariously through his experience. Had Rubashov taken the final step of acknowledging the fallacy inherent in communism, the reader would be left with a residual suspicion profoundly damaging to the work – that, as long as he was sending others such as Arlova, Loewy and Richard to their deaths, he remained firm in his allegiance to political doctrine; but the moment his own life is threatened, he deserts it. Such an ending would have been ruinous, any defiant condemnation of communism in his final speech, moreover, transforming the novel into a facile political tract instead of the moving account of a spiritual pilgrimage.

The solution Koestler offers is to leave Rubashov in the closing scene at the threshold of discovery, almost grasping the truth but not quite. The crucial word reiterated in his final meditation before execution is the hesitant 'Perhaps':

> What had he once written in his diary? 'We have thrown overboard all conventions, our sole guiding principle is that of consequent logica; we are sailing without ethical ballast.'
>
> Perhaps the heart of the evil lay there. Perhaps it did not suit mankind to sail without ballast. And perhaps reason alone was a defective compass, which led one on such a winding, twisted course that the goal finally disappeared in the mist.
>
> Perhaps now would come the time of great darkness.
>
> Perhaps ...

The message Koestler wished to convey has by now been fully transmitted to the reader, who at that point mentally contradicts Rubashov, recognising his remaining doubts as invalid, rejecting the 'perhaps' in his identification of a flaw which to us now appears a certainty.

Rubashov himself, therefore, remains one step behind, tragically bound, at least formally, to those ideals that, however false, had seemed for so long to justify his actions, his concern with the logic of a sweeping historical necessity to which the intrinsic value of the individual must be sacrificed. His search for the error within the system may not, for him, have reached the point of certitude, but the direction of his progress has been amply conveyed – that a totalitarian system based upon Darwinian principles, once it devalues the single member of society in its pursuit of the good of mankind, automatically disqualifies its own purpose.

Koestler is thus left subject to the tragic predicament of his generation, to a mournful recognition of the loss of human worth coupled with an inability to find any means of restoring it. Communism had, for a time, supplied him with an enheartening vision, an inspiring ideal that he could serve with devotion, a system imbuing the acts of each member with purpose and meaning; and to that system he devoted a number of years, repeatedly risking his life in the process. But the system had proved flawed and, relinquishing his belief in it, he was left with no alternative but to gaze back enviously at the biblical world-view that had indeed cherished the sacrosanctity of each human but to whose tenets he himself, as part of his twentieth-century conditioning, was unable to subscribe.

* * * * *

In contrast, Graham Greene, as a believing Catholic, did subscribe to that biblically derived concept of human sacrosanctity. One might have thought, therefore, that he would be immune to the problems posed by his age, confident of the inviolability of the human soul in a divinely ordered world. Yet he proved in fact not only sensitive to the challenge posed by the new configuration but a pioneer in coping with it, inaugurating in his novels from the 1940s a literary strategy that was to prove of central importance in mid-century fiction.

The collapse of the ethical precepts and socially approved paradigms of living upon which leading fictional characters had previously been constructed had left the writer in a quandary. The virtues of honesty, courage and compassion that had distinguished the nineteenth-century hero and the concomitant merits of modesty and constancy epitomising the heroine – either initially or after the correction of some minor failing in the course of the novel – had ensured in the past that such characters could serve as acceptable models for reader identification, representing as they did the ideals of which contemporary society approved. Elizabeth Bennet may be subject to prejudice and Darcy to inordinate pride, but by the end of the novel their moral integrity, discrimination and aesthetic sensibility win through to free them from those failings. Any serious deviation from the norms sanctioned by society had in those eras incurred automatic disqualification, even in novels seemingly critical of society's standards. Thackeray's *Vanity Fair*, satirising the folly of human affairs and prefaced with the claim that the book contained no moral lesson, observed those prerequisites nonetheless. The ostensible hero, George Osborne, although possessing all other traits associated with that role – handsome appearance, courage and masculine charm – forfeits that position the moment that he, as a married man, drops a *billet-doux* into Becky Sharp's bouquet. He must therefore be conveniently disposed of a few pages later by his death in battle. Although provocatively subtitled '*a novel without a hero,*' the book conforms closely to the nineteenth-century moral pattern. Dobbin, with his clumsiness and his large feet, may lack the physical grace of the traditional hero and Amelia may exasperate by her propensity for tears and her tardiness in recognising his sterling qualities, but it is clear that ultimately Thackeray approves of their conformity to the Victorian ideals of selflessness, compassion, loyalty and sexual purity. In contrast, the modern era, with its undermining of the traditional values upon which the appeal of the admired characters had rested, offered no acceptable basis upon which an author could construct a heroic image. With courage now defined as a covert suicidal tendency and adultery as an antiquated social taboo (witness D. H. Lawrence's *Lady Chatterley's Lover* of 1928), some new strategy needed to be developed for achieving reader approval and identification, a method dispensing in some way with dependence upon those outmoded norms.

Before investigating the carefully crafted genre of the anti-hero, it may be necessary to note how its distinctive qualities have been obscured by loose critical usage, the term being applied to so wide and varied a range of fictional characters as to make it almost meaningless. Among early instances identified as belonging within that category have been the disgruntled speaker in Dostoyevsky's *Notes from Underground*, bitterly railing at the world at large, as well as the diffident Prufrock of T. S. Eliot's poem. Both characters indeed represented a radical departure from the nineteenth-century tradition, but there is nothing remotely heroic in either. The term 'anti-hero' does not merely designate the absence of heroic qualities, nor, of course, does it characterise the antithesis of a hero for which we retain the term 'villain'. It denotes instead a fictional figure who is in some sense genuinely heroic despite characteristics that appear to incapacitate him for the role – timidity, unprepossessing appearance, self-doubt, or social ineptitude, together producing a propensity to failure – but who eventually wins the admiration of the reader despite, or because of, those seeming failings. To place Dostoyevsky's speaker in that category belies the definition. Spiteful and sadistic by nature, readily admitting the malevolence and viciousness with which he has treated the innocent Liza and his other mistresses yet revealing no remorse for his cruelty, he may arouse some minimal compassion for his twisted, perverted soul, for his revelation of the baleful forces at work within mankind, but he can evoke little approbation. Prufrock, in contrast, does possess a potential for heroism and artistic creativity. He is impelled by a craving for noble achievement as a creative artist in the tradition of Michelangelo, a yearning for religious commitment in emulation of John the Baptist ('though I have wept and fasted, wept and prayed'); but those proclivities lead in that poem only to lamentable frustration, indecision and, eventually, to the pitiable recognition that his moment of greatness has flickered and passed with nothing achieved. He captured the imagination of Eliot's contemporaries as a figure brilliantly embodying the impotence and paralysis of that generation, searching for vestigial values in the sterility of the modern world and attempting to ask the overwhelming question concerning the meaning of human existence. But he fails on all counts. Ultimately, he is a figure of pathos, devoid of the heroic, sinking in the final scene into escapist fantasies as he abandons all hope of self-fulfilment.

Attempts to identify the genre as it emerged a little later, during the mid-century, have been equally unsatisfactory, resulting in a mélange that merely blurs its features. Ihab Hassan, in his otherwise admirable study of the contemporary novel, *Radical Innocence*, included in that category so widely assorted a conglomeration of characters as to preclude the possibility of any precise definition. In fiction, he claimed:

> the unnerving rubric 'anti-hero' refers to a ragged assembly of victims: the fool, the clown, the hipster, the criminal, the poor sod, the freak, the outsider, the scapegoat, the scrubby opportunist, the rebel without a cause, the 'hero' in the ashcan and 'hero' on the leash.[14]

To place the criminal and the scrubby opportunist within the category is to debase the term, and to include, at the other extreme, Camus's 'absurd hero' (as Hassan does shortly after this passage) is to confuse it further, since in accordance with Camus's principle that to rebel *is* to exist, his Sisyphan character emerges in his estimation as a fully fledged hero. Sisyphus may be condemned, like the rest of mankind, to an utterly pointless world, he may be severely restricted in his ability to alter his condition, yet he courageously confronts his situation, determined to wrest from it the self-respect he deems essential for living.

The genre can, I believe, be defined with much greater accuracy, the most significant element in the emergent figure being not so much those factors disqualifying him for the traditional role, the failings and weaknesses that make him a misfit in society, but rather the subtle method employed by the author to ensure his ultimate elevation in the reader's estimation by the end of the novel, a recognition in him of qualities evoking in most instances an even higher degree of respect than that which had been accorded to his nineteenth-century predecessors. How widespread this new type became in the mid-century may be seen in the medium of the cinema, where such ruggedly handsome male leads as Clark Gable, Gary Cooper and Gregory Peck began to be replaced by a totally new type – Dustin Hoffman, Woody Allen, Gene Wilder and Dudley Moore, all short in stature, less prepossessing in appearance, generally representing the *schlemiel* in society; yet portraying characters who nevertheless emerge as ultimately more evocative of sympathy and respect, closer to the spectator's own situation, than the cellulose heroes of the past.

For the novelist, the situation in the 1940s had seemed especially bleak. The major attempt to cope with the contemporary disqualification of the traditional hero, the novel of the stream of consciousness, although it produced some fascinating results in the fiction of James Joyce, Virginia Woolf and William Faulkner, had by the forties led to a dead end.[15] Those authors had created a new form of reader-identification, based not upon the virtues or moral fibre of the central characters but on the opportunity which the technique of interior monologue afforded for penetrating into the minds of others, for observing anxieties, longings, mental associations and erotic thoughts hidden from the outside world and now revealed to the privileged reader. The intimacy established by that entry into the intensely private inner world of others served as an effective substitute for the embodiment of society's ideals that had previously distinguished the hero and did so in a manner that made moral principles irrelevant, the reader unconcernedly sharing Bloom's amorous interest in Gerty MacDowell's underwear or the uninhibited flow of Molly's erotically adulterous thoughts as she dozes off to sleep. Virginia Woolf was, however, to be proved correct when she foresaw that the innovations she and Joyce were introducing to the novel would not prevail for long, that they constituted only a passing, experimental phase:

> Ah, but I'm doomed! As a matter of fact, I think that we all are. It is not possible now, and never will be, to say I renounce. Nor would it be a good thing for literature were it possible. This generation must break its neck in order that the next may have smooth going. For I agree with you that nothing is going to be achieved by us. Fragments – paragraphs – a page perhaps: but no more. Joyce to me seems strewn with disaster. I can't even see, as you see, his triumphs. A gallant approach, that is all that is obvious to me; then the usual smash and splinters.[16]

The intellectual demands made upon the reader by the stream-of-consciousness technique, the page-long sentences representing the uninterrupted flow of ideas, the difficulty of grasping abstruse, unexplained allusions, and the lack of structural form intrinsic to an associative drift of thought made such novels eagerly discussed for their innovative experimentation but comparatively rarely read. Joyce's attempt to provide an artificial structural progression by means of sequential parallels to the Homeric epic assumed a detailed knowledge of that earlier work that few readers possessed, making it unlikely that they would recognise Cerberus in Father Coffey or identify in the fulminating Citizen in the pub an allusion to the Cyclopean Polyphemus without the assistance of the elaborate key provided some years later by Stuart Gilbert.[17] Accordingly, there were few who read *Ulysses* from cover to cover. And the same held true for their American counterpart, William Faulkner, whose books were often referred to but again rarely read. By 1945, as Malcolm Cowley has noted, not one of his seventeen novels remained in print, their sales reviving only after Faulkner had been persuaded to write a lengthy introduction setting out more intelligibly the chronology of events which are presented jumbled out of sequence in the novels themselves, where the characters' thoughts shift unpredictably back and forth from past to present. As a result, the novel of the stream of consciousness in effect disappeared from the literary scene in the forties, writers returning to a more conventional format, reinstating the authorial narrator and reinstituting structural unity, the technique of interior monologue being retained only as a subdued and minor element to indicate the flow of the characters' inner thoughts. The demise of the stream-of-conscious novel and the return to earlier forms left the author, therefore, once again confronting the problem of the invalidated hero, and needing to find an alternative method of evoking sympathy and respect for the central character while no longer reliant on the moral qualities previously endorsed by society.

In contrast to such reader-reception critics as Wolfgang Iser and Stanley Fish who, downplaying the authority of the text, have placed major emphasis upon the personal interpretations that each individual brings to the work, Hans Jauss has perceived the relationship between reader and text in terms of a two-directional discourse. If the reader brings to the work in each generation a referential framework derived in part from past tradition and in part from the codes embedded within contemporary culture, Jauss suggests that an innovative author aware of those assumptions, whether moral, philosophical, social or aesthetic, is obligated to wean the reader away from them and to construct new or modified values to replace them. For literary historians, he suggests, more important than a knowledge of the framework of a period should be a sense of the author's resistance to it, of the disparity between the reader's horizon of expectation and the ways in which the work satisfies, surpasses, disappoints or refutes the presumptions of its first audience.[18] In that context, there needs to be discerned within each work the process of seduction whereby the writer, by means of subtle manipulation from within the text, lures the reader away from his or her preconditioning, from the established conceptions brought to the work, and encourages the adoption of a new set of criteria by which the actions of the fictional protagonists are to be judged.

If we apply that insight to our present topic, it becomes apparent that a major requisite for weaning readers away from the contemporary antipathy to traditional heroes, the awareness that the basis of their supposed virtues has been disqualified in the new configuration, is to lull them into a sense of security, to dispel potential opposition as a prelude to winning eventual approval for the new fictional figure. Hence the anti-hero's initial presentation in these novels as a failure, unable to cope with the pressures of the modern world, a misfit in society, crushed by the demands placed upon him, a strategy providing assurance that the author is fully cognisant of the recent negations and responsive to the wasteland concept of the twentieth century.

In Greene's *The Power and the Glory* (1940), one of the earliest and finest examples of the genre, the problem of reader expectation faced by the author was twofold. In choosing to adopt Catholicism as a central theme in his fiction, novels which, in contrast to François Mauriac's, were directed in Britain to a predominantly non-Catholic readership, he needed, in addition to countering the potential distrust of the conventional hero, to circumvent or in some way overcome the widespread prejudice against the Catholic priesthood. It was a prejudice that he himself had witnessed in his Protestant youth, before his conversion:

> I had always, even when I was a schoolboy, listened with impatience to the scandalous stories of tourists concerning the priests they had encountered in remote Latin villages (this priest had a mistress, another was constantly drunk), for I had been adequately taught in my Protestant history books what Catholics believed.[19]

Accordingly, the nameless priest serving as the central figure is presented here in a manner calculated to disarm both of these potential antagonisms and thus may serve us here as a doubly effective instance of the confrontational or resistive quality of the new genre.

The priest, in contrast to the noble, dedicated martyr one might have expected in a pro-Catholic novel, conforms more closely to the unflattering stereotype as commonly conceived by detractors. Undistinguished in appearance ('a small man dressed in a shabby dark city suit'), he is, we soon learn, a wine-bibber or so-called 'whisky priest' as well as the father of an illegitimate child. There could be little opposition to such a central character either on the grounds of Catholic propagandising or on the grounds of the modernist rejection of traditional heroes, and the reader could feel secure in reading on. Moreover, the deliberate evocation of Eliot's *Waste Land* in the opening scene – the bleakness and seediness of the setting, the sterility of existence in a country impoverished by a harsh dictatorship, with Tench, the dentist, listlessly awaiting the pain-relieving canister of ether that he knows will never arrive – such drabness and despair leave no doubt of the author's familiarity with the spiritual quandary of his time in a manner designating him as admissible to readership by the intellectual avant garde. Vultures wait under the blazing Mexican sun for the humans to become carrion; Tench, with a faint feeling of rebellion, wrenches up a piece of the road with his splintering finger-nails, and tosses it feebly towards them though knowing that nothing will change the dreariness of his surroundings.[20]

That lulling of potential opposition has, however, led to a disturbing consensus among critics, a misunderstanding of a central element highly germane to the concept of the anti-hero both in this work and in subsequent instances of the genre. Instead of perceiving the priest's negative portrayal as only the initial stage in a subtly developing process during which the damaging aspects will gradually be discarded or their implications reversed, they have taken the disparagement at face value, as if it were the author's final evaluation. Roger Sharrock states unreservedly in his overall description of the priest,

> He is a drunkard and has broken his vow of chastity: more seriously he has not achieved anything: 'What an impossible fellow I am, he thought, and how useless.' The villagers are too terrified to shelter him: he cannot help his child: the American will not make his confession to him: he is caught in the end like a rat in a trap.

Francis Kunkel describes him categorically as 'a drunkard and a fornicator', employed by Greene to illustrate how God can use an imperfect human to attain his ends. In the academic journal devoted to criticism of Greene's work, Michael Higgins summarises the priest's spiritual unsuitability to his task: 'The hounded cleric in Mexico has long been unfit as Christ's representative,' quoting as substantiation a passage from the priest's meditation on his own failings:

> He was a bad priest, he knew it. They had a word for his kind – a whisky priest, but every failure dropped out of sight and mind: somewhere they accumulated in secret – the rubble of his failures. One day they would choke up, he supposed, altogether the source of grace. (p. 60)

And R.B. Lewis, in a widely respected study of the picaresque saint in the modern novel, after noting how badly the priest has broken the laws of his church, concludes that he is a rogue, a *picaro*, in several kinds of ways; his contradictory character includes much of the comical unpredictability of the traditional *picaro*; and the narrative Greene has written about him is perhaps the most patently picaresque of any we are considering – the lively story of the rogue on his travels, or better, on his undignified flights from and toward the forces of destruction.

To define the priest here as a rogue or *picaro* is, I believe, a travesty of criticism. With regard to the latter it would be difficult to find a single passage in the novel that hints at any comedy or comic unpredictability in his character that could identify him with the genre of the picaro, the experiencing of a series of amusing escapades. Even K.C.J. Kurismmootil, who has written one of the most sensitive studies of Greene, follows the same line. While admitting that the priest's character does gain depth as the novel progresses, he notes with some degree of puzzlement how unfit the priest was for his vocation:

> He is an anomaly of a priest and a scandal to the pious. A weakling and a brandy-bibber, corrupted with an ill-begotten child, he is by his own admission a coward. Nothing about him seems to measure up to the dignity we normally associate with the figure of a protagonist. He appears like a rogue, a *picaro*; as much unpredictable as he is ridiculous.[21]

Such comments abound in Greene criticism, usually followed by an admission that, by the end of the novel, the priest does, in some strange way, seem to redeem himself and to achieve at least the possibility of grace, although the means whereby he is even partially regenerated is, in such commentaries, left unspecified. I propose to argue that the reverse of this reading is true, that the priest does not progress or change, eventually achieving some hope of forgiveness but is, from the very opening of the novel and throughout the narrative itself, Greene's ideal of what a Catholic priest should be – not a model the Vatican would endorse but one, the author suggests, fundamentally more deserving of respect and admiration than the martyrs traditionally venerated in the church; and, moreover, that in this respect Greene provided a prototype not only for the figure of the anti-hero but also for the pattern of his presentation within the mid-twentieth-century novel.

M.M. Bakhtin revealed some years ago how, in the best type of novel, there exists a muted dialogue, a suppressed sub-text that undercuts, modifies and at times may even parody the surface theme, creating a coded ambivalence to which the sensitive reader is intended to respond, not always at the conscious level. That countertext is present invisibly, as an actualising background for creating and perceiving the ultimate theme. The two elements, text and countertext, represent respectively what Bakhtin terms the *centripetal* and the *centrifugal*, the centripetal appearing to reinforce contemporary attitudes while the centrifugal resists or modifies them, producing thereby a linguistic tension or heteroglossia:

> Every concrete utterance of a speaking subject serves as a point where centrifugal as well as centripetal forces are brought to bear. The processes of centralisation and decentralisation, of unification and disunification, intersect in the utterance; the utterance not only answers the requirements of its own language as an individualised embodiment of a speech act, but it answers the requirements of heteroglossia as well; it is in fact an active participant in such speech diversity.[22]

That concept is distinctly relevant to this novel. For if at the surface or ostensible level the priest is presented 'centripetally', in conformity with the unsympathetic view of the Catholic priesthood prevalent among contemporary readers, at the same time a concomitant 'centrifugal' impulse reshapes that impression, gradually encouraging a more charitable and appreciative response, a progressive and retrospective reassessment of the priest's supposed delinquencies. In effect, therefore, it is not the priest who changes but the reader's assessment of him, as the truth of his spiritual condition gradually emerges into the light.

The key to that process of reappraisal lies in a factor characteristic of the new anti-hero genre – the reader's gradual realisation, carefully directed by the author, that those self-condemnations upon which critics have so confidently based their negative interpretation of his character are in fact fundamentally suspect, that we are to learn in the course of the novel to dissociate ourselves from them as invalid. In the twentieth-century dispensation, with its profound doubts, scepticism and loss of direction, the traditional hero's self-confidence, his assurance of his moral rectitude has no place. To be acceptable, the protagonist must reflect the general despair of the age, he must be disillusioned, unsure of the ethical probity of his actions, incapable of coping with the pressures of living. He must be the embodiment not of exemplary virtues marred by some minor, impermanent flaw but (at least at the initial impression) of manifold deficiencies and inadequacies. Accordingly, the priest here is utterly self-deprecatory, not through false modesty but out of a deep conviction that he is indeed a total failure, irrecoverably damned for the sins he has committed, wearily living out his term until facing the inevitable and, he believes, censorious tribunal on the Day of Judgement. He is constantly aware of his own unworthiness which, as he puts it, rests at all times like a weight at the back of his tongue. 'I don't know a thing about the mercy of God,' he confesses to the lieutenant, 'I don't know how awful the human heart looks to Him. But I do know this – that if there's ever been a single man in this state damned, then I'll be damned too,' adding slowly, 'I wouldn't want it to be any different. I just want justice, that's all.' (p. 200) There are, indeed, more specific reasons for the reader's gradual rejection of such self-castigation, but even in general terms the fact that in Christianity pride constitutes the most reprehensible of sins and humility the cardinal virtue in itself creates from the beginning of the novel a submerged countertext, a silent contradiction of his statements alleviating our disapproval of his defects.

The more potent reasons for the eventual reassessment of the priest's character are conveyed in numerous hints earlier in the novel, hints that do not need to be traced individually here; but they reach their culmination in a single paragraph which conveys, not from his own unforgiving self-analysis but from what lies concealed within the passage, the true nature of those supposed sins and failures we so readily condemned earlier. It confirms our progressive recognition of the redeeming elements that he himself constantly misconstrues, our growing admiration for the virtues he has managed to preserve under such enormously difficult conditions. In conversation with the lieutenant shortly before his death, he recalls how, when commanded by the communist regime to break his vows of celibacy and to marry or suffer the penalty of death, the other priests (with the exception of Padre José, who chose to betray his priestly office) had elected to flee the country, leaving him in solitude:

'It was when [they] left I began to go to pieces. One thing went after another. I got careless about my duties. I began to drink. It would have been much better, I think, if I had gone too. Because pride was at work all the time. Not love of God.' He sat bowed on the packingcase, a small plump man in Mr Lehr's cast-off clothes. He said, 'Pride was what made the angels fall. Pride's the worst thing of all. I thought I was a fine fellow to have stayed when the others had gone. And then I thought I was so grand I could make my own rules. I gave up fasting, daily Mass. I neglected my prayers and one day because I was drunk and lonely well, you know how it was, I got a child. It was all pride. Just pride because I'd stayed. I wasn't any use, but I stayed. At least, not much use. I'd got so that I didn't have a hundred communicants a month. If I'd gone I'd have given God to twelve times that number.' (p. 196)

Throughout this passage, the countermanding subtext defined by Bakhtin is at work, taking precedence over the overt meaning of the priest's words as, through the sombre recriminations of the priest, can be discerned factors that in his simplicity and humility he totally ignores, factors not only mitigating but frequently justifying what might appear outwardly as vice or sin. One central point he entirely overlooks in that self-flagellatory passage is that, in contrast to the priests who fled, he had chosen to risk his life, to remain behind fulfilling his duty despite the very real threat of capital punishment. That act of courage he sees dismissively as arising from pride, an evaluation that no sensitive reader can accept. Moreover, there emerges at this point a major distinction between the new anti-hero and the conventional, often unbelievable hero of the past facing all dangers unafraid, secure in their knowledge of the rectitude of their actions. Instead, the priest is lonely and fearful, desperately needing to bolster his courage by an occasional sip of brandy, a practice that slowly takes its hold upon him ('I began to drink'). If he is a whisky priest, he has become one, we now learn, not through the self-indulgence traditionally associated with monks and clerics, a relish for the pleasures of wine-bibbing, but as a desperately needed aid in fulfilling the duties of his calling. If we are to weigh the dereliction of priestly responsibility evinced by his colleagues against the dedication of the priest in remaining, the occasional imbibing of a drink shrinks to insignificance, to a forgivable recourse in time of peril. That justification, however, does not prevent the priest from regarding his actions in the most damning light, seeing his remaining behind and the bolstering of his determination by drink as reprehensible weakness. And, one notes, almost all critics have accepted his self-condemnation, Michael Shelden writing, without the slightest support from the text, that his remaining behind

> gives him the chance to be the pope in one little corner of the world, to be the sole keeper of all the mysteries of his religion. But this grand ambition turns into nothing more significant than a personal surrender to petty vices. He drinks heavily, plays card tricks, sleeps with a woman and makes her pregnant ... Whenever he is required to perform the traditional functions of a priest, he reveals his incompetence.[23]

The same contrast between his self-condemnations and the positive implications to be derived from his actions holds true of the usefulness of his having remained in Mexico. He could indeed, as he claimed in that passage, have granted absolution to twelve times the number of communicants were he to have crossed the border; but he does not add, as the perceptive reader would, that in the neighbouring country there were at least twelve times as many priests to administer absolution, while here he was the sole resource for his communicants, risking his life every day to perform the rites of priesthood in a country deserted by his peers. In that same passage, he castigates himself for being neglectful in his duties, for having ceased fasting on the days assigned – at a time, as he omits to mention, when he was literally starving, when fasting, a practice intended to encourage abstemiousness, would have been an absurdity. As he remarked earlier,

> it was only one more surrender. The years behind him were littered with similar surrenders – feast days and fast days and days of abstinence had been the first to go: then he had ceased to trouble more than occasionally about his breviary – and finally he had left it behind altogether at the port in one of his periodic attempts at escape. Then the altar stone went – too dangerous to carry with him. He had no business to say Mass without it; he was probably liable to suspension, but penalties of the ecclesiastical kind began to seem unreal in a state where the only penalty was the civil one of death. (p. 60)

Again the subtext is powerfully at work, as the technical rituals of altar stone and breviary become nugatory beside the glowing fact of his courage in continuing, at the risk of his own life, to care for the spiritual needs of his parishioners. Even his reference to his attempt to escape, the scene depicted at the opening of the novel, reveals a man desperate to flee from a pursuit that has become unbearable yet turning back at the call for his priestly office from a supposedly dying woman, a call he knows from experience is almost certainly baseless.

Then there is the sin of his having fathered a child – a sin so grave in a priest that one might think it impossible to find extenuating circumstances. But those extenuating factors are provided later in the novel when we are informed, again obliquely, of circumstances that he, with his harsh self-appraisal, totally ignores. So far from having maintained a regular mistress as we are originally led to suspect, for having, as one critic recently put it, experienced a 'deplorable fall from grace' through drinking and fornication,[24] the priest, it transpires, fathered the child in a single, isolated incident under conditions so strongly mitigating as in effect to absolve him. Not only was he blindly intoxicated at the time, unaware of his actions as a result of having tried to fortify his courage, but, as we learn from her own lips, he was also the victim of a calculating peasant woman, eager for the celebrity of being known in the village as a priest's mistress, a woman who deliberately seduced him in his state of inebriation. As always, that alleviating factor is not mentioned by the priest; we learn of it only when she complains of the change in circumstances that has deprived her of the renown she had craved: 'When you-know-what happened, I was proud. I thought the good days would come back. It's not everyone who's a priest's woman. And the child ... I thought you could do a lot for her ... ' (p. 79).

There is, however, a further aspect to the priest's remorse over that incident. For his most grievous fault, he believes, a fault more serious than the crime itself, is his sin in loving the outcome of that deplorable event, his daughter Brigitta, when a truly repentant sinner should, he is convinced, abhor the proceeds of his crime:

> He said, 'I don't know how to repent.' That was true: he had lost the faculty. He couldn't say to himself that he wished his sin had never existed, because the sin seemed to him now so unimportant and he loved the fruit of it. (p. 128)

In the course of the novel he has remarked repeatedly that he is no theologian, only a simple village priest; and in regard to that act we are led to realise that he is guilty of a doctrinal error. While a thief, it is true, must, as a precondition for divine forgiveness, renounce the proceeds of his crime in addition to regretting the deed, that requirement is patently inapplicable when the outcome of the sin is a living child. On the contrary, the truest form of atonement in that situation is full acceptance of parental responsibility and unbounded love for the offspring, a love such as the priest does indeed experience for Brigitta, even at the price, he believes, of eternal damnation.[25] Once again, therefore, the anti-hero's condemnation of his actions is countermanded by the assessment to which Greene directs the reader, this discrepancy constituting one of the major characteristics of the genre at large, whereby the ultimate message of the novel is to be found not in the anti-hero's interpretation of his actions but in the dissent that they evoke from the attentive reader.

The priest, at least as I have characterised him, does not mature in the course of the novel – a factor that might appear to detract from the literary effectiveness of the novel – nor does he obtain deeper spiritual insights into his condition but, I would argue, remains essentially the same at the end as he was at the beginning. Yet the novel is far from static, since he evolves not within himself but through his gradual transformation in the reader's estimation. There is, indeed, support for this reading in a remark made by Greene. Dismissing the accepted critical interpretation of the priest as progressing from sinfulness to saintliness – a process described by Georg Gaston as his 'arduous journey from corruption to redemption' during which his Christian understanding gradually matures[26] – Greene declared unequivocally that, 'The priest and the lieutenant remained themselves to the end; the priest, for all his recollection of periods in his life when he was different, never changed.'[27] A distinction is of course to be made, as this comment acknowledges, between the priest as we meet him in this novel, struggling to fulfil his duties in a country under a vicious anti-Catholic regime, and his earlier career long before the story began when he had been utterly different, a self-satisfied clergyman complacently enjoying the good things of life, a fat youngish priest who stood with one plump hand splayed out authoritatively, as depicted in the photograph on the notice-board in the lieutenant's office. (p. 93) But such scenes are, as Greene noted, outside the parameters of the novel itself, recollections from a more distant past emphasising the contrast in living conditions as well as the profound change in his character that had followed the communist takeover. It is not a process of maturation occurring during the course of the novel. And the fact that, when he does eventually cross the border into safety, he finds himself subtly corrupted by that easy way of life, charging higher fees for baptismal rites, serves as a covert incentive for him to return to the battlefield, a recognition that the true purpose of priesthood is not to foster ladies' guilds or build expensive churches, but to assist the needy, comfort the suffering and lead the sinful to penitence.

Much critical attention has been focused in recent years on the principle of framing, the process whereby a painter, photographer or writer may deliberately exclude parts of a scene in order to stimulate the viewer mentally to extend its limits and to conjecture the hidden elements beyond.[28] Rubens' atectonic canvas *The Fall of the Rebel Angels*, with its myriad figures cascading down from heaven, reinforces the sense of infinite space by limiting it, by allowing the frame to slice through the bodies of those located at the edge, creating the impression of hundreds of similarly cascading bodies existent beyond the visual parameters. For literature, Hemingway had employed a similar principle of exclusion, declaring that a writer of prose 'may omit things that he knows, and the reader, if the writer is writing truly enough, will have a feeling of those things as strongly as though the writer had stated them.'[29] So in this novel, the omission of all mention of extenuating circumstances in the priest's self-accusations prompts us to search for those missing mitigating factors more diligently than if they had been supplied and, once we have perceived them, encourages us to place in those unstated elements more trust than if they had been specified.

Greene's creation of the mid-century anti-hero as a means of coping with the invalidation of the traditional hero and of combating the potential hostility of the Protestant reader finds its reverse strategy in his characterisation of the lieutenant. If the priest surprises us by his initially negative presentation in a patently pro-Catholic novel, the lieutenant, the representative of an oppressive, fiercely anti-religious and inhumanly totalitarian regime, emerges not as a sadistic torturer nor, in accordance with the usual stereotypes, as exploiting his rank to indulge in the luxuries denied to the proletariat but as an idealist, genuinely dedicated to alleviating the misery of the poor, selfless in his devotion to the task he has undertaken, and carrying within him 'his secret of love', prompting him at one point charitably to donate some of his own money to the unrecognised priest. At the end of the novel, despite his personal hatred of religion, he compassionately (and in direct contradiction of his own principles) attempts to find a confessor for the priest before the latter's execution. That he is in certain ways the priest's counterpart has long been noted. Unlike the *jefe*, he lives ascetically, spurning all luxury and comfort, indifferent to women, his room resembling a monastic cell, with Greene adding the further comment that there was something of a priest in his intent, observant walk, a theologian going back over the errors of the past. He is thus, it might seem, a fairly typical lapsed Catholic, disillusioned, as he says, by the white muslin dresses, the candles, and the laciness of a church reprehensibly impervious to the poverty of the peasants[30] yet, like many lapsed Catholics, unconsciously retaining, even after his defection, certain minor habits of his youth.

That authorial comment, however, points to a major aspect of the novel. Were he merely a disillusioned Catholic, a communist disgusted at the church's exploitation of the poor and at its demand for the payment of tithes out of the peasants' meagre earnings, whatever residue of his younger days he might unconsciously retain, such as his intent method of walking, he would surely reject consciously everything in his character and way of life that might resemble the theologian or priest he had come to detest. If, as was noted earlier, revolutionaries often unconsciously adopt certain elements of the traditions they are discarding, they do not normally retain the same way of life, such as the monastic, celibate existence the lieutenant preserves. There is the hint in Greene's description that the lieutenant functions here not as a foil to the priest,

the representative of a system opposed to Catholic values and principles –
the self-indulgent, exploitive *jefe* functions in that capacity – but, in a very
profound sense, as a mirror-image or alter ego of the priest. The basis for
apprehending this *Doppelgänger* relationship is embedded in one of the
earliest descriptions of him, where Greene is making a point intimately
related to the twentieth-century predicament we have been following:

> The lieutenant sat down upon his bed and began to take off his boots. It
> was the hour of prayer. Black-beetles exploded against the walls like
> crackers. More than a dozen crawled over the tiles with injured wings.
> It infuriated him to think that there were still people in the state who
> believed in a loving and merciful God. There are mystics who are said
> to have experienced God directly. He was a mystic, too, and what he
> had experienced was vacancy – a complete certainty in the existence of
> a dying, cooling world, of human beings who had evolved from
> animals for no purpose at all … (pp. 24–5)

The black beetles exploding against the walls like crackers are not inserted as
casual background description but as symbols, pointing to the lieutenant's
conviction of the utter pointlessness of the godless Darwinian world in
which he finds himself, where human beings 'who had evolved from
animals for no purpose at all' are subject to the same vagaries of an absurd
and capricious fate as those hapless insects. So far from being a confirmed
secularist rejecting religion as an outmoded set of superstitions, he is
essentially a mystic, one who had in his youth longed desperately for a
priestly vocation but had been denied it. At a crucial moment in his life, one
may assume from this passage, when he had been closest to fulfilling his
longing for a 'vocation', for a divine call to priesthood, the conclusions
intellectually arrived at within his twentieth-century setting had disqualified the promptings of his heart, in the manner so frequently experienced
by his contemporaries. His religious yearning had been transformed into a
dedication to the alternative messianic hope offered to his generation, the
apocalyptic vision offered by communism to which he now dedicates the
same priestlike devotion as he had hoped to pledge to the church. It
becomes clear in that context that his rabid hatred towards those who
continue to believe in a loving deity is a hatred born of envy and frustration,
a Freudian desire to kill elements in himself that he cannot eradicate. He is,
in fact, a *prêtre manqué*, a figure recurrent in Greene's novels, his day still
haunted by the regular pattern of 'the hour of prayer', of matins, nones and
vespers, a pattern to which he remains linked emotionally as he continues
to live, if in a different context, the life of a selfless ascetic.

The lieutenant is thus a mirror image of the priest in the sense of what the latter might have been had he, at that same vital moment in his life, succumbed to the pressures of twentieth-century secularism. They are both compassionately dedicated to relieving the suffering of the poor and the humble of this world, the lieutenant aiming at the economic and material advancement of the masses, the priest devoted to their spiritual or eternal well-being.[31] And if, it is implied, the priest chose his path through lack of academic learning, clinging simply to his faith unaware of those larger twentieth-century issues, the contrast between the two provides a structural strategy endowing with especial pathos the final scene, the debate between the two men shortly before the execution. That debate constitutes not only a dialogue between the contrasting premises of communism and Christianity but also, and perhaps more movingly, a silent inner dialogue between the lieutenant and his suppressed, unfulfilled self.

The crucial topic in that scene is, once again, the value of the individual in the light of modernist theory. The lieutenant, focusing like Gletkin on the distant fulfilment of the communist ideal, executes, however painful it may be to him, innocent peasants in the cause of achieving that end. In order to compel them to identify the priest, he announces that, should they refuse, he will randomly select a hostage to be shot, and he proceeds to carry out the threat. As they gaze sullenly at the ground, refusing to betray the priest, he remonstrates irritably that he too abhors killing, that in his eyes the peasants are worth far more than the priest, that he wishes to give them the world; but that sentiment does not prevent him, on their continued refusal, from selecting a young man for execution to the agonised protests of his mother. Hence the exchange in the final conversation with the priest: 'Those men I shot. They were my own people. I wanted to give them the whole world'; and the priest's reply, 'Well, who knows? Perhaps that's what you did.'

That reply is not a clever debating-point, a reminder that the priest believes in a world-to-come whereas the lieutenant acknowledges nothing beyond the terrestrial. It marks rather the culmination of a theme developed as a *leitmotif* throughout the course of the novel – Greene's claim for the sacrosanctity of each person, however nugatory, despicable, or unequivocally evil he or she may appear to human eyes. For the lieutenant, the individual must be sacrificed for the good of the cause and ultimate benefit of the majority, while the priest's concern at all times is not with the body but with the soul, with the enormous responsibility he bears for the eternal fate of each person, whether parishioner or non-parishioner. He will return from safety across the border, fully aware that he is walking into a trap that will cost him his life, if there is even the faintest chance that the murderous gangster may repent at the final moment, so that he will be there to administer extreme unction, the ritual condition for salvation in Catholic belief. The soul even of so contemptible a creature remains to him of immense significance.

In the hostage scene, one may wonder momentarily why the priest declines to identify himself and thereby sacrifice himself to save others after the model of Christ. Once he surrenders, the others will be allowed to go free. Is it cowardice on his part? The text unequivocally allays that suspicion. It reveals how much he longs to take that course, to disclose his identity and save the others. He approaches, indeed, as close to such self-surrender as possible – 'lieutenant … I'm getting too old to be much good in the fields. Take me.' But that is the furthest he may go. He recognises that, were he to reveal himself as the priest, he would be depriving of eternal salvation any peasant preferring death to betraying him, robbing the faithful of the eternal bliss ordained for martyrs; and that he must not do. It is that concept that prompts his comment that by killing the hostages the lieutenant may have unintentionally given them the whole world.

The concept of the sacrosanctity of the individual is central to the priest's faith, as Greene points out repeatedly in the novel. The most repulsive figure next to the gangster is the half-caste, a character enacting the role of Judas to the priest's unconscious portrayal of Jesus. Malicious, greedy, deceitful, planning to betray him to the police for the few pesos offered as a reward, the mestizo would seem deserving of hatred and contempt, above all by his intended victim. But the feelings he evokes in the priest are very different:

> at the centre of his own faith there always stood the convincing mystery that we were made in God's image. God was the parent, but He was also the policeman, the criminal, the priest, the maniac, and the judge. Something resembling God dangled from the gibbet or went into odd attitudes before the bullets in a prison yard or contorted itself like a camel in the attitude of sex. He would sit in the confessional and hear the complicated dirty ingenuities which God's image had thought out, and God's image shook now, up and down on the mule's back, with the yellow teeth sticking out over the lower lip, and God's image did its despairing act of rebellion with Maria in the hut among the rats. He said, 'Do you feel better now? Not so cold, eh? Or so hot?' and pressed his hand with a kind of driven tenderness upon the shoulders of God's image. (p. 101)

As he remarks elsewhere, 'When you visualised a man or woman carefully, you could always begin to feel pity – that was a quality God's image carried with it. When you saw the lines at the corners of the eyes, the shape of the mouth, how the hair grew, it was impossible to hate.' (p. 131) And again in line with that older tradition, with the Christian ideal of humility, the priest, recalling what he unforgivingly terms his own 'despairing act of rebellion with Maria', evaluates himself as morally inferior even to the mestizo.

That self-deprecation carried with it a certain danger of which Greene was cognisant. The humility of the priest could carry with it an impression of complacency, a suspicion that he is aware at some subdued level that his actions could lead to martyrdom and glory. Even a hint of such self-interest on the priest's part could militate against his effectiveness in the novel. Greene employs two methods of dealing with the problem; the first, less important, is the priest's genuine incredulity at any mention of his candidacy for martyrdom, a fear, indeed, that, were he to be caught and executed, dying in the name of his religion and thereby qualifying technically as a martyr, such status would bring shame instead of honour on the church. Hence the priest's involuntary response to any mention of such absurdity:

> The priest giggled: he couldn't stop himself. He said, 'I don't think martyrs are like this.' He became suddenly serious, remembering Maria's words – it wouldn't be a good thing to bring mockery on the church. He said, 'Martyrs are holy men. It is wrong to think that just because one dies ... no. I tell you I am in a state of mortal sin.' (p. 126)

More fundamental, however, was the element in this novel that made it theologically unacceptable to the Catholic authorities, at least in its present form. In 1953, Cardinal Pizzardo, after examining the novel on behalf of the Vatican's censors, informed the archbishop of Westminster of his adverse response, concluding his report:

> I am therefore writing to beg Your Eminence to inform Mr. Graham Greene with your accustomed tact of the unfavourable verdict of the Holy See on his book, and to exhort him to be more constructive from a Catholic point of view in his writings, as all good people expect him to be. As for the book in question, Your Eminence will not fail to ensure that the author does not allow further reprints or translations of it to be published without his introducing into it the necessary corrections that the foregoing remarks would suggest.[32]

Fortunately, Greene ignored the advice, leaving the novel unchanged on the excuse that the copyright lay with the publishers. The Vatican's opposition arose in large part from the method he adopted for treating the danger outlined above, namely the contrast he provided between his anonymous priest and the holy martyrs or saints of the church as they had been and continued to be traditionally venerated. Where Catholic hagiography, both in its official accounts and in the versions produced for educational purposes, had consistently emphasised the imperturbable faith, the untroubled devotion and the unhesitating courage of saints as they laid down their lives for their beliefs, in the new dispensation where psychological investigation had penetrated beyond outer appearances to the medley of traumas, anxieties and hidden terrors operative within, far more admirable for the modern reader was the martyr's struggle to overcome an instinctive dread of physical torture and death, to stifle fears and to suppress, however falteringly, a powerful and very natural impulse to flee.

To convey that aspect of the priest's character, Greene provides a tale within the tale, the account of Juan's martyrdom reverently read to Luis and his sisters by their mother, a story that highlights by contrast the traits within the priest which we will learn to admire. The foil or true contrast to the priest is not the lieutenant but this traditional martyr who, in this acknowledgedly Catholic novel, is presented as revoltingly smug. No-one, she reads to them, was 'more amused than Juan' when chosen to play Nero in the school play. That remark, intended by the author of the educational tract to display Juan's good humour and youthful sense of fun, is, to the perceptive reader, the first in a series of comments exposing what to Greene was an insufferable element in such hagiographic accounts, a revelation of Juan's deplorable arrogance, his conviction (even though the story informs us that he was known for his humility and piety) that the saintliness of his character makes him the clear choice for the role of the noble martyr in the play and not that of the evil Nero. The recurrence, in such accounts authorised by the church, of the saint's awareness of his own piety would seem, as Greene so rightly perceives, to betray instead the cardinal sin of pride. Such complacency constitutes the antithesis to the priest's dismay at Maria's jeering comment:

> She said, 'Suppose you die. You'll be a martyr, won't you? What kind of a martyr do you think you'll be? It's enough to make people mock.'
>
> That had never occurred to him – that anybody would consider him a martyr. He said, 'It's difficult. Very difficult. I'll think about it. I wouldn't want the Church to be mocked.' (p. 79)

The contrast the inner story affords reaches its culmination when the priest in this novel, having attempted to bolster his courage with whisky, desperately trying to keep up a bold front as he is led to his execution, finds his legs involuntarily buckling beneath him; while Juan, supremely confident of his own saintliness and certain of the joys awaiting him in heaven, happily (and nauseatingly) asks the jailer if the latter has come 'to lead him to the banquet'. His martyrdom, such comment reveals, is motivated not by altruistic self-sacrifice but by the promise of his celestial reward.

Analogous to this abhorrence of religious complacency is Greene's treatment of the consciously 'pious' in the novel, the only type of person with whom the priest and, by extension, Greene, find it difficult to empathise. For the nineteenth century, Browning's expression of contentment, 'God's in his heaven / All's right with the world,' while it may not have suited all moods in that period, was accepted as a basically valid viewpoint for Christian trust in a benevolent deity. But for the twentieth century, with its revelation of the cruelty of nature, such sentiments seemed grossly inappropriate. Religious faith, where it was retained, needed now to be a faith *despite* human suffering, an attitude exemplified in the title of Paul Tillich's theological tract, *The Courage To Be*. In such a setting, the priest can feel genuine affection and forgiveness for the prisoners in the jail, even when they are covertly indulging in sexual intercourse, but he finds it almost impossible to feel the same for the woman he meets there who self-righteously condemns them, or for the communicant across the border who, when urged by him to confess her real sins instead of her minor infractions concerning abbreviated prayers or fasting, replies with astonishment, 'But I'm a good woman, father!'

> He had always been worried by the fate of pious women. As much as politicians, they fed on illusion. He was frightened for them: they came to death so often in a state of invincible complacency, full of uncharity … He said in hard accents, 'I have a child.' (p. 127)

Such attacks on the supposedly devout within the church and on those selected to serve as exemplars of the faith were unlikely to endear Greene to the church authorities, especially with the unstated corollary that to be fully cognisant of one's faith, one needs to have experienced sin. The priest comes to realise that venial sins such as impatience, a trivial lie or having eaten on a fast day – the kind of sin usually recited by the pious in the confessional – could cut one off from grace more effectively than the worst malefactions. He himself, he comes to recognise, when comfortably installed in his parish before the revolution had really loved no-one, while now, after having fathered a child, he had learnt to empathise with the sinners of the world, to feel a profound kinship with and love for the supposed dregs of humankind of which he saw himself to be a member.

That contrast between the martyr Juan and the priest, especially in the scenes of their execution, parallels in its essence the difference between the nineteenth-century hero, assured of his moral standards and of his own impeccable devotion to them, and the anti-hero, scared, diffident, vulnerable and self-deprecatory, convinced he has failed to fulfil his ideals. Dickens's Nicholas Nickleby, on witnessing Squeers's brutality towards the schoolboys in his charge, sees himself as the representative and defender of society's noble principles:

> 'Wretch,' rejoined Nicholas, fiercely, 'touch him at your peril! I will not stand by and see it done; my blood is up, and I have the strength of ten such men as you. Look to yourself, for by Heaven I will not spare you, if you drive me on.' ... Concentrating into that one moment all his feelings of rage, scorn, and indignation, Nicholas sprang upon him, wrested the weapon from his hand, and, pinning him by the throat, beat the ruffian till he roared for mercy.[33]

For the modern reader, those assumptions now seem simplistic – not his attempt to rescue the boys, but his confident adoption of the role of justicer meting out punishment to a 'ruffian' in the name of moral uprightness. We require today a questioning of social values, a dissatisfaction with simple divisions of right and wrong, an agonised probing of self to determine one's real, hidden motivation, a sense, indeed, of the complexity of the human situation. If, therefore, Nicholas's response evoked the unhesitating approval of the nineteenth-century reader who identifies with the hero's sentiments, the end of this novel, in contrast, assumes the reader's dissociation from the priest's thoughts, a mental abjuration or disengagement from his convictions, not through disapproval of his actions but through a perception of his under-estimation of his own virtues and his unforgiving censure of his own supposed failings:

> What a fool he had been to think that he was strong enough to stay when others fled. What an impossible fellow I am, he thought, and how useless. I have done nothing for anybody. I might just as well have never lived ... He felt only an immense disappointment because he had to go to God empty-handed with nothing done at all. (p. 210)

If we may return at this point to the critical consensus concerning the novel, it is, I trust, apparent at this stage how far from the mark are those statements cited earlier in this chapter, the view that the priest is 'a picaresque rogue on his travels', that he is 'unfit as Christ's representative' that he is, at the conclusion 'caught like a rat in a trap', that there 'is, of course, only a small difference' between the priest and the dying American gangster,[34] evaluations citing as textual substantiation passages from his self-condemnations. Even the view that the novel recounts the maturing of a fallen figure into an eventual recipient of divine grace – Marie-Béatrice Mesnet maintains that 'this poor, corrupt man, who is little better than a thief, finds his vocation at the eleventh hour with the help of brandy'[35] – may be seen to fall short, since in fact he never changes. Intrinsic to the new genre of the anti-hero, then, not only in this novel but in the genre as it was to develop, is a movement from an initial impression of failure and despair towards the reader's gradual discernment of his superiority to those around him, to the perception that he has indeed a claim to heroic stature, not through a process of self-improvement in the course of the novel but as a quality inherent in him from the opening scenes.

There may be discerned, moreover, a developmental change in the novel in its treatment of a character's mental processes. In the nineteenth-century tradition, the author's disclosure of the thoughts passing through a character's mind was, whatever outward pretence or façade that character may have adopted, understood to be a disclosure of his or her true feelings. Thus we learn of Hetty Sorrel in *Adam Bede*: 'How she yearned to be back in her safe home again, cherished and cared for as she had always been ...' Freud, by depriving conscious thoughts of their ultimate authenticity and transferring such validity to the concealed fears, longings and traumas of the repressed self, had prompted novelists such as Woolf, Joyce and Faulkner to concentrate instead upon the borderline where the subconscious rises to make contact with, to affect and even to control the associative flow within a character's mind. The reader is impelled in such writings to search for the incestuous desires lurking behind Quentin's frenzy at his sister's marriage or the mother fixation disturbing Stephen Dedalus, to perceive underlying motivations of which the character is himself unaware. But now the genre of the anti-hero, while continuing to cast doubt on the validity of conscious thought, focuses not on the gap between conscious and subconscious thought, but on the contrast between the anti-hero's self-condemnation and the reader's perception of the laudable qualities unperceived by him and raising him above the moral level of his peers.

If it has been generally accepted that 'the anti-hero must summon up courage and reserves for a challenge he is inadequate to fulfil,'[36] one suspects, both from the instance of the priest and from other examples we shall be examining, that he emerges ultimately as far from inadequate to the task. Physically such anti-heroes may be defeated – executed, confined to a sanatorium or otherwise penalised by society – but spiritually they prove not only eminently qualified to address the challenges of the time but function as models for the way the author believes such challenges should be confronted. In brief, the anti-hero emerges not as social failure, picaro or rogue, nor even partial hero, but as an exemplar of moral integrity in a world that has lost its ethical and spiritual standards, his social ostracism exemplifying not an inferiority to his peers but a more refined ethical sensibility. By his innovative use of the genre, Greene not only circumvented the disqualified tradition of the hero but also, and perhaps more importantly, restored, despite the pessimism that won him the appellation of 'grim Greene', a sense of the potential nobility and dignity of the individual in the bleak surroundings of the twentieth century.

I would like briefly to examine one of Greene's later novels, still within this mid-century period, in order to reveal the subtlety and sophistication with which he developed his use of the anti-hero. *The Comedians* (1966), undertaken initially to protest against the brutal dictatorship of Papa Doc Duvalier in Haiti, emerged as a literary work of far wider and more durable quality, illustrating with especial effectiveness this technique of constructing positive standards in a world that seemed to have annulled them. In the setting of that regime, there might seem little room for the comedy suggested by the title. There is indeed, as usual in Greene's work, a vein of wry humour, usually in the minor scenes, but that is not the reason for the title. By employing at times the French form of the word, *comédien*, which in that language comprises all types of actors, serious as well as comic, he focuses upon the kind of comedy that approximates to tragedy, to the absurdity of the human condition as conceived in the twentieth century in a world ruled, if ruled at all, by a Being who, as Brown remarks, can be regarded only as a practical joker:

When I was a boy I had faith in the Christian God. Life under his shadow was a very serious affair; I saw Him incarnated in every tragedy. He belonged to the *lacrimae rerum* like a gigantic figure looming through a Scottish mist. Now that I approached the end of life it was only my sense of humour that enabled me sometimes to believe in Him. Life was a comedy, not the tragedy for which I had been prepared ... [37]

Embracing his mistress on their reunion, Brown comments that 'the corpse in the pool seemed to turn our preoccupations into comedy. The corpse of Doctor Philipot belonged to a more tragic theme; we were only a sub-plot providing light relief.' (p. 57)

That sense of cosmic absurdity permeates no less the drab opening scene, with its rusty cargo boat ironically named *Medea* in an age in which, as Krutch had foreseen, high tragedy was no longer viable, and bearing in its passenger list a confidence trickster claiming the dubious title of 'Major' Jones, a one-time marginal candidate for the American presidency ludicrously representing the vegetarian vote, his unworldly, eccentric wife, and the narrator, a nondescript Mr. Brown despondently returning to the empty hotel he owns in Haiti and to an almost equally empty love affair. The commonplace names – Jones, Smith and Brown – are, he notes, interchangeable, 'like comic masks in a farce.' On reaching Port au Prince and discovering his mistress Martha waiting in her car at their usual meeting-place, he assumes at once that she has an assignation with some new-found lover; while in the cry she utters on recognising him he hears gloomily only 'the kind of tone she might have used for a recurrent fever'. With so sordid or fatuous a cast, there seems little opportunity for an assertion of heroic values, for recording noble achievements, or for justifying Brown's strange opening statement that the modest stone on Jones's grave bears comparison with the finest sepulchral monuments in London, a stone that Brown is personally proud to have helped raise. That process of evaluative reversal as the characters, dismally aware only of their failings, rise in our estimation from contemptibility to grandeur forms one of the most fascinating and critically ignored aspects of the novel.

The title provides a key to the underlying theme of the work. For each of the main characters, it transpires, is a *comédien* in a special sense, acting out a fictitious role in order to disguise an underlying despair, adopting a mask as the only means of living through the agonising trial of mortal existence. Martha's husband, the ambassador, cognisant of his wife's infidelities, acts as though ignorant of her liaisons, attempting by such pretended insouciance to preserve their empty marriage. Brown's mother, unable to believe that her black paramour Marcel could really love so elderly a woman and hence assuming he is pursuing their affair only in hope of a legacy, writes him a note begging him to continue playing the roles of lovers they have undertaken:

> I know I'm an old woman and as you say a bit of an actress. But please go on pretending. As long as we pretend we escape. Pretend that I love

you like a mistress. Pretend that you love me like a lover. Pretend that I would die for you and that you would die for me. (p. 253)

Similarly, Brown, attempting to obtain Jones's release from prison, comments sarcastically of his action:

I thought of my mother's words to me, when I saw her for the last time, 'What part are you playing now?' I suppose I was playing a part – the part of an Englishman concerned over the fate of a fellow-countryman, of a responsible business man who saw his duty clearly and who came to consult the representative of his Sovereign. (p. 103)

This pattern of role-playing is Greene's altered version of the anti-hero mode. For if, in *The Power and the Glory*, the discrepancy between the statements of the anti-hero and the reader's evaluation had arisen from the priest's humility, here the theme has become universalised, the discrepancy emerging from the characters' attempt to create façades (to 'prepare a face to meet the faces that we meet') behind which they can hide their lugubrious view of the purposelessness of their existence and live out their lives with a modicum of efficiency. The parallel to the discrepancy between priest and reader in that earlier novel is to be found here in a different form. For however false such masking may be in the eyes of the actors themselves, however bitterly conscious they are of the gap between their true condition and the 'heroic' part each is acting out, gradually we are led to perceive that they eventually rise to merge into their adopted roles, fulfilling the heroic elements in the highest degree in their real lives. Marcel may be 'playing' the part of the lover, participating in an agreed make-believe; but on his mistress's death he hangs himself in despair, prompting Brown's surprised reflection, 'perhaps he was no *comédien* after all. Death is a proof of sincerity.' (p. 253) The ambassador, contemptible as he may seem in his pretended ignorance of his wife's disloyalty, ascends in our estimation as we come to learn that by that imperturbable insouciance he is in fact preserving the marriage for the sake of their child. And at a moment of emergency, that supposed insouciance leads him generously to offer a potential rival, Jones, refuge in his ambassadorial home. Smith, claiming the title of Presidential Candidate despite the preposterousness of that past attempt and, in that role, gravely attempting to establish a people's vegetarian centre under a regime where none of the populace could ever afford meat or fish has, nonetheless, by the end of the novel won Brown's unhesitating admiration for the nobility and courage with which he pursues his ideals:

'Perhaps we seem rather comic figures to you, Mr. Brown.'
'Not comic,' I said with sincerity, 'heroic.'

That praise holds true for the wife too, ludicrously advocating Yeastrel and Barmine as panaceas for world violence, fixed in her past role of demonstrator for human rights for the downtrodden blacks in Nashville, yet rising magnificently to a true defence of human rights in a manner crossing the black/white divide. Outraged to discover a black Tonton Macoute officer torturing Brown, she attacks Concasseur so ferociously, so imperiously, and so unexpectedly in her demotic French that he is impelled to call off his men in dismay. These, however, although valuable pointers to the central theme of the book, remain extraneous elements. It is the development of that pattern in the central characters, most notably in Brown himself, that is most revealing.

A remark appearing in Greene's much earlier novel, *The Ministry of Fear* (1943), provides a foretaste of this pattern, suggesting that he had already been thinking of producing a work embodying the idea. He wrote there:

> One could laugh at day-dreams, but so long as you had the capacity to day-dream, there was a chance that you might develop some of the qualities of which you dreamed. It was like the religious discipline: words however emptily repeated can in time form a habit, a kind of unnoticed sediment at the bottom of the mind until one day to your own surprise you find yourself acting on the belief you thought you didn't believe in.

And in this novel, the primacy of that pattern for the development of the story is confirmed in its epigraph, the lines from Thomas Hardy: 'who *seems* / Most kingly is the King.'

For 'Major' Jones the reader can have nothing but contempt in the opening scenes. He is, we learn, a cheat, a briber, and a fraud, pursued by the international police for criminal activity, and engaged at present in some form of shady arms deal. His claim to senior military rank, to having served with distinction in Burma is, we discover, utterly baseless. Yet by degrees he rises in our estimation, winning our sympathy first by his endearing humour, and then by the compassion aroused as we learn of his background – born out of wedlock to an unknown father, condemned to survive unaided in a hostile world, resorting to any expedient that would keep him from starvation, he yet retains throughout a cheerful resilience to misfortune. More significantly, his pose as an ex-officer, adopted in the hope of obtaining respect from others, blends into reality at the end of the novel when, totally ignorant of warfare, unable even to fire a gun, he agrees to lead a Haitian rebel force in a dangerous expedition. Despite his conviction that his military incompetence will soon be exposed and that his innate cowardice will betray him at the vital moment, he in fact wins his men's unhesitating admiration and respect, dying courageously and selflessly in the course of the abortive coup.

So bald a summary does scant justice to the subtlety of the gradual evaluative reversal but may suffice for our present purposes. The aspect so frequently missed in critical assessments of the novel is the intimate relationship between Jones and Brown, not merely in their similar backgrounds but, more importantly, in this process of Greene's reassertion of positive moral values. In the same way as the fringe characters had prepared the way for our understanding of Jones' merger into his adopted role, so Jones functions, like Gloucester in *King Lear*, as a simplified reflection of the central character's spiritual odyssey, a structural parallel from which we may learn to reassess Brown. Despite the patent contrasts between the two, Jones lacking the intellectual ability and emotional range of the narrator, they are close in their experience of life. Both are, we learn, illegitimate and fatherless, cast into the world to fend for themselves, both confidence tricksters, Brown having at one period supported himself by selling paintings bearing the forged signatures of well-known artists – a source of income redeemed, as he says, by the fact that it was harmless, the fake signatures giving pleasure to the purchasers while not depriving financially artists long dead. And they are both lapsed Catholics.

The initial negative impression of Jones had been produced by his covert actions, including his attempt to bribe the steward to change his cabin. But Brown's depressing condition we learn from his own lips, as the narrator of the story. His life is, he informs us, a total failure. The inheritor of a hotel deprived of its clientele by the dictatorship, he knows he will find no buyer for it. He is a cynic, has lost faith in everything, even Martha's love for him evoking from him no joy but the bitter premonition that her disloyalty to her husband bodes future disloyalty to himself: 'even your mistress's most extreme embrace is a proof the more that love doesn't last.' A paradigm of non-commitment, he has renounced all principles and ideals: 'somewhere years ago I had forgotten how to be involved in anything. Somehow, somewhere I had lost completely the capacity to be concerned.' Yet as with all anti-heroes, such self-assessments must be viewed with suspicion. We discover that he too is unforgivingly harsh in his self-condemnations, placing the worst possible interpretation on his actions in sour assumption of his moral and spiritual bankruptcy.

It comes as a surprise to realise, as Martha eventually perceives, that beneath that non-committal exterior and despite the illicit love affair, Brown is, of all things, again a *prêtre manqué*, a failed priest, one who had in his youth longed desperately for a vocation but, to his profound disappointment, had felt himself unworthy of the privilege of holy orders. Unlike the lieutenant of the earlier novel, his abrogation of the priesthood results not from an intellectual conflict but from a bitter conviction of unworthiness, a belief that he has not been found suited to the task.[38] As other boys fought with masturbation, he recalls, he had fought with faith at the seminary, but no inner voice had come to assure him of election. By now, he believes, all such ambition has been left behind him, his last vestige of faith having been blown away when, having arranged the expulsion that would free him from the hopeless struggle, he left the seminary. But it is a belief patently contradicted by the dream he continues to experience during the period covered by the novel, a dream symbolising his immense disappointment at having been denied a vocation:

> I fell asleep and dreamt I was a boy kneeling at the communion-rail in the college chapel in Monte Carlo. The priest came down the row and placed in each mouth a bourbon biscuit, but when he came to me he passed me by. The communicants on either side came and went away, but I knelt obstinately on. Again the priest distributed the biscuits and left me out. I stood up then and walked sullenly away. (p. 207)

In conformity with the new genre, his failure to achieve his ideal, the conviction of his unsuitability for priestly selection, arises not from weakness but from the loftiness of his standards, in this instance the deep respect he has for the priesthood and for the immense responsibility in undertaking holy orders. With that quality perceived, all his actions within the account that he provides as narrator demand reader reassessment, the uncharitable construction he places on them rejected, to be replaced by the truth we perceive hidden beneath. It is a task made more challenging by the fact that our only source is Brown himself. If in the passage quoted earlier he scornfully saw himself as 'playing the part' of an Englishman concerned over the fate of a fellow-countryman, we understand retrospectively the heroism implicit in that act, an act that could, as he well knew at the time, result in his own murder or torture at the hands of the Tontons Macoutes. More important is the striking contrast between his own version of the events climaxing the novel and the more valid interpretation of them towards which Greene has been leading us.

The motive that had prompted him to trap Jones into agreeing to lead the rebels Brown himself defines unequivocally as arising from his envy of Jones's success with Martha, his suspicion that the two are engaged in a love affair, and his desire therefore to remove his rival from proximity to her. As one critic remarks naively, accepting Brown's statement as authentic, 'his sole impulse is jealousy he has lost completely the capacity to be concerned.'[39] But, as always in these novels, there is a marked discrepancy between his harsh self-analysis and the truer evaluation to which the author directs us. Never will Brown admit to his real purpose, his hatred of tyranny and his commitment to the rebel cause whereby he will risk his life to smuggle Jones across the border and to provide the rebels with a leader. The author's suppression of that positive moral impulse compels the reader to discover and mentally assert it despite Brown's disavowal, a process endowing the impulse with a forcefulness and validity that could not be achieved overtly within the negative atmosphere of the mid-century.

In the final scenes of the novel, Brown's true motivation is revealed by means of a mirror technique in which Jones, functioning as Brown's *alter ego*, reflects through his own frank admissions the hidden elements motivating his companion, the threads of their discourse intertwining. Jones, no longer the brash figure he had attempted to project, feels a need to unburden himself before embarking on the campaign, disclosing to Brown his fear of going into battle. Unlike the fearless nineteenth-century hero, the anti-hero struggles with a very natural terror on the eve of the military expedition. In a scene patently echoing the confessional, a scene in which Brown finds himself ironically cast in the role of priest, Jones' confidences confirm the hints we have received concerning Brown's character. 'It was like meeting an unknown brother,' Brown realises as he listens to Jones's disclosures: 'Jones and Brown, the names were almost interchangeable, and so was our status. For all we knew, we were both bastards.' The relevance to Brown's own condition is patent as Jones, admitting his frustrated longing to be an army officer, poses the plaintive query: 'You can feel a vocation, can't you, even if you can't practise it?' Brown is prompted to wonder (with patent reference to himself) 'whether perhaps in his devious life [Jones] had been engaged on a secret and hopeless love-affair with virtue, watching virtue from a distance, hoping to be noticed, perhaps, like a child doing wrong in order to attract the attention of virtue.' (p. 267) When Jones divulges the second dream that haunted him, that of becoming the opulent owner of an elite golf club, Brown muses: 'Making money had been my dream also. Had there been another? I had no wish to search so far back.' He may decline to search back but the allusion to his days in the Jesuit seminary is clear. It is a dream persistent despite his denials, as reflected in the brass coffin paperweight marked with the letters 'R.I.P.' that he kept on his desk, a *memento mori* recalling, like the skull in a monastic cell, not only his own eventual death but also the need to perform for others the priestly rites of extreme unction and Christian burial.

Although the theme of priesthood lends a specifically Catholic aspect to the novel, Greene had, since his earlier novel, broadened his conception to provide a more humanistic range reaching beyond the sectarian. If Brown here is the central character on whom rests the primary focus, the choric figure who delivers the main message of the work is the avowed communist, Dr. Magiot.[40] It was he who had recognised the heroism of Brown's mother and it is he who now perceives the courage motivating Brown's actions. The letter he writes to Brown as he himself calmly awaits his death at the hands of the Tontons Macoutes carries Greene's final message:

> 'Communism, my friend, is more than Marxism, just as Catholicism – remember I was born a Catholic too – is more than the Roman Curia. There is a *mystique* as well as a *politique*. We are humanists, you and I. You won't admit it perhaps, but you are the son of your mother and you once took the dangerous journey which we all have take before the end. Catholics and Communists have committed great crimes, but at least they have not stood aside, like an established society, and been indifferent . . . I implore you – a knock on the door may not allow me to finish this sentence, so take it as the last request of a dying man – if you have abandoned one faith, do not abandon all faith. There is always an alternative to the faith we lose. Or is it the same faith under another mask?' (p. 286)

As the novel draws to its close, we are prompted to reassess the opening paragraph of the novel; for Brown's laudatory tribute to so unlikely a hero as Jones is now seen to apply to himself no less. Drifting purposelessly in a world that seemed to have lost all meaning, involved in a depressingly unsatisfactory love affair, bereft of ideals and moral principles, he had seemed unworthy of respect. If at the end he does not, like the priest in *The Power and the Glory*, achieve sainthood, he has, as we learn through the veil of his unforgiving self-deprecation and self-contempt, proved to be dedicated to far finer ideals than he will admit to, courageously resisting evil whatever base motives he may attribute to his actions, and emerging as worthy of praise similar to that which he had bestowed on his alter ego. Both had possessed their Edenic dreams, Jones his green golfcourse, Brown his vision of a naked girl swimming in the pool of his hotel; but both had suppressed or failed to acknowledge dreams of a more noble nature, Jones secretly in love with virtue and Brown with dedication to a sacred office. If they assume that their conscious dreams are unattainable, beyond the reach of such miserable failures as they conceive themselves to be, unknowingly they achieve in their own lives a dignity and integrity surpassing such dreams.

Characteristic of the critical reading of this novel is the assumption that its conclusion is negative, depicting the moral impotence of twentieth-century man. According to A.A. DeVitis, Brown, although fully aware of the evil palpable in Papa Doc's Haiti, is unable to commit himself either ideologically or emotionally to any rebel group, simply fleeing from the horror at the end. Grahame Smith, oblivious of the parallel offered by Jones and seeing nothing of Brown's heroism, quotes his final remarks as conclusive evidence of his failure. Michael Gorra, taking at face value Brown's statement 'We are the faithless,' assumes he remains passive in the final scenes, lacking belief in any moral imperative. But in reaching that conclusion Gorra overlooks the irony in the passage immediately subsequent to the quotation, a hint that reverses the self-condemnation: 'The argument interested me. I daresay it eased the never quiet conscience which had been injected into me without my consent, when I was too young to know, by the Fathers of the Visitation.' (p. 279) Brown himself may believe that he no longer succumbs to the urgings of that conscience, but the comment is an authorial pointer not to be missed, restated by Greene a page or two later for the benefit of the myopic:

> I remembered Martha saying, 'You are a *prêtre manqué*.' How strangely one must appear to other people. I had left involvement behind me, I was certain, in the College of the Visitation: I had dropped it like the roulette-token in the offertory. I had felt myself not merely incapable of love – many are incapable of that, but even of guilt. There were no heights and no abysses in my world – I saw myself on a great plain, walking and walking on the interminable flats. Once I might have taken a different direction, but it was too late now. When I was a boy the fathers of the Visitation had told me that one test of belief was this: that a man was ready to die for it. So Doctor Magiot thought too, but for what belief did Jones die?

We, however, do know by now for what belief Jones died, having learnt of the genuine courage and altruism motivating him to lay down his life to cover his men's retreat. And we perceive through that parallel Brown's own situation, his continued longing, despite his denial, for a life of dedication to others and, by the readiness he shows in risking his life for Jones, his very real commitment to a belief for which he is willing to die.[41]

To define Brown as in desolation at the end, experiencing the pain of a life beyond amendment, is to miss not only the grandeur of the novel as a whole but also the allusion supplied so deftly in the final sentence. However ironic the office may appear to him, Brown finds himself at the end employed in a task close to that of the priest, the burial of the dead. The paperweight in the form of a coffin, the macabre joke whose disappearance had nevertheless so disturbed him, was a reminder throughout the novel of the priestly duties he had been denied. The word 'call' in the final sentence of the novel subtly informs us that, in a certain sense, he has at last received the 'vocation' he had always longed for:

> The ringing of the telephone woke me – I had overslept. The call came, so far as I could make out, from Mr Fernandez who was summoning me to my first assignment.

In such contrasting authors as Koestler and Greene may be perceived the shared impulse that was to animate literature of the mid-century, their perturbation at the dwindling of the individual into insignificance and the need somehow to reassert the dignity of what appeared to have become a mere statistic in the sweeping advance of history. Koestler's desertion of the messianic movement of communism, ostensibly dedicated to improving the welfare of the poor and downtrodden, derived from his eventual realisation that inbuilt into its philosophy was a contradictory assumption, an acceptance of the evolutionary principle of callously discarding or liquidating those members of the community whom the party decided were 'unfittest' to survive. It was, he contended, a principle denying the sanctity of the individual which, he believed, should have formed the basis of its programme, reflecting the compassion that had impelled Rubashov and Koestler to join the movement initially. Such sanctity, however, belonged to a biblical ethos to which he himself could not subscribe. Greene began from the opposite angle. While believing that each person did indeed bear within the image of God and hence was of eternal significance, he was nonetheless aware of the predominant twentieth-century view and of his need to resist it. As a means of weaning his reader away from such 'horizons of expectation', he provided one of the first instances of the mid-century anti-hero, a figure seemingly a failure in all aspects of his life yet emerging retrospectively as a man worthy of deep respect and admiration. Motivating both authors was the recognition that a fundamental reassessment of the human condition was required to combat the individual's reduced significance, the search for an ideal that could offer hope *despite* the apparent aridity of existence, *despite* the cruelty, injustice or apathy of the cosmic patterns that had been so depressingly revealed.

3
The Adolescent Rebel

The child or adolescent, identified for so long with the idea of an innocence as yet uncorrupted by the dissimulations of adulthood, bringing into this world recollections of the truths and ethical principles existent in the eternity it had so recently left, could no longer function in the new dispensation. The basic savagery of human instincts, chillingly revealed by Freud's *Totem and Taboo*, and powerfully reinforced by Frazer and Conrad, had exposed how far the supposedly civilised societies of the West were motivated by the same greeds, cruelties, superstitions and lusts for power as had animated the most primitive tribes – promptings not inculcated in adulthood but now seen as innate in the human condition, waiting only for the tools and facilities that maturity would provide. That concept animated William Golding's *Lord of the Flies* (1954), which constituted in many respects a re-enactment of the story of Cain and Abel, the scriptural account of the results of original sin, but transferred to a setting in which the gradual eruption of human savagery takes on Freudian and Darwinian undertones. Unlike Defoe's imagined island where Crusoe must rely upon his intelligence and resourcefulness to survive, theirs is an almost idyllic setting, with food and water in plentiful supply, perfect weather and excellent beaches for bathing. The enemy they must face is the emergent brutality of their inner selves as the restraints instilled by their upbringing fade away, and fierce tribal rivalries, culminating in a craving for blood and a crushing of the weaker members of society take hold. The only adolescent horrified at the barbarity, struggling like the anti-hero in loneliness against society's evils, is, by the end of the novel, in the process of being hounded to his death by his peers, saved only by the arrival of adult rescuers. The conclusion, with its echo of Conrad, offers a dismal picture of the mid-century concept of human depravity:

The tears began to flow and sobs shook him. He gave himself up to them now for the first time on the island; great, shuddering spasms of grief that seemed to wrench his whole body. His voice rose under the black smoke before the burning wreckage of the island; and infected by that emotion, the other little boys began to shake and sob too. And in the middle of them, with filthy body, matted hair, and unwiped nose, Ralph wept for the end of innocence, the darkness of man's heart ...[1]

The allusion to Original Sin in this novel was not an isolated instance. While the centrality of Catholicism in Graham Greene's fiction might appear attributable to an entirely personal factor, namely his religious conversion in 1926 when he was still an unpublished writer,[2] an overview of the mid-century reveals an emergence of religious themes in the leading literary works of that period. Evelyn Waugh, a personal friend of Greene and, like him, a convert to Catholicism, in 1944 suddenly abandoned the mordant secular satire of his earlier novels in favour of a religious topic. In the earlier part of his *Brideshead Revisited*, the Catholic interest is subdued, seemingly peripheral, but gradually Charles Ryder's friendship with Sebastian and his romantic attachment to Julia, which had seemed to constitute the main themes, recede into the background as the concealed sub-stratum of the novel, the need for religious belief in the wasteland of the modern world, comes to the fore. Ryder's interest in architecture, expressed professionally in his water-colour paintings of the great country houses of England, becomes symbolic as the monumentality and grandeur of the Flytes' aristocratic home, Brideshead – a structure improved and added to over the years by successive generations – comes to represent to him the Catholic faith of its owners. Billeted there as an officer during the war, several years after his relationship with the family has ended, he discovers a lamp burning in its chapel, a source of comfort to him after the empty materialism represented by his adjutant, Hooper:

The builders did not know the uses to which their work would descend; they made a new house with the stones of the old castle; year by year, generation after generation, they enriched and extended it; year by year the great harvest of timber in the park grew to ripeness; until, in sudden frost, came the age of Hooper; the place was desolate and the work all brought to nothing; *Quomodo sedet sola civitas.* Vanity of vanities, all is vanity.

And yet, I thought ... something quite remote from anything the builders intended has come out of their work, and out of the fierce little human tragedy in which I played; something none of us thought about at the time: a small red flame – a beaten-copper lamp of deplorable design, relit before the beaten-copper doors of a tabernacle; the flame which the old knights saw from their tombs, which they saw put out; that flame burns again for other soldiers, far from home, farther, in heart, than Acre or Jerusalem. It could not have been lit but for the builders and the tragedians, and there I found it this morning, burning anew among the old stones.[3]

Retrospectively, one understands the significance of other supposedly peripheral elements in the novel – Rex Mottram's conversion-of-convenience so delightfully ridiculed there, Sebastian's gradual movement towards a saintly, altruistic celibacy, the spiritual revelation Julia experiences at her father's bedside, and the repercussions of these events upon Ryder himself, led by them to a change in his own religious allegiance.

If the shared Catholic interest of Greene and Waugh has long been noted, the broader interest in religious themes among major writers of that time is no less noteworthy, an interest somewhat surprising in the light of the burgeoning secularism of the generation at large and the growing alienation of the public from its traditional loyalty to the church – surprising, that is, unless one bears in mind the growing discontent with the supposed intellectual and spiritual autonomy that twentieth-century changes had effected, and the increasing sense that an ethical void had resulted. As Marcel Arland had foretold in 1924 in an article published in *Nouvelle Revue Française*, the most urgent motivation of modern writers would be their search for ways of replacing or restoring lost values and faiths: 'Morality will be our first concern. I cannot conceive of literature without an ethic. No doctrine can satisfy us, but the total absence of doctrine is a torment to us.'

T.S. Eliot's formal adoption of the Anglican faith in 1927 had been a lonely pilgrimage, as he recalled in his poetic account of it in *The Journey of the Magi*, the need he had felt to 'travel at night' because of the voices in his ear proclaiming that this was all folly.[4] But by the mid-century, the nostalgia for religious faith had become more widely felt. Auden, after having been lionised by the Left for his attacks on capitalism, began to turn to Christian themes. His *For the Time Being* (1942), a Christmas oratorio intended for reading or recitation rather than for a musical setting, depicted with patent reference to the spiritual condition of his own generation, the period of exhaustion and despondency that had preceded the birth of Christ. The chorus chants there its melancholy lament:

Alone, alone, about a dreadful wood
Of conscious evil runs a lost mankind

concluding with the protest, 'We who must die demand a miracle.'

Perhaps because of the solemn effects of the war, as John Wain has recalled from his own experience, the influence of Christianity at Oxford during the 1940s was paramount: 'Everybody to whom an imaginative and bookish youth naturally looked up, every figure who radiated intellectual glamour of any kind, was in the Christian camp,' C.S. Lewis being among the most prominent after the wide interest aroused by his *Screwtape Letters* of 1942. In 1941, the BBC invited Dorothy L. Sayers to prepare a series of twelve plays forming, in the tradition of the medieval mystery drama, a cycle on the birth, crucifixion and resurrection of Jesus. Entitled *The Man Born to Be King*, the series became the centre of public debate, eliciting wide praise among the public at large in a way unlikely to be paralleled in our own day. Dylan Thomas's collection of poems, *Death and Entrances* (1946), extensively adopted Christian myth and symbolism. Christopher Fry's *Moses*, performed at the Edinburgh Festival in 1948, was followed by a second verse play on biblical themes, his *Sleep of Prisoners*, which, no doubt in response to the religious mood then prevalent among academics, had its first performance in 1951 within the university church of Oxford.

In the United States, Archibald MacLeish provided at that time a similar re-enactment of biblical events transferred to a modern setting. Some years earlier, he had written a verse play, *Nobodaddy*,[5] the title intended as a rebuttal of Bernard Shaw's use of that term in his preface to *Back to Methusaleh* (1922). Shaw recounted there how, at a party he attended, participants had viewed with scepticism the story that the atheist Bradlaugh had once taken out his watch and challenged God to strike him with a thunderbolt within five minutes if He disapproved of atheism. In the face of their disbelief in the Bradlaugh incident, Shaw offered to repeat the experiment there and then, to the consternation of believers and atheists alike:

> In vain did I urge the pious to trust in the accuracy of their deity's aim with a thunderbolt, and the justice of his discrimination between the innocent and the guilty. In vain did I appeal to the sceptics to accept the logical outcome of their scepticism: it soon appeared that when thunderbolts were in question there were no sceptics.

At the urgent request of his host, who saw his party rapidly breaking up, Shaw was persuaded to forgo the experiment; but his point had been triumphantly made. Sheer superstition apart, it was obvious that God would not have accepted the challenge; ergo there was no God.

In MacLeish's *Nobodaddy*, Adam and Eve, after eating from the tree, fearfully await, like Shaw's companions, the dreadful thunderbolt from the skies; but they are met only with the enormous indifference of heaven. MacLeish had reversed the argument: the very absence of divine manifestation in this world was, in a sense, God's means of manifesting himself, a response to mankind's transformation of the divine Somebodaddy into, for them, a mere Nobodaddy. It was a theme expressed in his sonnet 'The End of the World,' depicting humanity engaged in frivolous activities as if in some circus tent, but suddenly confronted with the vast vacuity of a godless universe, a cosmos they had emptied of its divine essence:

> ... while the drum
> Pointed, and Teeny was about to cough
> In waltz-time swinging Jocko by the thumb –
> Quite unexpectedly the top blew off:
>
> And there, there overhead, there, there hung over
> Those thousands of white faces, those dazed eyes;
> There in the starless dark the poise, the hover,
> There with vast wings across the cancelled skies,
> There in the sudden blackness the black pall
> Of nothing, nothing, nothing – nothing at all.

In 1956, that theme received further prominence in his drama *J.B.*, which filled the theatres of America and Europe in its first season, evoking a storm of protest and acclamation, and keeping audiences hours after a performance immersed in discussions of its problems and message.[6] The play was a staging of the book of Job in contemporary terms, with the three false comforters represented here by a communist, a psychiatrist and a doctrinaire clergyman. But there was within it a reversal peculiarly relevant to our present concerns. In the biblical account, the innocent Job, seeking agonisingly to reconcile the patent lack of justice in this world with his longing to believe in divine order, is repeatedly assured by the false comforters of the doctrine of retribution, urged by them to acknowledge the grave sin he must have committed in order to have deserved the loss of his sons, of his possessions and of his health. Only after he has admitted his culpability, they argue, can he be forgiven. In the twentieth-century version, the message of the comforters has been transformed to its antithesis, as they insist that personal guilt is a chimera, a fantasy, a trivial figment of the imagination. The communist (in line with Koestler's Ivanov) declares that, in the context of 'historical necessity', the supposed innocence of the individual is totally irrelevant to the forward march of history, and therefore all sense of personal liability for moral action superfluous.

> Innocent! Innocent!
> Nations shall perish in their innocence.
> Classes shall perish in their innocence.
> Young men in slaughtered cities
> Offering their silly throats
> Against the tanks in innocence shall perish.
> What's your innocence to theirs ?
> God is history. If you offend Him
> Will not History dispense with you?
> History has no time for innocence.

The psychiatrist, in line with Freud, sees guilt as a mere neurosis, the residue of primitive taboos devoid of any moral implications:

> Come! Come! Come! Guilt is a
> Psychophenomenal situation –
> An illusion, a disease, a sickness:
> That filthy feeling at the fingers,
> Scent of dung beneath the nails ...

And the theologian, arguing that all mortals are automatically guilty by reason of the Fall of Adam, concludes that individual culpability is inconsequential: 'All mankind are guilty always!' These contentions J.B. passionately rejects, insisting on assuming full personal responsibility for his actions despite the modern attempt to deprive him of such accountability:

> I'd rather suffer
> Every unspeakable suffering God sends,
> Knowing it was I that suffered,
> I that earned the need to suffer,
> I that acted, I that chose,
> Than wash my hands with yours in that
> Defiling innocence.[7]

Yet the general pessimism of the twentieth-century changes the ending of the drama. Where the biblical story ended with Job's reconciliation with God and his restoration to wealth, security and the blessing of a new family – 'in all the land no woman was found as fair as the daughters of Job' – the modern view is less sanguine. The scoffers jeer at his acceptance of restitution, and on a darkened stage symbolising the devastation of Hiroshima, his wife Sarah whispers the closing message of the play, the very limited comfort to be found in the desolation of the modern world:

> Blow on the coal of the heart.
> The candles in churches are out.
> The lights have gone out in the sky.
> Blow on the coal of the heart
> And we'll see by and by

Around the fifties, a new group of writers emerged on the American scene, none of whom could be regarded as in any sense traditionally religious, whether in their personal lives or in their fictional themes, but that aspect haunts their writings nonetheless. There is the oft-cited conclusion to J.D. Salinger's *Franny and Zooey*, where Franny, obsessively reciting 'the Jesus prayer' in the course of a nervous collapse resulting from her search for meaning in a seemingly meaningless world, is at last consoled by an insight provided by her brother, Zooey. He reminds her how their late older brother Seymour had always urged them to shine their shoes before participating in their radio quiz programme even though their shoes would not be seen by the audience, adding cryptically that it was an act to be performed 'for the Fat Lady'.

> 'I'll tell you a terrible secret. Are you listening to me? *There isn't anyone out there who isn't Seymour's Fat Lady* ... Don't you know that? Don't you know that goddam secret yet? And don't you know – now *listen* to me, now – *don't you know who that Fat Lady really is?* ... Ah, buddy. Ah, buddy. It's Christ Himself. Christ Himself, buddy.'[8]

Here again, despite the generally secular nature of the work, the validity of the individual in a world which seemed to have turned humankind into mere statistics is reaffirmed by reliance upon biblical tradition. And such Christ allusions recur throughout Salinger's work, coupled with his fascination with Zen Buddhism, both elements indicating a predisposition to a mystical faith in the transcendental that was at variance with the pragmatism ostensibly prevalent in his generation. Then there appeared a group of Jewish writers who began to dominate the literary scene, among them Bernard Malamud and Saul Bellow – writers not merely Jewish by birth but incorporating the theme of their Hebraic heritage as a major constituent of their novels and achieving broad appeal among a readership that was overwhelmingly non-Jewish, in the same way as Greene had achieved prominence though his readership was over-whelmingly non-Catholic. And the reason for their success lay in large part in their sense of the overarching scriptural ethos that leads its central characters to move from the barrenness of their contemporary egocentricity into an awareness of an ever-present obligation to their fellow men and women.

Such instances of thematic convergence, when writers, painters and artists in related media are drawn to the same topic, often unaware of a similar tendency in their peers, can serve as valuable pointers to the underlying concerns of the day, to some contemporary impetus to which the creative urge was prompted to respond. One recalls among leading painters of this time a similar tendency to choose religious themes. There was Graham Sutherland's *Crucifixion* (1946), Salvator Dali's *Christ of St John of the Cross* (1951), Stanley Spencer's *Resurrection* (1950), while in architecture, Le Corbusier designed with considerable reverence his impressive Notre-Dame-du-Haut at Ronchamp (1954), speaking of the work as 'a sacred task' and declaring that he wished to create in it 'a place of silence, of prayer, of peace, of spiritual joy'. Erwin Panofsky has shown how even the predominance of geometrical forms in certain eras can have profound implications for our understanding of the mental processes or predilections of the time, noting the figural similarity between the Gothic cathedral on the one hand, with its ramified transepts and side-aisles emanating from a central nave and, on the other, the scholiast's passion for rational articulation, for logically ramified argument, as in the schematic divisions and subdivisions of Aquinas's *Summa Theologiae*.[9] In this present instance, we may suspect, therefore, that the mid-century surge of interest in religious themes was not fortuitous. Such writers were independently motivated by their disturbance at the loss of ethical values attendant upon the new theories, their perception that, with all its apparent advantages, the new-found liberation from the dominance of religion in the Western world, from the dictates of social conservatism, and from conformity to established convention, had left the thinking individual deprived of direction, impotent to take effective action and profoundly frustrated. The result was an attempt on their part to reinstate or replace in some way the missing factor, the set of discarded moral imperatives; or, if they could find no means of replacing them, at the very least to lament their absence and acknowledge the need for some alternate set of values that could compensate for the loss. They did so in different ways, but there was this coordinating factor in their work.

* * * * *

In J.D. Salinger's *The Catcher in the Rye* (1951), that disenchantment with the freedom attained by rejecting conventional values serves as a primary motif. The book's enormous popularity with the younger generation of the fifties and sixties (a popularity that alienated many belonging to the older generation) stimulated among youth a break with the past, a rejection of the crew-cut, career-oriented lifestyle prevalent until then, and a desire for the kind of rebellion against the establishment being simultaneously advocated by Jack Kerouac and the Beat generation. Holden Caulfield's whimsical desire to hitch-hike his way out west offered a welcome, idyllic alternative to what youngsters now saw as the crass materialism cultivated by their urban middle-class parents:

> What I'd do, I figured, I'd go down to the Holland Tunnel and bum a ride and then I'd bum another one, and another one, and another one, and in a few days I'd be somewhere out west where it was very pretty and sunny and where nobody'd know me and I'd get a job ... I didn't care what kind of a job it was, though, just so people didn't know me and I didn't know anybody.[10]

Throughout universities and highschools, Holden's provocative reversing of his peaked cap became adopted as a symbol of the students' opposition to the establishment, their overthrow of convention, and their acceptance of a new set of values incorporating self-determination, freedom in matters of sex, allegiance to Zen Buddhism and a return to simpler standards of living. Even Holden's language, interspersed with 'damns' and 'goddams' (an ingredient that caused the book to be banned from certain school libraries) encouraged a fresh way of talking, its undisciplined spontaneity evincing a contempt for the proprieties of grammatical precision and social acceptability, and proving especially attractive to a disaffected generation.[11]

Among critics, the response was less generous. Christopher Parker complained that Holden had no real ideas of his own to substitute for the false values of society against which he railed and charged him with being guilty of the very phoniness he condemned. Albert Fowler, deploring the same contradictory element, charged that, with such confused standards, he had no escape except relegation to a mental institution. Hugh

Maclean, while admiring Holden's repudiation of the fraudulent pretentiousness dominating twentieth-century society, similarly deduced that his philosophy was, in the final analysis, entirely negative, an 'Everlasting No'; while Ihab Hassan, although refuting Holden's supposed lack of values, was disturbed at the fact that his aspirations were full of unresolved ambiguities, unmodified by any other viewpoint expressed in the novel. In one of the most hostile responses to the work, Maxwell Geismar described Holden contemptuously as a sad little screwed-up hero' with no real standards to live by, concluding: 'If this hero really represents the nonconformist rebellion of the fifties, he is a rebel without a past, apparently, and without a cause.'[12] That negative evaluation may seem exaggerated but it was repeatedly echoed, as in Gerald Graff's influential study, *Literature Against Itself*, which classed Holden with Jimmy Dean and Elvis Presley as youthful rebels lending a certain heroism to aimless youngsters of the fifties, but whose rebellion was ultimately without a cause – 'a-historical, a-political, and non-ideological'.[13]

Such critics have, of course, a perfect right to express their personal dissatisfaction with the novel and to censure its supposedly negative quality. But there is a uniform quality in their analyses that casts considerable doubt on the validity of their criteria, namely that (as in the critical response to Greene's priest) each cites as evidence for their evaluation Holden's own statements about his failings; they accept them uncritically, at face value, at no time considering the possibility of a marked discrepancy between his self-condemnations and the response that Salinger intends to elicit from the reader. It is a critical limitation that has significantly affected the interpretation of Holden's moral stand as well as the general evaluation of the novel. For, once the principle has been recognised upon which the genre of the anti-hero is based, it becomes apparent that the values to which he aspires constitute, despite the impression created among younger readers and generally reinforced by the critics, not a rebellion against traditional morality but the reverse – a longing to reaffirm and reinstate a morality that has, to his dismay, been forsaken by his peers and mentors.

Perhaps I should offer one example before examining that aspect in any detail. Duane Edwards, pointing to what she regards as Holden's grave deficiencies as a person, deduces from his scene with the prostitute the existence within him of a serious psychological inadequacy, an 'inability to relate sexually to females'. Ernest Jones similarly concluded that he was 'afraid to make love to the prostitute supplied by an obliging bellboy'.[14] It is true that, in the manner characterising the anti-hero of this period, Holden readily admits to a weakness in that regard, confessing that something always goes 'wrong' when he is with a girl. But his accounts of such incidents, although he himself sees them as personal deficiencies, should appear very different to the alert reader. They arise, as the text confirms, not from inadequacy on his part but from an innate and admirable respect for the girl's sensitivities. Holden recalls of such episodes in his life that whenever they approach their climax

> she keeps telling you to stop. The trouble with me is, I stop. Most guys don't. I can't help it. You never know whether they really want you to stop, or whether they're just scared as hell, or whether they're just telling you to stop so that if you do go through with it, the blame'll be on you, not them. Anyway, I keep stopping. The trouble is I get to feeling sorry for them. (p. 97)

As he remarks later in the novel, again castigating himself for what he sees as an infirmity:

> You know what the trouble with me is? I can never get really sexy – I mean *really* sexy – with a girl I don't like a lot. I mean I have to *like* her a lot. If I don't, I sort of lose my goddam desire for her and all. Boy, it really screws up my sex life something awful. My sex life stinks. (p. 153)

Peter Shaw states unambiguously in this connection, as did the previously quoted critics, that Holden suffers from a hangup, that his anger with Stradlater arises from the fact that he himself 'is frozen at a painful stage of development', having never reached further than the kissing stage with Jane.[15] In our own day, after the advent of feminism with its demand that women should never be regarded merely as sexual objects but should be respected as personalities with their own needs, desires and preferences, Holden's supposed hangups emerge as especially laudable, as well as remarkably anticipatory of ideas that were to become accepted only in subsequent decades. Those principles stand, moreover, in marked contrast to the popular view of the novel among its younger readers, their supposition that it advocated casual promiscuity in sexual affairs as part of its rebellion against the establishment.

The more detailed examination of the scene with the prostitute, cited so often as evidence of his sexual impotence, offers a perfect instance of those principles in action. Forced into an assignation by the overbearing Maurice, Holden hesitantly assumes that the event might, after all, be for the best, offering him an opportunity to have some of the experience which, he has been assured by his more knowledgeable friends, is a healthy preparation for marriage and which he has so far been lacking. But the moment she enters the room, he instinctively relates to her as an individual, compassionately noting her youthfulness, her unexpectedly childish expressions such as, 'Like fun you are.' He asks her name, and begins empathising, wondering what it must be like to belong to such a profession:

> I took her dress over to the closet and hung it up for her. It was funny. It made me feel sort of sad when I hung it up. I thought of her going in a store and buying it, and nobody in the store knowing she was a prostitute and all. The salesman probably just thought she was a regular girl when she bought it. It made me feel sad as hell – I don't know why exactly. (pp. 100–1)

Holden may not know why, but the reader surely cannot miss the reason, his sympathy for the young girl as a fellow human being, a sensitivity that leaves him commendably incapable of exploiting her sexually. For his idea of sex, in contrast to those around him, an idea confirmed repeatedly throughout the novel, is not self-gratification but (however old-fashioned the concept may be) the consummation of a deeply personal relationship based upon mutual regard and affection.

If that scene with the prostitute occupies a comparatively minor place in the novel, there is another scene relevant to this aspect whose centrality cannot be overemphasised, a scene which, though no critics refer to it, is the real reason for Holden's frenzied search for meaning. His flight from Pencey Prep, his distraught search for a refuge from the wasteland of the twentieth century – pathetically symbolised by his desire to know where the ducks go when the lake is frozen – is precipitated not by dissatisfaction with the school, contributory though that may have been, nor even by a general distaste for his situation there. He had known for some time that he would not be readmitted to Pencey Prep at the end of the Christmas vacation after having failed four subjects and after his irresponsibility in the matter of the fencing foils, neither factor disturbing him unduly, as he had had a long history of such school dismissals. The sudden determination to leave before the vacation and, indeed, his entire 'madcap' journey is, in fact, prompted by a specific incident, an incident that goads him almost to distraction.

His discovery that Stradlater is dating Jane Gallagher is not in itself the cause, nor, one should note, is his violent response to that fact provoked by personal jealousy. Although Jane was a friend of Holden's, a companion for whom he felt a special affection, their relationship involved no proprietary rights on his part. His affection for her had been aroused by sympathy for the problems she had been experiencing with her lewd stepfather and by his admiration for such endearing individual traits as the way she plays checkers. But she is not his special girlfriend and he has no claim upon her of exclusivity that would prevent her from dating any other young man. The aspect that horrifies him in that incident is quite different, namely the discovery that Stradlater is dating her *without even knowing her name* – the classic symbol for the twentieth-century loss of identity, echoed in his own need to know the prostitute's name. For Stradlater, Jane is not a person, only, in the world of the survival of the fittest, an object for gratifying his personal lusts, a 'date' vaguely recalled by him as being the room-mate of someone's girl-friend:

> 'Who is your date if it isn't Fitzgerald?' I asked him, I sat down on the washbowl next to him again. 'That Phyllis Smith babe?'
> 'No. It was supposed to be, but the arrangement screwed up. I got Bud Thaw's girl's room-mate now . . . Hey, I almost forgot. She knows you.'
> 'Who does?' I said.
> 'My date.'
> 'Yeah?' I said. 'What's her name?' I was pretty interested.
> 'I'm thinking . . . Uh, Jean Gallagher.'
> Boy, I nearly dropped dead when he said that.
> '*Jane* Gallagher,' I said. I even got up from the washbowl when he said that. I damn near dropped dead. (pp. 34–5)

At the climax of his fight with Stradlater a little later – in which, as anti-hero, he is inevitably the loser – the motivation for his frenzied anger emerges unambiguously. The incident maddens him by its revelation of the selfish exploitation and corruption of others, a discovery that will drive him on a crusade, however impractical, to rescue children from growing up into such a repugnant world:

> 'Get your lousy knees off my chest,' I told him. I was almost bawling. I really was. 'Go on, get offa me, ya crumby bastard.'
> . . . I can hardly even remember what all I said to him. I told him he thought he could give the time to anybody he felt like. I told him he didn't even care if a girl kept all her kings in the back row or not, and the reason he didn't care was because he was a goddam stupid moron . . . 'You don't even know if her first name is Jane *or June*, ya goddam moron!'[16]

From that moment the frenzy seizes him, the urge to leave Pencey Prep immediately, not waiting for the end of the term but quitting it at once in tormented search for an alternative to the world of crude egocentricity that Stradlater and his fellow Penceyans represent, a world in which other people function merely as exploitable objects. *'Sleep tight, ya morons!'* he sardonically bids farewell, including them all in the same category.

The fact that his fevered flight is prompted by revulsion at the collapse of individual worth is re-echoed throughout the work, symbolised in Holden's dread that his own existence as a distinguishable entity is slipping dangerously away. Early in the novel, he had experienced the first signs, if at that stage more mildly. He recalls how, on the way to visit Mr Spencer, 'I felt like I was sort of disappearing. It was that kind of crazy afternoon ... you felt like you were disappearing every time you crossed a road.' But towards the end, when the pressures and frustrations have built to a climax, that feeling of disintegration is intensified, expressed in a desperate, recurrent plea to his dead brother to help him retain his selfhood and to prevent him from vanishing into the void:

> Every time I'd get to the end of a block I'd make believe I was talking to my brother Allie. I'd say to him, 'Allie, don't let me disappear. Allie, don't let me disappear. Allie, don't let me disappear. Please, Allie.' And then, when I'd reach the other side of the street without disappearing, I'd *thank* him. Then it would start all over again as soon as I got to the next corner ... (p. 204)

In a sense Holden does fall into the void, failing to find any escape from the debilitating conditions of his time; and for that he has been repeatedly censured. It has become a commonplace to declare, citing his sister Phoebe, that he likes nothing, that he can only rail impotently at the phoniness around him, offering no valid alternative, hence helplessly ending his odyssey in a sanatorium. If Holden is to be condemned for finding 'no escape except a mental institution', as Albert Fowler and others have claimed,[17] we may well enquire why so many other anti-heroes of the mid-century share this quality with him and whether they too should be castigated for their failure. In fact, the nervous breakdown of the anti-hero becomes in this era a badge of distinction, Holden's collapse being essentially the same as that experienced by Saul Bellow's Herzog, by the unnamed sergeant in Salinger's moving story, 'For Esmé in Love and Squalor,' by Querry in Greene's *The Burnt-Out Case* and, by extension, by the characters in Ken Kesey's *One Flew Over the Cuckoo's Nest* and Peter Weiss's *The Persecution and Assassination of Jean-Paul Marat: as performed by the inmates of the Asylum of Charenton.* In Kesey's novel, the mental institution serves, until the arrival of the new nurse, as a refuge from the insanity of the real world or as a penance imposed upon the inmates as misfits refusing to conform to the inanities of modern society; while the enormously impressive play by Weiss, like Kesey's novel, poses the question whether the world of the supposedly sane is any more rational than that of the supposedly deranged. The convergence on that theme in this period suggests once again that we are dealing not with an isolated phenomenon but with a shared, underlying concern of the time.

The phenomenon is indeed fascinating, a twentieth-century variation on the function of madness in *King Lear*, where supposed insanity is not a failing but the path to spiritual redemption, a route which, with all its agony, eventually endows the sufferer with an enhanced ethical perception. It is a variation also of the biblical prophet enunciating moral principles unsavoury to the public of his day and hence frequently regarded by his contemporaries as deranged.[18] In the form adopted in the anti-hero genre, there are both differences and similarities.[19] In its twentieth-century setting, the madness becomes, as one would expect, translated into a psychological neurosis, a paranoia or mental collapse with obsessional symptoms – such as Holden's fear of disappearing, Herzog's urge to compose unsent letters to the living and the dead, and Eli's fixational donning of the greenhorn's black garments in Roth's story 'Eli the fanatic'. The similarity to Lear lies in the positive function assigned to such madness, the nervous breakdown of the anti-hero resulting neither from weakness nor from a blemish in character, even though such may be the initial impression. The collapse arises from a quality that elevates him above his peers, his heightened moral sensitivity which prevents him from coming to terms with the cruelty, perversion, corruption and selfishness epitomising the contemporary world. In that context, the neurosis comes to represent the anti-hero's nobler set of values, contrasting him with what Bellow has called the Reality Instructors around him, so that the breakdown in that context eventually earns the reader's sympathy and respect.[20]

On the other hand, if Lear does eventually win through to a truer understanding, learning to distinguish genuine love from flattery, to kneel for forgiveness before Cordelia, and to reject the autocratic pride that had marked his period of kingship, what deeper understanding does the anti-hero achieve when he is, like Holden committed to an asylum, like Eli forcibly injected with a hypodermic tranquilliser or like Kesey's Randle chillingly compelled to undergo a lobotomy? The difference may well lie in the nature of tragedy and Krutch's claim that there can be no place for tragedy in the modern world once the sense of a benevolent deity and divine order has disappeared. Lear may suffer appallingly, but he has, by the end, achieved a nobility that to some extent has made the suffering worthwhile. It has reconciled him with the world, not least endowing him with the realisation that he himself was ultimately responsible for the troubles that befell him, and with that recognition, the knowledge that there is, after all, divine justice in the world. As order is restored, his successor Albany closes the play with the assurance:

> All friends shall taste
> The wages of their virtue, and all foes
> The cup of their deservings.[21]

In the desolation and alienation of the twentieth century, there can be no such final comfort. But that does not mean total negation. For there is, in much of the writing of the time, at least a pointer to the direction we must travel, to standards that can perhaps be attained. And in the anti-hero genre, those standards are generally perceived in the discrepancy between the seeming failure of the central character and the more positive concepts to which the author has directed the reader. If in tragedy the hero dies having learnt too late the error of his ways, the audience is privileged to live on, bearing from the theatre the insights that the hero had gained. So here, the anti-hero may be confined to a sanatorium, unable to solve his crisis, but the author, the figure felt at all times as existent behind the character, has transmitted to the perceptive reader the lesson to be learned. The madness has been transposed in our era into neurosis, but little faith is placed here on psychiatry or psychoanalysis as means of salvation. Salinger, like Bellow's *Herzog*, adopts the psychiatrist's couch as the framework for the novel. Holden relates his story as a confessional monologue in the sanatorium, having been requested by his psychological counsellor to set his experiences down in writing. Herzog, 'from his sofa in New York', contemplates his recent experiences, trying after his breakdown to justify and make sense of it. No salvation will come from the psychiatrist. It is the sufferer himself who must make sense of his confusion and find his own form of salvation, or the author who must suggest to the reader the direction to be taken.

The way those positive moral principles are conveyed is fascinating to watch, contradicting the common charge that Holden likes nothing, that he has no positive alternatives to offer for the phoniness around him. He, of course, admits to the truth of the allegation, failing to answer Phoebe's accusation and lamely confessing that he could not concentrate at that moment, his mind roaming to other matters. But that is, as usual, the self-condemnation that we are meant to discard. For what Holden sees embarrassedly as mere irrelevancies and digressions, we, in contrast, are led to see as pointers to the values he does embrace:

> But the trouble was, I couldn't concentrate. About all I could think of were those two nuns that went around collecting dough in those beat-up old straw baskets. Especially the one with the glasses with those iron rims. And this boy I knew at Elkton Hills named . . . James Castle. (p. 176)

The altruism of the nuns, devoting themselves to the good of others, free from the complacency and self-aggrandisement characterising his aunt's charitable activities, coupled with the courage of James Castle, standing by his principles and staunchly refusing to submit to bullies, have, even though Holden does not consciously acknowledge their significance, come to symbolise for him the kind of world for which he yearns.

The literary strategy behind this reader dissociation operates slightly differently here from the way it functioned in Greene's work, that distinction illuminating an aspect of Holden's character that has again invited negative criticism. Although Greene's priest frequently acknowledges that he is of peasant origin and that his theological learning is limited to that of a village incumbent, he is nonetheless a mature individual. The reason we absolve him of the sins that so gravely trouble him emanates from our recognition of his extraordinary humility and of the severity with which he constantly condemns himself for failings that we come to see as virtues. In Brown's case, his conviction that he is unworthy of the priestly call betokens a similar humility, leading him to misinterpret his actions and see his courage and dedication as a form of corruption. For Holden, the mitigating factor is his adolescence, his striving to reach out to ideals which are, by any standards, beyond the grasp of a sixteen-year-old. He may symbolically have a streak of grey in his hair, representing the mingling of maturity and immaturity that marks his character; but the appealing unaffectedness of his speech – the schoolboy jargon, the ungrammatical colloquialisms, the adolescent exaggerations, and, not least, his repeated recourse to the vague term 'phoney', together with such impractical dreams as living as a deaf-mute or becoming a catcher in the rye – are indications that he remains, for all his aspirations, a teenager incapable of coping with the intimidating problems he confronts. Salinger the author, however, is not an adolescent, and it is from that shadowy authorial presence behind Holden's account that the message of the novel emanates.

Those positive values emerging through the mists of this juvenile exploration are substantial, even if only hazily recognised by Holden himself and dismissed by him as part of his craziness. His hatred of the victimisation of others, especially the weak and vulnerable, extends beyond the context of Stradlater's behaviour towards women. One major reason for his dislike of Pencey Prep, as we learn from his conversation with Phoebe, is the boys' treatment of Ackley as a pariah, excluding the latter from the secret fraternity he longs to join because of his pimply unattractiveness. Holden, no less conscious of those unsavoury characteristics, sees them as a reason not for ostracism but for compassion: 'That guy had just about everything. Sinus trouble, pimples, lousy teeth, halitosis, crumby fingernails. You had to feel a little sorry for the crazy sonuvabitch.' (p. 43) Holden makes no effort, one notes, to be moved out of the room he shares with Ackley, and in fact resigns from the fraternity in protest when the latter is refused membership.

An experience of such exploitation of the defenceless which was to prove momentous for Holden is his awakening in Antolini's apartment to find his past schoolmaster patting his forehead. It is a scene that has, like the incident with the prostitute, been widely misread. Warren French, in a well-known reading of that scene, attributes the fault to Holden, maintaining that the vehemence of his response arises from his own pathological sensitivity to being touched; while Duane Edwards offers a more ingenious if, to my mind, extraordinarily inept explanation, that 'he is projecting his desire for homosexual expression onto Antolini'. Others have similarly interpreted the scene as reflecting on Holden's weaknesses, with the suggestion that his fierce reaction was totally unfounded.[22] As usual, they have Holden's own comment to rely on, his remark shortly after the incident, 'I wondered if just maybe I was wrong about thinking he was making a flitty pass at me. I wondered if maybe he just liked to pat guys on the head when they're asleep.'

Apart from the heavy sarcasm in that final remark, the text itself offers ample hints to alert the reader to the justice of Holden's response. We are made cognisant that Antolini and his wife, the latter a much older and wealthier woman, have a strange relationship, avoiding being in the same room together, those elements suggesting that it was a marriage of convenience based on financial advantage and excluding sexual relationship, with the implication that Antolini finds his satisfactions elsewhere. There is the significance of Antolini's parting remark before Holden falls asleep, 'Good night, handsome'; and most notable of all, the fact, carefully mentioned in the story, that Antolini had 'forgotten' to lend Holden pyjamas – all this quite apart from the totally uncalled-for visit at night and the patting on the head. What outrages Holden, however, is not so much the implied homosexuality but the abuse of trust involved. Antolini was the only adult in whom he had been able to place his faith, the sole teacher who had had the decency to cover James Castle's body, who had tried to dissuade D.B. from going to Hollywood, and who had attempted to develop Holden's character. He was, moreover, the only person to have offered him any sound advice, his quotation concerning the difference between the mature and immature man – that the latter wishes to die for a cause, the former to live nobly for one. Holden's condition on arrival at Antolini's apartment had been desperate. He was seeking in his past teacher the only refuge he could find in a bleak and hostile world. And the discovery that the sole admired adult left to him was as selfishly exploitive of his vulnerability as all the rest is devastating, destroying any residual faith he has in humankind.

It is unnecessary to list here in any detail the many positive values to which Holden subscribes, the moral and aesthetic principles arising from his dissatisfaction with the condition of the twentieth-century world. There is his longing for a truer form of art, an art to be performed for its own sake, not for applause or fame (a principle that Salinger himself was to live by in his reclusive avoidance of all media attention after the celebrity bestowed upon him by this novel). There is his hatred of the use of cars as status symbols, his love of digression in essays and his rejection of the instruction to 'stick to the point', seen by him as a repression of individuality. And there is his dislike of the cinema for having created a fantasy-world of macho heroes remote from reality. Here too, Holden has been accused of inconsistency, the contradiction between his sweeping condemnation of the movies and his own attempt, after being punched by Maurice, to play the role of the male lead in such films. The scene he visualises of himself staggering down the stairs after having been shot reveals, we are told, a covert or subliminal desire to model himself on Humphrey Bogart.[23] But the scene is, surely, a delightful parody, a humorous attempt not to imitate but to satirise the absurdity of contemporary movies in their distancing from reality, films in which courageous heroes, impervious to bullet wounds, continue to play handsomely to the cameras. After Maurice has punched him in the stomach, leaving him gasping for breath, Holden manages to reach the bathroom:

> But I'm crazy. I swear to God I am. About half way to the bathroom, I sort of started pretending I had a bullet in my guts. Old Maurice had plugged me. Now I was on the way to the bathroom to get a good shot of bourbon or something to steady my nerves and help me *really* go

into action ... I'd walk downstairs, instead of using the elevator. I'd
hold on to the banister and all, with this blood trickling out of the side
of my mouth a little at a time. What I'd do, I'd walk down, a few floors –
holding on to my guts, blood leaking all over the place ... (p. 109)

Holden is, in fact, perfectly consistent in the ideals he has adopted. In a
society hostile to such notions, it is inevitable that, as a young teenager,
he senses the impossibility of changing the adult world that awaits him,
his quest ending in failure to find any solution, in his being committed to
a sanatorium and in his ultimate inability to answer with any confidence
whether he will apply himself when he returns to a new school in the fall.
But does Holden's failure to solve his problem constitute, as has so often
been charged, a failure in the novel itself? John Seelye condemns the
novel for shying away from any positive message, arguing, with echoes of
Freud, that Holden is motivated ultimately by a death-wish negating all
viable solutions: 'There is, of course, only one way to escape growing up
and that is Allie's way, which is why the book can be read as a lengthy
suicide note with a blank space at the end to sign your name.' Or, as John
Aldridge concludes, after the flight 'no recognition follows, and no
conversion. He remains at the end what he was at the beginning – cynical,
defiant, and blind,' inviting, Aldridge suggests, some degree of identification but offering no insight.[24]
It may be legitimate to enquire, on the other hand, how far Holden's
inability to answer his advisors at the conclusion of the novel is in itself a
deficiency, quite apart from whether that inability involves the failure of
the novel as a whole. As regards that latter point, the disqualification of
the novel as a whole, we may well ask what solution to the twentieth-
century predicament is offered by Beckett's *Waiting for Godot*, and
whether the absence of any corrective impairs it as a literary work. Surely
one perfectly valid function of an artist is to express the leading concerns
of the age without necessarily providing solutions. Malcolm Bradbury has
noted correctly that twentieth-century literature in general no longer aims
at asserting a coherent wisdom, preferring to express the uncertainties of
human existence.[25]
More importantly, perhaps, we should enquire whether, at the final
point in this novel, we as readers would indeed wish Holden to 'apply'
himself – to conform to the selfish, unprincipled, status-seeking,
acquisitive world that his visitor D.B. represents? Are we in favour of his
heeding the advice of an older brother who has, in Holden's view, debased
his enviable literary talents for financial gain, predictably arriving at the
sanatorium in the company of a curvaceous movie-star intended to

impress onlookers with the material and macho success of his Hollywood career? Those are standards which in the course of the novel we have learned to deplore. In the light of Holden's youthfulness, both his breakdown and his inability to produce any valid remedy become eminently forgivable, the advent of the crisis itself redounding to his credit, distinguishing him from his peers who lack the perspicacity to perceive the corruption and hypocrisy around them. Moreover, if he may not know in which direction to proceed, he does know what pitfalls to avoid, and that, for an adolescent, is a notable achievement.

It has been rightly remarked that this novel in certain ways echoes *Huckleberry Finn*, with its somewhat inarticulate teenager, there limited to the vocabulary of an uneducated rustic, yet discerning in his society moral blemishes of which his contemporaries are oblivious. On the other hand, Edwin Bowden is correct in noting a fundamental difference between the two, that, although Huck may deliver an occasional remark on the depravity of the human race, he maintains a generally detached view, having long become conscious of the cruelty and perversity of the adult world and hence being rarely shocked by the instances he encounters.[26] As the child of an alcoholic wastrel, a viciously abusive father, Huck represents in contrast to Tom Sawyer (and to Holden) the suffering minority of society who, as part of that upbringing, has developed an admirable resourcefulness in coping with crises. In the harsh environment into which he has been born, he has achieved the attributes of a survivor, reacting inventively to unexpected challenges, such as spontaneously feigning an infectious illness to protect Jim from his pursuers. Moreover, he has, unlike Holden, found in the character of Jim and, to some extent in Tom Sawyer, models he wishes to imitate. He may express at the end a desire to light out for the territory but one has the impression that, if he does, he will manage there very competently. In contrast, Holden exemplifies the irremediability of the twentieth-century predicament, his sense of alienation in a tainted world, and his despair at ever achieving spiritual fulfilment. The only valid models he has are either dead (Allie and James Castle), the nuns (who have opted out of society) and Phoebe, whose innocence and purity will, he is grimly convinced, become contaminated as she is absorbed into the adult world. Hence his affection for the museum where everything remains just as it was, the emblem of a Phoebe never deserting her uncorrupted state; and hence too the title of the novel, reflecting his longing to rescue the young before they fall into the abyss of warped adulthood.

If Holden fails to produce any viable solution to his crisis, to condemn the book for that supposed flaw is to miss, once again, a central characteristic of the anti-hero genre. For instead of offering a fictional hero incorporating the author's positive standards – a Tom Jones gradually maturing into a second Squire Allworthy, or the Pip of *Great Expectations* learning loyalty and gratitude – the author in each of these mid-twentieth-century novels presents us with a figure embodying above all the sense of deprivation and disillusionment in the contemporary scene, unable to conform to the norms of a society that either has lost its principles or has exchanged them for a selfish preying upon others that parallels the cruelty now seen to motivate the amoral world of Nature. But to deduce from that inability the failure of the novel as a literary work, to assume that, since Holden is unable to conform to society's demands, the novel collapses is to confuse the author with his fictional character. Holden may have taken no positive action to resist the crisis, but Salinger did – he wrote the novel, with its advocacy of the standards to which society ought to aspire.

In line with the distinction we have been making, the author constantly impels the vigilant reader to move beyond his protagonist's frustrations or admissions of weakness towards a set of ethical and aesthetic values implied by Holden's thoughts and actions, to ideals which, if not easily attainable in the depressed condition of the modern world, do at least offer some direction, some hope, however limited, for reinstating a respect for the individual, for restoring integrity to art-forms that had become debased and commercialised, and for establishing a set of criteria by which it might be possible to live. That twentieth-century concern with the value of the individual in an era which seemed to have nullified it finds confirmation in the final lines of the novel: 'About all I know is, I sort of miss everybody I told about. Even old Stradlater and Ackley, for instance. I think I even miss that goddam Maurice'. Holden, disillusioned as he may have been by the selfishness, brutality, and hypocrisy of those surrounding him, acknowledges nonetheless the human bond that links him to each character whatever his personal disapproval of their traits.

* * * * *

The sudden prominence on the American scene of Jewish writers during the fifties was not fortuitous. Unlike authors such as Norman Mailer who merely happened to be Jewish, Bernard Malamud and Saul Bellow afforded a centrality to the Jewish experience in their literary work, a centrality that attracted the interest of the public at large, introducing into the vocabulary of gentile reader and critic alike such words as *schlemiel*, *pogrom* and *shtetl* as those novels topped contemporary book sales. The time was fitting. The harrowing scenes of Nazi concentration camps, only recently revealed to the Western world, made the Jew ideally suited to the role of victim, a symbol of the suffering human caught up in the cruelty of vicious forces over which he has no control, a twentieth-century Sisyphus who, in the guise of Malamud's Fixer, falsely accused by an antisemitic Russian government, must struggle against enormous odds to assert his individuality and his will. But there were additional elements pertinent to the American scene that provided those writers with unique qualifications. The first was their background. The sons of immigrants to a country that prided itself on its multi-racial origins, they possessed as members of that society the right to review and, where necessary, to censure its characteristics.[27] Yet at the same time, as partial outsiders, heirs to the Old Testament ethic upon which the Puritan founders of America had built their concept of the New World, they could to some extent fulfil the function of the biblical prophet separated from his peers by his hairy mantle, viewing the contemporary scene *sub specie aeternitatis*, and admonishing or condemning when he saw them straying from the true path. The Christian legend of the Wandering Jew embedded in the Western tradition had depicted him as condemned not merely to journey from country to country throughout eternity but also to testify. Like Coleridge's Ancient Mariner based upon that legend, he could calm the agony within him only by unburdening himself of his message, by acting as a moral gadfly for the society of which he formed part. Bellow's Herzog is more than a troubled American intellectual. Urged repeatedly in his youth to become a rabbi, he is dogged by the inescapability of his moral conscience. The mental breakdown he experiences, the neurotic collapse that constitutes the central theme of the novel, takes the form of a moral revaluation both of his own spiritual condition and of the society in which he lives. 'Late in the spring, Herzog had been overcome by the need to explain, to have it out, to justify, to put in perspective, to clarify . . .' Feverishly he scrawls off letter after letter to personalities of past and present, to public figures, friends, names he has chanced upon in newspapers, all these missives correcting, reproaching, analysing, qualifying and questioning the ethical standards and values of his cultural milieu. To General Eisenhower he writes:

> *The more political our society becomes . . . the more individuality seems lost. Seems, I say, because it has millions of secret resources, More plainly, national purpose is now involved with the manufacture of commodities in no way essential to human life, but vital to the political survival of the country. Because we are now all sucked into these phenomena of Gross National Product, we are forced to accept the sacred character of certain absurdities or*

falsehoods whose high priests not so long ago were mere pitchmen, and figures of derision ...

On the other hand, there was a significant difference between the modern gadfly and the biblical. The mid-twentieth-century version of the prophet-figure is no longer a devout, morally upright spokesman for the divine but, in a manner approximating to the genre of the anti-hero, is a failure, something indeed of a buffoon or *schlemiel*,[28] infected by the false values around him, needing to acknowledge his own errors and only through their exposure to offer an example for his peers. He wears the mantle of the Old Testament prophet uncomfortably as he senses his own deficiencies, his inability to live up to that tradition, but aware nonetheless that the demands made upon him by the imperatives of the past cannot be ignored. Ever-present in Herzog's mind is the recognition that he could have been 'a patriarch, as every Herzog was meant to be. The family man, father, transmitter of life, intermediary between past and future, instrument of mysterious creation.' At the height of his pursuit of the American dream – the attainment of a beautiful wife, a country home in the Berkshires, and the gratification of his materialistic desires – while in the process of trying on a new summer outfit in a fashionable clothing store, he suddenly perceives himself in the mirror as 'gruesomely unlike a rabbi now in the trunks and straw hat, his face charged with a heavy sadness, foolish utter longings of which a religious life might have purged him.' Betrayed by a spiritually castrating wife, cuckolded by his closest friend, deceived by his own lawyer, Herzog's nervous breakdown expresses itself as an urgent need to reorient his life, to restore it to a more honourable form. Almost destroyed by the acquisitive egocentricity around him, he comes at last to recognise not only his own distorted values but also the moral decay of society at large from which they have derived, to discern, by enlarging his perspective, the duty incumbent upon each individual to contribute in some way to the moral progress of mankind:

Survival! he noted. *Till we figure out what's what. Till the chance comes to exert a positive influence.* (Personal responsibility for history, a trait of Western culture, rooted in the Testaments, Old and New, the idea of the continual improvement of human life on this earth. What else explained Herzog's ridiculous intensity?) *Lord, I ran to fight in Thy holy cause, but kept tripping, never reached the scene of the struggle.*[29]

Fundamental to that impulse is his perception of the need for personal responsibility for history, for a type of survival contrary to that advocated by the Darwinians, a responsibility which, like other writers at this time, he sees as deriving ultimately, perhaps exclusively, from the biblical source.

In a similar way, the central characters both in Malamud's short story, 'The Lady of the Lake', and in his novel, *The Fixer*, must learn through suffering to renounce their desire to assimilate into the warped society around them and to return instead to the ethical responsibilities of their Old Testament heritage, that message, it is suggested, being no less applicable to the non-Jewish members of an American society rooted in the ethical traditions of its Puritan founders. In the short story, Freeman (the name symbolising his 'liberation' from religious allegiance) repeatedly denies his Jewish origin to the beautiful Italian girl with whom he has fallen in love, only to be rejected at the end as she reveals the concentration-camp number tattooed on her flesh, explaining, 'My past is meaningful to me. I treasure what I suffered for.' Too late, he realises his error: ' "Isabella – " he cried brokenly. "Listen, I – I am – " '; but she has disappeared, never to return. In *The Fixer*, Yakov Bok, having attempted to discard the bonds of his faith, recognises towards the close of the novel the urgent need to identify with his Jewish fellow-victims, representative of the suffering members of humankind at large. Generously, he acknowledges his wife's illegitimate offspring as his own son, explaining 'what suffering has taught me is the uselessness of suffering. *Rachmones*, we say in Hebrew – mercy, one oughtn't to forget it, but one must also think how oppressed, ignorant, and miserable most of us are in this country, gentiles as well as Jews'.[30]

It will be noted that from the group of Jewish writers mentioned above who dominated American fiction in the fifties and sixties I omitted one of the most prominent, Philip Roth. To include him in a group whose characters rededicate themselves to the ethical imperatives of the Bible would seem patently absurd. His novels provoked fierce hostility from the Jewish community for their derisive depiction of its social norms, while for the public at large the attraction of his writing, most notably of *Portnoy's Complaint* (1967), lay in its often hilarious portrayal of an adolescent Jew's rebellion against all moral and religious constraints, against what he saw as an oppressive, intolerant and outmoded Judaism. The rebellion was described there in flagrant contravention of established rules of propriety (especially those of the sixties) as Roth, in confessional guise, relates the masturbatory and other sexual indulgences of his central character and ridicules the primitively obsolete dietary laws, protesting:

> instead of crying over he-who refuses at the age of fourteen ever to set
> foot inside a synagogue again, instead of wailing for he-who has turned

his back on the saga of his people, weep for your own pathetic selves, why don't you, sucking and sucking on that sour grape of a religion!,[31]

The writing was so intensely personal in its vigorous hostility and the author so clearly involved in Portnoy's experiences that he became, inevitably, identified with his protagonist. Since that semi-autobiographical aspect has some bearing on this present chapter, it should perhaps be noted that Roth's repeated attempts to dissociate himself from his leading characters are patently ingenuous. He may claim wittily that in *Portnoy* he wrote 'a novel in the guise of a confession [which] was received and judged by any number of readers as a confession in the guise of a novel', but it is he who bears responsibility for the assumption.[32] The specific escapades narrated in *Portnoy* and the other novels may not have occurred in his own life, but the fact that Roth invariably locates his protagonist's upbringing in his own birthplace of Newark, New Jersey, and inserts so many details patently applicable to himself (such as having published a novel deeply shocking to the Jewish community) were clearly intended to invite that identification.

For many, the book proved deeply offensive not only for the forth-rightness whereby the sexual scenes were described but, in marked contrast to Malamud and Bellow, for the hostility he expressed to his religious heritage. Where those authors, however far they or their fictional figures may have diverged from observance of the tradition, had come eventually to recognise the compassion, selflessness, and moral rectitude demanded by the biblical code, Roth not only rejoiced in deriding its restraints and obligations as hopelessly obsolete but in the course of doing so attributed to his less savoury Jewish characters, both in this book and in his other writings, the kind of behaviour previously associated with the most blatant forms of anti-semitic caricature. They are portrayed as scheming draft-dodgers, as racist exploiters of black workers, as money-grabbing indus-trialists, in a manner that led the respected historian, Gershom Scholem, to accuse Roth in a widely-read article of having traitorously provided ammunition to the gentiles for the worst kind of Jew-baiting:

> Here in the centre of Roth's revolting book ... stands the loathsome figure whom the anti-Semites have conjured in their imagination and portrayed in their literature, and a Jewish author, a highly gifted if perverted artist, offers all the slogans which for them are priceless.

Marie Syrkin commented in similar vein that 'under the cartoon of the Jewish joke leers the anti-Jewish stereotype. Portnoy polluting his environment is one such ... like Julius Streicher's satanic Jewboy lusting after Aryan maidens'; while the editor of *Commentary*, Peter Shaw, condemned Roth for 'fanaticism in the hatred of things Jewish'.[33]

This present book is not concerned with anti-semitism but with the broader spiritual crisis of the era; and it is in that connection that I have chosen to examine Philip Roth here. For his writings provide, I would argue, a remarkable expression of the central spiritual disturbance of the time. Where Koestler had approached the problem of his generation in the context of Marxism, and Graham Greene within the framework of Catholicism, Roth may be seen as responding to that same contemporary dilemma in terms of the American-Jewish experience.

The most striking aspect of his writing, the one that captured public attention from the first, was the sense it offered of longed-for release from the constrictive taboos of the past. Like Salinger, he chose as his central character an adolescent, in order to represent the new generation needing to confront and struggle with the implications of modernism. But if Holden detested the crass materialism and profligacy of modern society, Alexander Portnoy was deeply enamoured of it. His flight from Judaism and all it entails, accompanied by a series of incidents related in order to shock by their contravention of the established code – lurid accounts of sexual prowess, a frenzied pursuit of non-Jewish females recalled in full physiological detail, and a bold denial of the existence of God – that rebellion is prompted by a fervent desire to escape into the enticing twentieth-century world of bodily and spiritual freedom and to flee the burdensome restrictions his parents constantly try to impose on him as part of their religious identity. Located within the American-Jewish setting, he marks the culmination of the liberating impulse resulting from the writings of Darwin, Frazer and Freud, the desire to eschew the oppressive dictates of previous eras and to advance into a rationally based world untrammelled by outmoded prohibitions and superstitions. The tale is related with buoyant vivacity and humour, while revealing beneath the hilarity the opposition he encountered in his bid for independence, in his break from the prohibitions and taboos imposed by his family:

> this is my life, my only life, and I'm living it in the middle of a Jewish joke! I am the son in the Jewish joke ... Please, who crippled us like this? Who made us so morbid and hysterical and weak? Why, why are they screaming still, 'Watch out! Don't do it! Alex – *no!*' ... what do you call this sickness I have? Is this the Jewish suffering I used to hear so much about? Is this what has come down to me from the pogroms and the persecution? (pp. 36–7)

Accused by his father of denying his religious heritage without ever having understood it, of refusing to acknowledge his Jewish responsibilities, Portnoy responds unequivocally:

A Jew. No! No! An *atheist*, I cry. I am a nothing where religion is concerned, and I will not pretend to be anything that I am not! I don't care how lonely and needy my father is, the truth about me is the truth about me, and I'm sorry but he'll just have to swallow my apostasy whole! (p. 72)

Were that all, there would be little to interest us here, since that element of rebelliousness against the past was shared by so many other writers. But beneath the surface theme, not only of *Portnoy* but of Roth's other works too, may be perceived a powerful counter-movement, a movement corresponding to the stage subsequent to scientific optimism. It marked the awareness of the spiritual emptiness created by liberation, the recognition that such freedom from the past carries as its price a recognition of the purposelessness of the individual in a vast, impersonal universe, and, together with that void, the loss of a defined set of ethical values. For there are, it would seem, two aspects of Philip Roth in conflict within him, and expressed within his writings. Before returning to *Portnoy*, it might be helpful to examine briefly the first of his books, the collection of short stories entitled *Goodbye Columbus* that won him the National Book Award in 1960.

The first story, which gave the book its title, was a devastating exposure of the Jewish *nouveau riche*, capturing with extraordinary flair the nuances of Jewish middle-class dialect, and attributing to his characters the ingrained prejudices and materialistic ambitions that Roth saw as characterising their way of life. Paralleling his portrayal of Grossbart in 'The Defender of the Faith' and his hostile depiction of Rabbi Binder in 'The Conversion of the Jews', both included in this collection, that first story did indeed reveal a marked distaste for and disloyalty to his community. Those were the aspects that aroused such angry opposition in the Jewish community. But few have commented on the final story in that collection – a masterly piece of writing from a purely literary point of view – which offered in direct contrast to those other tales a sense of the rich spiritual tradition that was being so thoughtlessly discarded by the assimilationists (himself included), a story written in a manner leaving no doubt where the author's sympathies lay, at least during the course of its composition.

The setting is Woodenton, a progressive suburban community shortly after the Second World War, whose assimilated Jews live in apparent amity with their gentile neighbours, largely by having sacrificed (as they fondly imagine) everything that might distinguish them as Jews. To their dismay, a bearded Jew with sidelocks, a broad-brimmed, black 'Talmudic' hat and long gabardine coat mysteriously appears on Main Street – symbolically an invasion by the past endangering their calm, peaceful integration into modern America. Two such bearded males, it transpires, have purchased a house on the outskirts of the town as a Yeshivah or religious boarding school for refugee children rescued from Auschwitz. The Jewish community, feeling its very existence threatened, commissions one of its members, Eli Peck, an attorney recently recovered from his second nervous breakdown (the inevitable mark of the anti-hero), assigning to him the task of forcing the Yeshivah to close on the grounds that it transgresses municipal zoning laws.

No brief account of Eli's gradual transformation can serve as a substitute for the subtle delineation achieved in the story, but we can at least glance at the allegorical implications. He is, even before the arrival of the Yeshivah, already a potential anti-hero, sensitive to the selfishness, cruelty, and absurdity of contemporary society, false standards with which he is unable to come to terms, the problem affecting him professionally as well as in general.

> Sometimes Eli found being a lawyer surrounded him like quicksand – he couldn't get his breath. Too often he wished he were pleading for the other side; though if he were on the other side, then he'd wish he were on the side he was. The trouble was that sometimes the law didn't seem to be the answer, law didn't seem to have anything to do with what was aggravating everybody. And that, of course, made him feel foolish and unnecessary.[34]

His wife, Miriam, intensifies his sense of isolation by applying to him those psychological labels that had come into fashion by that time. University-trained, she fixes him in formulated phrases, overwhelming him with solicitous diagnoses of his every move in a manner intended to ensure his well-being but driving him to nervous distraction. He winces at the maddening prospect that, in her terminology, his moral dilemma is simply a 'reaction formation' to be dealt with hygienically by the family psychiatrist – a perfect instance of the way Freudian ideas had come to neutralise ethical ideals, identifying any longing for justice or compassion as sublimations of personal repressions. The neurosis into which he is driven symbolises, as with most anti-heroes, his inability or refusal to conform to the debased standards of behaviour represented by his peers. While it invites the derision or condescending pity of the successful businessmen and robust professionals around him, it singles him out as the twentieth-century seer, the visionary whose real reason for failing to come to terms with society is his perception of its hollowness.

In Eli's first exchange with Tzuref, the head of the Yeshivah, Roth contrasts two sets of law or social standards, the American legal system to which Eli owes a professional allegiance, created to protect property values for the wealthy Woodenton residents, and that of the Old Testament with its injunction to heed the cry of the needy, the widow and the orphan. That latter code impels Tzuref to provide parental care, comfort, security and education for the destitute children rescued from Nazi concentration camps, each of whom is, in his eyes, a being of inestimable worth. Eli, in explaining the legal basis for his clients' demands, finds himself confronted by a set of values drawn from a totally different world:

> 'It's a matter of zoning ... '
> 'The law is the law,' Tzuref said.
> 'Exactly!' Eli had the urge to rise and walk about the room.
> 'And then of course' – Tzuref made a pair of scales in the air with his hands – 'the law is not the law. When is the law that is the law not the law?' He jiggled the scales ... 'And vice versa.'
> 'Simply,' Eli said sharply. 'You can't have a boarding school in a residential area.' He would not allow Tzuref to cloud the issue with issues. 'We thought it better to tell you before any action is undertaken.'
> 'But a house in a residential area?'
> 'Yes. That's what residential means.' The DP's English was perhaps not as good as it seemed at first. Tzuref spoke slowly but till then Eli had mistaken it for craft – or even wisdom. 'Residence means home,' he added.
> 'So, this is my residence.'
> 'But the children?'
> 'It is their residence.'
> '*Seventeen* children?'
> 'Eighteen,' Tzuref said.
> 'But you *teach* them here.'
> 'The Talmud. That's illegal?'
> 'That makes it a school.'
> Tzuref hung the scales again, tipping slowly the balance.

Eli's initial attempt at compromise – the suggestion that when visiting the vicinity of Woodenton the bearded assistant should wear modern clothing – elicits a one-line reply from Tzuref: 'The suit the gentleman wears is all he's got.' Eli, interpreting the reply in the financial terms of the world he lives in, assumes that the man lacks money for a new suit; and at once pulls out his billfold, offering to cover the cost. But he has missed the tragic import of the reply – that, as a victim of Auschwitz, the sole possession left to the man is his ancestral faith, of which the Talmudic clothes are the symbol. Tzuref finds that he needs to explain:

> 'But I tell you he has nothing. *Nothing.* You have that word in English? *Nicht? Gornisht?*'
> 'Yes, Mr. Tzuref, we have the word.'
> 'A mother and a father?' Tzuref said. 'No. A wife? No. A baby? A little ten-month-old baby? No! A village full of friends? A synagogue where you knew the feel of every seat under your pants? Where with your eyes closed you could smell the cloth of the Torah?'

With the first symptoms of another breakdown, Eli, selecting his best green suit from the rack, feverishly thrusts it, together with shoes, hat, tie and underwear, into a cardboard box which he leaves on the Yeshivah porch under cover of darkness. It is his first act of involvement, an embryonic recognition of the need for commitment rather than flight. Next day, he is confronted on the street by a reflection of himself, the bearded refugee ludicrously decked out as an American citizen. The vision, an alter ego representing what Eli might have been had he been born in Europe, piteously questions Eli with his eyes as they pass each other: *'The face is all right, I can keep it?'* – must his identity be totally submerged by assimilation to the gentile world or may he keep some last vestige of his individuality?

The final step remains to be taken. As Eli sits brooding at home, his wife having left for the hospital where she is about to give birth, he hears a noise at the back door. The man, he assumes angrily, has taken the cowardly step of returning the suit. But as he opens the box left there, he discovers to his shock the 'Talmudic' suit within. And in the grip of an irresistible urge, he dons the clothing – the black hat, the black suit, even the one white garment, the fringed prayer shawl, which he sees as the flag of his voluntary surrender to Judaism. Eager for the approval of his alter ego, he races to the Yeshivah; but there the man points silently towards Woodenton. A public recantation is required; and to the consternation of his neighbours, both Jewish and gentile, Eli walks demonstratively down

Main Street in his black garb and on to the hospital where he must make his declaration before his newborn son, the future generation. As he stands before the crib, planning in due course to have the suit cut down to fit his son, and ready now to fulfil his patriarchal responsibilities in assuring a return to Talmudic faith, a male nurse summoned urgently by his neighbours, who assume he has again 'flipped' into a nervous breakdown, slips under his skin the needle of a sedative-syringe. The drug, Roth concludes, 'calmed his soul but did not touch it down where the blackness had reached' – the blackness representing here the spiritual life associated with the 'Talmudic' suit.

It would be hard to find anywhere in modern literature so uncompromising a reaffirmation of Old Testament morality, the reader's sympathies being directed throughout the story away from the brash, complacent Jews of suburbia and towards the scriptural values of compassion and personal responsibility which, Roth suggests, can alone make Eli's life meaningful. If we view it in the larger context, it marks, in parallel with Greene's Catholic grappling with the twentieth-century crisis or Koestler's political version, a recognition of the principles that had been lost in the process of discarding ancient traditions and standards. As in previous instances of this mid-century genre, even though the anti-hero may himself be prevented from fulfilling those ideals as a warped society places him in an asylum or tranquillises him with a sedative, the insights he has achieved serve as the author's pointer to the path we should follow.[35]

Such revalidation of the Hebraic tradition would be irreconcilable with the flagrantly profligate Portnoy or with a Nathan Zuckerman exulting in his overthrow of conventional beliefs were it not for the ambivalence that pervades the novels in which those characters appear, the existence of a submerged counter-theme undercutting the surface rebellion, a heteroglossia such as Bakhtin had identified. The facetious self-mockery of Portnoy's struggle to free himself marks, as has long been noted, a hopelessly belated attempt to cut the umbilical cord, to break away from the smothering influence of his mother. His onanism is, as he himself recognises, a childhood gesture of defiance, an attempt to repulse the smothering affection of his mother. His philandering bachelorhood is a deliberate refusal to provide grandchildren for that masterful maternal figure who has insinuated her meddlesome presence into the most intimate areas of his life. Each humiliating conquest of a gentile girl – and it is their humiliation he seeks more than his own sexual gratification – constitutes a protest against that symbol of his own arrested development, the 'Yiddische Mamma', to whom he will always remain a little boy in need of coddling. For the outside world he may have achieved television coverage as a successful lawyer already appointed to a leading post in the New York City administration, but for her, all that matters is that he wear a warm vest and take care of his weak knee.

There is, I suspect, an allegorical substratum to this relationship, especially as the family described here was, in fact, entirely fictional, fundamentally different from the actual family in which Roth grew up. Roth's father was, for example, in no way offended by the unflattering description of the fictional father, offering his son every encouragement to continue writing such novels despite its condemnation by the Jewish community; and Roth himself declared that the story had been based not on his own family but on a neighbouring family with whom he sometimes stayed.[36] Roth's substitution, his replacement of his own parents in a work so obviously autobiographical in its basis, suggests that he needed the fictional figures for a specific purpose. Indeed, the recurrence in American-Jewish literature of the stereotype to which Sophie Portnoy belongs, endlessly fussing and worrying over her children's welfare, implies a symbolic significance needing examination. It has long been assumed that the Yiddische Mamma in literature represents everything traditionally Jewish – chicken soup, beigels, maternal concern – and that the rebellion against that figure in so much of modern Jewish writing reflects the effect of the Enlightenment, an urge to break away from the past and to enter the twentieth-century world. But the reverse, I would suggest, is true, as a close reading of the texts embodying such characteristic accounts confirms. For the figure of the Yiddische Mamma emerging at the turn of the century is in fact a symbol in open contradiction of Jewish tradition, negating the markedly patriarchal emphasis stretching unbroken from the earliest history of Judaism to the late nineteenth century. From the time of Abraham, through the kings and priests, and on through the generations of rabbis who followed, it was the bearded paterfamilias seated at the head of the table who constituted the family's unquestioned spiritual and religious authority, the wife occupying a respected but subordinate position in the household hierarchy, deferring to the learned head of the household in all matters pertaining to Jewish law, whether of a moral or a ritualistic nature. And so the tradition remained in the Jewish townships or *shtetls* of Europe until the Russian pogroms of the nineteenth century sent waves of emigrants westwards to the United States. Nor was it the rise of feminism that changed that picture.

The impact of the refugees' entrance into the New World shattered the religious framework. In a country caught up in a race for financial prosperity in which the poverty-stricken immigrants needed urgently to find a foothold, the roles of mother and father became reversed. The motivating ideal of Judaism became transferred from the spiritual to the material sphere, the father's concern with transmitting the moral teachings of Judaism to his sons shrinking to insignificance, to be replaced by the newly domineering mother's insistence on physical survival – plying her children with hot chicken soup to ensure their bodily health, bundling them up in sweaters against the cold, driving them towards professional success as doctors and lawyers and, above all, urging them towards the wealthy marriages that were to serve as the guarantees of success. So here, depicted in humorously exaggerated terms, Sophie Portnoy reproves her recalcitrant bachelor son:

> 'Do you remember Seymour Schmuck, Alex? ... Well, I met his mother on the street today, and she told me that Seymour is now the biggest brain surgeon in the entire Western Hemisphere. He owns six different split-level ranch-type houses made all of fieldstone in Livingston, and belongs to the boards of eleven synagogues, all brand-new and designed by Marc Kugel, and last year with his wife and his two little daughters, who are so beautiful that they are already under contract to Metro, and so brilliant that they should be in college – he took them all to Europe for an eighty-million-dollar tour of seven thousand countries, some of them you never even heard of ...' (p. 99)

In the literature produced within this immigrant Jewish community at the time of Roth's youth, literature typified by Clifford Odets' play, *Awake and Sing!* of 1935, that figure of the prodding, goading Yiddische Mamma achieves prominence, with the bewildered father seated at the side helplessly stirring a glass of tea (the lemon-flavoured Russian version symbolising the *shtetl* which, mentally, he cannot leave) as his wife nags him mercilessly for his inability to cope with the unfamiliar world into which he has been thrust. The patriarchal tradition is replaced by a materialistic matriarchal unit; and in *Portnoy*, the helplessness of the father is translated, in Roth's usual unsavoury toilet imagery, into the chronic, paralysing constipation from which he permanently suffers.[37]

The interpretation of the symbolism offered here suggests a reading of the novel very different from the norm. Could it mean that Portnoy, the sexual profligate overthrowing everything traditional, was, in his rebellion against his interfering mother, protesting not against Judaism itself but against the subversion of Judaism dictated by the career-oriented society to which it had been transplanted? Like those thankfully overthrowing the strictures of the past only to find unhappily that they have nothing with which to replace the jettisoned values, Portnoy here would thus be really rebelling against the *usurpation* or discarding of the patriarchal tradition – and one recalls here the profound respect accorded to the bearded, Talmudic figures in the story of Eli. He would be decrying the expropriation of authentic Judaism by a grossly acquisitive philosophy represented in the mother.

The theory seems a little far-fetched, perhaps, until one returns to the text. At a moment of intense exasperation at the unremitting maternal badgering and pestering, Portnoy protests:

> if my father had only been my mother! and my mother my father! But what a mix-up of the sexes in our house! Who should by rights be advancing on me, retreating – and who should be retreating, advancing! Who should be scolding, collapsing in helplessness, enfeebled totally by a tender heart! And who should be collapsing, instead scolding, correcting, reproving, criticising, faultfinding, without end! Filling the patriarchal vacuum! (pp. 41–2)

That *cri de coeur*, his longing to see the father-figure reinstated in the place of honour, suggests that, like a child screaming 'I want ...' who deep within is hoping to hear his parents' firm, authoritative 'No!', so Portnoy's tirade against his mother is an attack not on the Hebraic religion but on its contemporary perversion on the American scene, on the repression of the morally authoritative voice of his father that should be scolding, correcting, and improving. Among the few scenes of quiet family pleasure recalled by Portnoy are the times when, in his youth, he used to accompany his father to the bathhouse, a place free from women, a locality whose atmosphere reminds him of 'some sloppy watery time before there were families such as we know them'.

It requires no psychologist to perceive in Portnoy's orgiastic ventures, in his unabashed and exhibitionist accounts of his sexual licence a desperate attempt to cauterise something within himself. As Bernard Rodgers rightly notes, the guiltier he feels, the more frustrated he becomes; the more frustrated he becomes, the more vehement is his obscenity and his sexual promiscuity, all directed towards countering the mother-figure[38] – although the symbolism of that mother-figure may not be quite what Rodgers imagines. One may note here in broader terms how that powerful figure, smothering the son's desire for self-expression in American-Jewish literature, is symbolically updated for the next generation by a version more suited to changed conditions but performing essentially the same function, a wife similarly undercutting the male's paternal authority, spiritual aspirations and moral yearnings. In Bellow's novel, Herzog, driven to distraction by his wife's duplicity, regards her as the primary force destroying his religious and spiritual potential. He sees himself as:

> a man tempted by God, longing for grace, but escaping headlong from his salvation, often close at hand. This Herzog, this man of many blessings, for some reason had endured a frigid, middlebrow, castrating female in his bed, given her his name and made her the instrument of creation, and Madeleine had treated him with contempt and cruelty as if to punish him for lowering and cheapening himself, for lying himself into love with her and betraying the promise of his soul. (p. 228)

Eli in Roth's story had, we have seen, experienced a similar form of uxorial castration, his young wife having advanced beyond the chicken-soup-and-sweater stage to the more modern refinements of psychoanalysis, continually subverting thereby his search for moral justification. So for Portnoy, the sexual indulgences aimed at defying his mother arise in large part from his desire for a reassertion of those same moral and spiritual codes he seems so eager to overthrow. As Roth himself noted in the pseudo-psychological analysis attributed to Dr Spielvogel on the opening page of the novel – and since it is, of course, written by Roth himself, it is of especial value in suggesting his own interpretation of Portnoy's actions – the latter experiences not only sexual urges but also 'strongly-felt ethical and altruistic impulses' perpetually at war with those urges: 'Acts of exhibitionism, voyeurism, and fetishism are plentiful; as a consequence of the patient's "morality", however, neither fantasy nor act issue in genuine sexual gratification, but rather in overriding feelings of shame and the dread of retribution'. In the same way, the epigraph Roth chose for this novel, the Yiddish proverb 'The heart is half a prophet', would appear singularly inappropriate to the blatant rejection of Judaism normally attributed to Portnoy were it not for this recognition of the contrary urge, partially submerged, his yearning for a revalidation of the moral imperatives associated with the biblical prophet but now subverted in the career-oriented setting in which he finds himself. If half his heart is libertine, half remains loyal to traditional morality.

In one of Roth's rare comments on the novel, during an interview published in the *New York Times*, he offered significant substantiation of this view in a comment deserving of more attention than it has received. Rebutting the charge that the book is full of dirty words because such is the way people talk, he remarks that such a reason would be one of the least persuasive motives for introducing obscenity in fiction. Instead, he explains that Portnoy

> is a man speaking out of an overwhelming obsession: *he is obscene because he wants to be saved.* An odd, maybe even mad, way to go about seeking personal salvation; but, nonetheless, the investigation of this passion, and of the combat that it precipitates with his conscience, is what's at the center of the novel. Portnoy's pains arise out of his refusal to be bound any longer by taboos which, rightly or wrongly, he experiences as diminishing and unmanning. The joke on Portnoy is that for him, *breaking the taboo turns out to be as unmanning in the end as honoring it.*[39] [My italics]

If consciously Portnoy rejects the 'taboos' of Jewish tradition in order to assert his manhood, he needs to learn, Roth maintains, that it is his rejection of those taboos that deprives him of his virility, a virility which, the novels reveal, is intimately connected to his ability to function as patriarch. Elsewhere, Roth recorded how deeply impressed he had been in his youth by an early essay of Philip Rahv's which distinguished two main schools among American writers – the so-called redskin type such as Mark Twain, expressing the aggressive vitality of an expanding country, and the paleface type such as T.S. Eliot, who 'continually hankers after religious norms.' Roth locates himself not within the redskin group as might have been expected but within the group of writers emerging on the American scene subsequent to those authors, younger writers who embody both tendencies in uneasy association:

> The point here is that the weakening of social and class constraints accelerated by World War II, and the cultural exchanges thus encouraged, has produced a number of writers, many now in their forties, who have to some degree reconciled what Rahv described as this 'disunity of the American creative mind', though not in any way necessarily congenial to Philip Rahv, or even to the writers themselves. For what this 'reconciliation' often comes down to is a feeling of being *fundamentally ill at ease in, and at odds with, both worlds.*[40] [Roth's italics]

That ambivalence, the mingling of rebellious breakaway with a nostalgic desire to return, remains a central theme throughout his writings, achieving one of its most impressive expressions in his later novel *The Counterlife* of 1986, skilfully adapting this central concern to the new critical principles of deconstructionism. Although that novel lies outside the chronological limits of this present study, I should like to glance at it briefly since it throws considerable light on his earlier work. In *Portnoy*, Roth had amusingly burlesqued the contemporary fad for psychoanalysis by presenting Alexander Portnoy's confessional narrative as if it is being delivered from the analyst's couch to a gravely Teutonic, note-taking Dr Spielvogel; and he had forestalled any disdainful response by readers versed in Freudian jargon by providing as the novel's epigraph the mocking, pseudo-psychoanalytical definition of his protagonist's condition, of 'Portnoy's complaint'. It marked the growing distrust of psychiatry as a solution for modern ills. In *The Counterlife*, the target of his parody has shifted to postmodern literary theory, especially the identification of unresolved conflicts within texts. Roth was clearly familiar with Bakhtin's concern with the conflicting 'voices' or tongues that he termed *heteroglossia* and with Derrida's concept of *aporia*, both highlighting the mutually exclusive discourses embedded in literature, and the impossibility of reconciling such contradictory messages;[41] and Roth mischievously saw in that widely accepted approach to literature a strategy that he, as an author, could apply in his own writing in a manner that would deprive the postmodernist critic of the need, or of the opportunity, to deconstruct them. It provided also a perfect vehicle for expressing Roth's conflicted dual personality as discernible in the earlier writings.

In burlesquing deconstructionism, Roth produced a novel in which the various chapters or sections dismantle the plot as it unfolds. The opening section, in traditional narrative form, introduces the unsuspecting reader to Henry Zuckerman, about to undergo a dangerous bypass heart operation. It proceeds to relate his death on the operating table and the arrival of his brother Nathan from Newark to participate in the funeral. The next section, with no authorial comment or explanation, changes to a Henry who has successfully survived the heart operation and has left Newark for Israel; while in a subsequent chapter, again with no authorial comment, Roth casually transposes the characters, as we learn that it was Nathan who died in cardiac surgery, leaving Henry to mourn him. The brothers' lives interchange in their peripherals too, Maria portrayed sometimes as Henry's mistress, sometimes as Nathan's, in a manner ensuring that the contrastive accounts remain totally irreconcilable, precluding any possibility of an integrated plot.

That deliberate confusing of the fraternal roles has an especial relevance both to our present theme and to an aspect of critical theory concerning the modernist era that has emerged in recent years. As Michael Levenson has shown, the recurrence of *Doppelgänger* figures in twentieth-century literature, evidenced by the Marlow–Kurtz relationship in Conrad's *Heart of Darkness* or by that of the priest and lieutenant in *The Power and the Glory*, reflected in part the plurality of modernism. The individual, no longer able to appraise life from a single authoritative standpoint, moral or otherwise, becomes disturbingly aware of manifold, often contrasting norms that compel him to project himself into a second figure, into an alternative vantage-point. It was a phenomenon, one may add, that found similar expression early in the century in Synthetic Cubism, in the process the Cubists termed 'simultaneity' whereby multiple viewpoints were superimposed on a single canvas, all angles of vision now being regarded as equally valid or invalid. It occurred too in Aldous Huxley's *Point Counter Point*, where, as the title indicates, for every seemingly authoritative standpoint there is now revealed a second or even a third authoritative standpoint that contradicts or nullifies it, leaving no single angle of vision as reliable. This sense of the divided self became a focus of concern for Jacques Lacan. Extending Freud's theory of narcissism, Lacan saw as especially significant the moment when a child first perceives itself in a mirror, the previously unified self being suddenly observed from without. From that moment onward, he suggests, the individual begins to define himself dually, in terms both of self and of 'Other', the latter constituting a contrast to or elaboration of personal identity. And Michel Foucault, adopting Bentham's Panopticon as the most pertinent image for the twentieth century – a form of prison in which a guard situated aloft in a tower is able to watch all the inmates while remaining hidden from them – noted how each prisoner within a cell develops a twofold conception of self: he becomes simultaneously conscious of his personal identity while at the same time aware of the way he is being viewed from outside.[42]

In Roth's version, this bifurcation of self takes on the fictional form of two brothers representing the polarised aspects of Roth's 'ill-at-ease' being, the transition back and forth ensuring that they evoke equal and alternating reader sympathy. Nathan, depicted as the author of a novel that had infuriated the Jewish world by its 'disloyal' exposure of the less palatable aspects of Jewish life, is most obviously a surrogate for the Roth most people recognise, rejecting allegiance to Judaism in favour of absorption into the modern American scene. Urged by a friend to commit himself to the Zionist cause, Nathan responds in the language of the classic assimilationist:

> My landscape wasn't the Negev wilderness, or the Galilean hills, or the
> coastal plain of ancient Philistia; it was industrial, immigrant America –

Newark where I'd been raised, Chicago where I'd been educated, and New York where I was living in a basement apartment on a Lower East Side street among poor Ukrainians and Puerto Ricans. My sacred text wasn't the Bible but novels translated from Russian, German and French into the language in which I was beginning to write and publish my own fiction – not the semantic range of classical Hebrew but the jumpy beat of American English was what excited me. (p. 57)

But if the character of Nathan offers Roth the opportunity of expressing his disdain for the faith he deserted, Henry provides an equally effective vehicle for formulating Roth's regrets, his yearnings in the opposite direction. Henry, in the course of the novel, returns passionately to his Jewish roots, leaves the United States for Israel, joining there a bearded Orthodox rabbi to settle in the disputed territories on the West Bank. Rejecting the comfortable lifestyle he had enjoyed as a successful dentist and the pleasures of an extramarital relationship with his female assistant, he undertakes with fervour his dedication to the heritage he had ignored for so long. His defence of his new stance is both vigorous and intense. On visiting the 'Talmudic' area of Jerusalem, with its bearded patriarchal figures, Henry declares, 'I actually don't care how it sounds to you or to anyone. I am not *just* a Jew, I'm not *also* a Jew – *I'm a Jew as deep as those Jews.* Everything else is nothing.' (p. 65). And when Nathan himself travels to Israel in an attempt to persuade Henry to return, the conversations with him, with the settler rabbi, with a young female teacher, offer a fascinating two-sided presentation, the secularist egocentrically determined to integrate into the American scene versus the committed Jew returning to his spiritual roots and dedicating himself to the ideals of brotherhood and morality. Indeed, so effective is the two-sidedness that one tends to forget that Roth is the author of both sides of the disputation, of Henry's and Rabbi Lippman's ardent devotion to the religious-Zionist cause as well as of Nathan's whole-hearted rejection of it. Roth's caustic criticism of himself in those exchanges is at times startling in its frankness, as when Henry castigates Nathan's continual recourse to slick psychoanalytic terms as a means of belittling his brother's every move and at the expense of respect for the most fundamental issues of life:

There's a world outside the Oedipal swamp, Nathan, where what matters isn't what made you do it *but what it is you do* – not what decadent Jews like you think but what committed Jews like the people here do! Jews who aren't in it for laughs, Jews that have something more to go on than their hilarious inner landscape! Here they have an outer landscape, a nation, a world! (p. 144)

If, on visiting the religious settlers, Nathan had treated them with carping, mordant cynicism, on the plane home he admits to a covert admiration for the settler-rabbi, a recognition that

> It's Lippman, after all, who is the unequivocal patriot and devout believer, whose morality is plain and unambiguous, whose rhetoric is righteous and readily accessible, and to whom a nation's ideological agenda is hardly an object for sardonic scrutiny. (p. 166)

Perhaps the most telling comment on the duality within Roth's personality is a remark about Nathan's anti-Jewish novel, *Carnovsky* (an obvious allusion to *Portnoy's Complaint*) delivered by a eulogist at Nathan's funeral – and again we need to remind ourselves that Roth penned those words too:

> The book, which I, like most people, believed to be about rebellion is actually a lot more Old Testament than that: at the core is a primitive drama of compliance versus retribution. The real ethical life has, for all its sacrifices, its authentic spiritual rewards. Carnovsky never tastes them and Carnovsky yearns for them. Judaism at a higher level than he has access to does offer real ethical rewards to its students, and I think that's part of what so upset believing Jews as opposed to mere prigs. Carnovsky is always complying more than rebelling, complying not out of ethical motives, as perhaps even Nathan believed, but with profound unwillingness and in the face of fear. (p. 213)

Similarly, in an interview with George Plimpton in 1969, in which Roth attempted to defend himself against the charge of anti-semitism, he insisted that, despite the impression he sometimes gave of eagerness to break away from the moral restraints of his Jewish background,

> the fact is (and I think there's even a clue to this in my fiction) that I have always been far more pleased by my good fortune in being born a Jew than my critics may begin to imagine. It's a complicated, interesting, morally demanding, and very singular experience.[43]

Even Nathan, one notes, in the section where he himself is the cardiac sufferer, decides to undergo the operation and thereby restore his infertility because of a sudden and inexplicable desire to become the patriarch, a desire he attempts to explain away on psychological grounds but that impels him to undertake the risk nonetheless.

> Why suddenly do I want so passionately to become a father? Is it entirely unlikely that far from the latent paterfamilias coming to the fore, it's the feminised part of me, exacerbated by the impotence, that's produced this belated yearning for a baby of my own? I just don't know! What is driving me on toward fatherhood, despite the enormous danger it poses to my life? (p. 207)

Thomas Huxley's optimistic assurance that the traditional moral code would be replaced by rationally based ethical standards had, as the next generation regretfully concluded, proved baseless.

> 'Standards', Krutch had remarked, 'are imaginary things, and yet it is extremely doubtful if man can live well, either spiritually or physically, without the belief that they are somehow real. Without them society lapses into anarchy and the individual becomes aware of an intolerable disharmony between himself and the universe. Instinctively and emotionally he is an ethical animal. No known race is so low in the scale of civilisation that it has not attributed a moral order to the world, because no known race is so little human as not to suppose a moral order so innately desirable as to have an inevitable existence. It is man's most fundamental myth, and life seems meaningless to him without it.[44]

For Salinger's adolescent Holden, the desire to reinstate the lost moral values was paramount as, in his flight from Pencey, he searched desperately for some principles on which to base his life, rejecting the dog-eat-dog world of the Stradlaters, the Darwinian-based entity ruled by the pursuit of self-gratification and reproduction, from which compassion, altruism and genuine love seemed to have disappeared. Philip Roth's adolescent, Alexander Portnoy, might seem to approximate more closely to the pattern emanating from Sir James Frazer's work as he contemptuously jettisons the religious traditions now revealed to him as merely primitive taboos and outdated superstitions; but beneath that surface rebellion and countermanding it throughout Roth's writings is a second impulse very similar to Holden's, a recognition of the ethical principles and ideals that have been discarded in the process of achieving the right to assimilate into the materialist world of America, and the consequent need to reconstruct or reclaim moral standards by which to live more nobly.

4
Innovative Drama

The main reaction to the modernist dilemma in Britain within the realm of poetry had come from the American expatriates within its midst. Stylistically, the crabbed allusiveness of T.S. Eliot's *The Waste Land*, with its broken images, split persona and disorienting contiguity of incidents disparate in time and space, had created a new model for verse far removed from the lyrical modes of Tennyson and Browning, a poetic style eminently suited to the new configuration and to the fragmentation of the individual; and Ezra Pound's Imagist movement, closely allied to Eliot, with its conception of poetry as needing to possess 'hardness, as of cut stone. No slop, no sentimentality,' had furthered this cultivation of an essentially new style.[1] Its influence, however, was to be not only far-reaching but also to some extent stifling, and by the 1950s there was a concerted reaction. The word 'concerted' may seem inappropriate, for although the reaction was shared by a number of leading poets, by friends who came to be known informally as 'The Movement', like many creative artists they resented being grouped in any category, tending to deny the existence of any unifying element.[2]

The facts, however, do point in the direction of a common endeavour. Philip Larkin, Kingsley Amis and John Wain, who had met as undergraduates at Oxford, formed the nucleus, soon to be joined by D.J. Enright, Donald Davie and Thomas Gunn who were then students at Cambridge, disciples of F.R. Leavis. One element unifying them was their determination to distance themselves from involvement in world problems. Ezra Pound's deplorable identification with Italian fascism had served as a warning, strengthening within the group an antipathy to verse devoted to national or any other contemporary concerns, including the general spiritual quandary of their time. Gunn stated forthrightly:

many literary commentators seem to think that the trouble with my generation is that it does not have a 'cause' – as if we were wrong for not nosing round after one. But there is no mass unemployment now, the unions are as powerful as they could wish to be, National Health has been around for ten years, and the village squires are all dead. The agony of the time is that there is no agony.[3]

Donald Davie, accused of avoiding engagement in the anti-militaristic movement or in any other form of action, wrote in his 'Rejoinder to a Critic':

You may be right: 'How can I dare to feel?'
May be the only question I can pose ...
And yet I'll quote again, and gloss it too
(You know by now my liking for collage):
'Alas, alas, who's injured by my love?'
And recent history answers: half Japan!
Not love, but hate? Well, both are versions of
The 'feeling' that you dare me to ... Be dumb!
Appear concerned only to make it scan!
How dare we now be anything but numb?

As the quality of this poem indicates, their rebellion against the type of verse introduced by Eliot and Pound included a stylistic preference as well as a thematic. They discarded the compressed, often cryptic language and imagery that had continued to dominate the poetic scene, D.J. Enright accusing Eliot's followers of cultivating obscurity merely in order to impress or to fill a gap. Whenever a poetaster, he claimed, 'can't go on meaning any longer, he can always slip in a stanza or two of non-meaning, which relieves him of the strain genuine poets must occasionally suffer under'.[4] One notes the word 'occasionally' here, suggesting that, for this group, poetry was no longer the challenging, agonising task it was normally assumed to be, its composition now demanding effort only from time to time. Davie's widely read *Purity of Diction in English Verse* of 1952 claimed openly that it was time for a return to clarity in verse, and Wain, reviewing *Oxford Poetry* for 1948, wrote: 'I have combed the book for evidences of what used to be called "contemporary sensibility", but there are almost none. Pylons, nylons, pistons, cisterns, all are banished ...'[5] The opening of the BBC radio service's Third Programme during this period furthered the attempt to make poetry available to a wider public, John Lehmann deciding to experiment with radio as a means of encouraging a broadening of response and ending the élitism that had characterised much of the century's verse. Wain, then a lecturer at Reading University, was invited by him to prepare a broadcast series entitled *First Reading*, aimed at introducing the writings of lesser-known contemporary poets to the average citizen. The type of theme characterising their verse was no longer the despair of the individual in a spiritually barren universe or the search for ethical values to replace those that had been invalidated but a cultivation of the mundane, a focus upon the trivial interests of everyday life. Amis, in deliberately colloquial terms, described his own dislike of the social and political embroilment of the previous generation, lightheartedly personifying such calls to responsible action as the wearisome visits of 'Major Courage':

> Trim in his boots, riding-breeches
>   And threadbare Norfolk jacket,
> He watched me, frowning, bawled commands
>   To work hard and enjoy it.
>
> I asked him once why I was there,
>   Except to get all dirty;
> He tugged his grey moustache and snapped:
>   'Young man, it's your duty.'
>
> What duty's served by pointless, mad
>   Climbing and crawling?
> I tell you, I was thankful when
>   The old bore stopped calling.[6]

All this has a considerable bearing on the theme of this present chapter. For the conscious mood of non-involvement among these poets produced in their prose-writing an essentially new kind of fiction, at the centre of which was not an anti-hero struggling to come to terms with the corruption around him but a figure closer to the tradition of the picaro – the irrepressible, often amoral scamp alien to the norms of society. Charles Lumley in John Wain's *Hurry on Down* of 1953, despite his university education, shuns the constrictions of a professional career, fecklessly progressing in the course of the novel through a series of such menial employments as window-cleaner, chauffeur and (lest anyone imagine the existence of a moral impetus to his rebellion) even drug-trafficker, ridiculing, often amusingly, the pretensions and complacencies of those around him. His satirical barbs, however, are no longer aimed at the hypocrisy, crass materialism or false values of society but at such minor irritations as the shrewish nagging of a landlady or the foul-smelling smoke from an old man's pipe. For an England still predominantly conservative in its traditions at that time, the novel seemed delightfully refreshing, warmly received by critics as marking a turning-point in the genre of the novel, especially when it was closely followed by Amis's far more successful *Lucky Jim*, with its hilarious spoof of socialised Britain. Amis's novel included a farcical satire on the 'red-brick' universities then being established in the provinces, seen here as mindlessly aping the centuries-old traditions of Oxford and Cambridge and, not least, parodied the supposedly scholarly research being pursued at these new institutions. The doctoral dissertation Jim Dixon has embarked upon in the hope of obtaining tenure in the history department, a thesis entitled *The Economic Influence of the Developments in Shipbuilding Techniques, 1450 to 1485*, he himself acknowledges with withering scorn as utterly worthless:

> It was a perfect title, in that it crystallised the article's niggling mindlessness, its funereal parade of yawn-enforcing facts, the pseudo-light it threw upon non-problems. Dixon had read, or begun to read, dozens like it, but his own seemed worse than most in its air of being convinced of its own usefulness and significance. 'In considering this strangely neglected topic,' it began. This what neglected topic? This strangely neglected what? ... [7]

The surprise and to some extent the pleasure for the reading public, particularly its younger members, was the reversal of expectation involved – that these authors, the first beneficiaries of the Welfare State, generously granted free university tuition so that members of the working class could have access to professional careers and enjoying a period when unemployment was almost nil, instead of expressing gratitude to the state for the opportunities offered them, were responding with scorn, burlesquing the middle-class mentality of England, the small-mindedness of its puritanical attitudes to sex, the drabness of the postwar scene, and the depressing lack of direction in society at large. Some of the older generation were horrified, Somerset Maugham remarking (with considerable justice, if with notable lack of humour) that the behavioural standards of these new characters were reprehensible:

> They do not go to university to acquire culture, but to get a job, and when they have got one, scamp it. They have no manners, and are woefully unable to deal with any social predicament. Their idea of a celebration is to go to a public house and drink six beers ... They will

write anonymous letters to harass a fellow undergraduate and listen to a telephone conversation that is no business of theirs. Charity, kindliness, generosity are qualities which they hold in contempt.[8]

But by the public at large such novels were welcomed as gratifyingly new in the stodgy environment of mid-century Britain. With the staging of John Osborne's *Look Back in Anger* at the Royal Court Theatre in London in 1956, the picture seemed complete, this innovative cluster of writers now being unanimously labelled 'The Angry Young Men'.[9]

Despite the wide acceptance of that term and its continued use by historians in application to this group of writers, there is, it seems to me, a basic fallacy in placing them within the same category. Two of them, Wain and Amis, had been members of the 'Movement' mentioned above, poets with a declared determination to avoid involvement in serious problems whether on the world scene or the national, and it was a principle that found equal expression in their prose writings in a manner that would seem to nullify the applicability of the term. Their novels incorporate no tragic quality, no angst, no deep spiritual disturbance, the main theme of Amis's novel being the lively pursuit of a spectacularly beautiful young lady whose hand Jim, of course, wins at the end. They were refreshingly amusing, not least in their irreverent flippancy towards the establishment. But to see in them any fundamental challenging of the contemporary scene, any deep-seated anger at the condition of the younger generation, is to endow them with a seriousness they did not possess and, moreover, with a seriousness they made no claim to possess. Amis dismissed as absurd the various critical attempts to read sociological implications into his fiction, insisting that his aim had simply been to amuse.[10]

Indeed, in British literature at large that refusal to face universal problems was paramount, the focus being primarily on the class-changes that were taking place on the English scene, with no real equivalent in America where class distinction had never been as deeply embedded. The profound social revolution occurring at the end of the war had deposed Churchill despite his enormous personal popularity, in favour of a Labour government that would implement the social programme of the Beveridge Report.[11] Among the recommended changes, free university education for qualified working-class youth provided an opportunity of professional advancement and consequent acceptance into the upper-middle class. That upward movement was to form the central theme of many British novels appearing at this time, notably by provincial writers, among them being John Braine's *Room at the Top* (1958) and *Life at the Top*

(1962), exploring the problems involved in adapting to the unfamiliar status and conventions of newly acquired wealth, and Alan Sillitoe's *Saturday Night and Sunday Morning* (1958) recounting, from the viewpoint of one who had escaped it, the drab, unrelieved life of the working class in his native city of Nottingham. They were concerned with local matters.

That freedom from commitment to causes did not apply, however, to Osborne's play. There were, indeed, superficial similarities to encourage his inclusion in the group of the Angry Young Men. There was Jimmy Porter's decision to reject the opportunities opened to him by his university degree and to operate instead a sweet stall in the market in partnership with his working-class friend Cliff; there was his trumpeting, both literally and metaphorically, in the face of the establishment, as well as his mordant comments on contemporary England as he and Cliff read through the Sunday papers in the opening scene. Alison's brother, the typical representative of England's upper-middle class, he sees as the straight-backed, chinless wonder from Sandhurst who has, somewhere at the back of his mind, 'the vague knowledge that he and his pals have been plundering and fooling everybody for generations'. He scoffs at remarks about nuclear armament by the Bishop of Bromley and, with regard to puritanical sexual mores, ridicules the female correspondent who wishes to know whether her boyfriend will lose all respect for her if she gives him what he asks for. But there is no passion or festering outrage in such remarks, as the stage directions confirm: '*He looks up at both of them for reaction, but Cliff is reading, and Alison is intent on her ironing.*'[12] He is trying merely to enliven a dull Sunday morning, to provoke a response from the others that might produce a spirited discussion, scuffle or argument to relieve his boredom before the play embarks on its more serious theme.

Both the motivation and the target of Jimmy's anger, including his often vicious treatment of his wife Alison, have aroused widespread controversy among critics, their suggestions providing a plethora of conflicting explanations. The views of the first-night critics, hastily set down to meet a newspaper deadline, need not, perhaps, be taken too seriously. Patrick Gibbs of the *Daily Telegraph*, unable to determine the nature of Jimmy's predicament, thought simply that he should have been sent to a psychiatrist; Stephen Williams in the *Evening News* determined that he was a character who could 'only be shaken into sense by being ducked in a horse pond or sentenced to a lifetime of cleaning latrines'; while Eric Keown defined him in *Punch* as 'an exhibitionist wallowing in self-pity'.[13] Yet even if one turns to later critics who had time to examine the text more closely and to reach more sober judgements, the motive for Jimmy's anger continued to be puzzling, some of the wilder conclusions indicating their frustration, their inability to pinpoint any relevant cause for his anger. He was (in all seriousness) identified in articles appearing in various academic journals as suffering from an unresolved oedipal complex, as tormented by a suppressed homosexual impulse, and as being (in current psychological jargon) 'an orally fixated neurotic who projects his own psychological shortcomings onto the external environment'; while so eminent a scholar as Muriel Bradbrook gave up the search for the object of his wrath, declaring that his self-pity and impulse to hurt 'have no particular target'.[14] The main motivations were, however, generally seen to be either Jimmy's class sensitivity, driving him to act sadistically towards his wife as a form of revenge on her middle-class background or, alternatively, a sexual incompatibility between them, the play portraying a particular kind of unhappy matrimonial relationship.[15]

Even those advocating such interpretations, however, admitted to difficulty in explaining the powerful impact the play had on audiences and its undoubted contribution to a major change in the direction of the theatre. All agreed on the 'electric tension' and sense of immediacy it produced on audiences, one very experienced theatregoer and critic commenting on those performances at the Royal Court that 'no evening in the theatre since has seemed quite as stirring.'[16] The British stage, still dominated at that time by the light, frothy plays of Noel Coward and Ian Hay, suddenly turned serious, taking on a new type of social concern that had not been seen since the time of Shaw's dramas. Critics could only conclude, somewhat lamely, that the impact of Osborne's play was fortuitous, that it 'just happened to set off or coincide with a theatrical chain-reaction'.[17] There was, moreover, the further problem that even those hostile to the play – seeing Jimmy as an unchivalrous maladjust, ranting at everyone because his sexual energy was bottled up and festering within him, or attributing the play's success to the appeal it held to the suppressed sadism of the audience – were troubled by the contradiction to those explanations implied by the warm affection and loyalty he so clearly aroused in Cliff, in Alison and in Helena, as well as by the heroic quality perceived in him by the audience despite, or perhaps because of, his fulminating. Such contradictory elements suggest that there were aspects of Jimmy's character that did not accord with the definition of him as a 'conscienceless sadist' – a comment from a review in the *New York Herald Tribune* considered so apt that it appeared for many years on the cover of the leading paperback edition of the play.[18]

I should like to leave the play for a few moments to focus upon an aspect of the broader cultural scene that has, I believe, considerable bearing on its theme. The novel of the stream of consciousness, by concentrating upon the unformalised thoughts and associations passing through the human mind in a sequence dictated by intimately personal experience, had constituted one very notable attempt during the course of the century to counter the sense of human insignificance in an alien universe. The emotional concerns of each character, individualised by the specific childhood experiences, traumas and ambitions relevant to his or her life, militated against the uniform psychological patterning that had undermined faith in the self, thereby reasserting the markedly independent personalities of such characters as Stephen Dedalus or Leopold Bloom. In directing attention away from the physical world, the empirically verifiable reality, to the interior mental processes of the mind, the mundane events of plot and the details of location or setting had tended to shimmer away into triviality beside an inner existence revealed with fascinating vitality and credibility. For Virginia Woolf's protagonists, physical actuality becomes an unwelcome intrusion upon that rich inner life, their gaze averted from it whenever possible or transforming it into misty, unsubstantial background images:

> They had reached the gap between the two clumps of red-hot pokers, and there was the lighthouse again, but she would not let herself look at it. Had she known that he was looking at her, she thought, she would not have let herself sit there, thinking. She disliked anything that reminded her that she had been seen sitting thinking. So she looked over her shoulder, at the town. The lights were rippling and running as if they were drops of silver water held firm in a wind. And all the poverty, all the suffering had turned to that, Mrs Ramsay thought. The lights of the town and of the harbour and of the boats seemed like a phantom net floating there to mark something which had sunk.[19]

Partly through that avoidance of actuality, the novel of stream of consciousness had, as was noted in an earlier chapter, been unable to hold its own, the intellectual strain of a narrative devoid of structured plot and often of chronological sequence proving too daunting for the average reader.

The emergence of the anti-hero in fiction formed a very different attempt to cope with the problem of loss of individuality, this time not avoiding but confronting the outer world, depicting the individual's search for integrity in a corrupt material reality. But within that genre, there was a marked vein of pessimism. Whatever pointers might be offered by the author, hints at a valid way of living that could serve as a model for combating the crisis, the anti-hero himself, even if he did succeed in preserving his integrity, did so at the price of nervous collapse or social ostracism. He might, like Herzog, eventually overcome his crisis but then only by partial surrender, reconciling himself to the dominance of the so-called Reality Instructors, the vulgar, manipulative exploiters with whom he must reluctantly come to terms.

Existentialism, in contrast, entering literature from the realm of philosophical speculation normally of little interest to the general public, supplied in the mid-century a powerfully attractive method of contending with the spiritual dilemma central to the time. The resumption of cultural contact with the European continent at the end of the Second World War, by introducing Britain and (initially, with less enthusiasm) the United States to a new generation of French intellectuals – to Sartre, Simone de Beauvoir and Camus, whose philosophy had been created in part by their experiences in the Resistance movement under Nazi occupation – provided a vibrantly positive method of resisting the meaningless suffering of the human condition as they strove to reverse the implications of the twentieth-century crisis. And it is there, I believe, that the source of this play's attraction is to be found.

It has become traditional to trace back the origins of existentialism to the early nineteenth century, a factor that might seem to disqualify it as arising from problems specific to the twentieth. But a basic principle of historical investigation is relevant here. Indebtedness to earlier sources, even when openly acknowledged by writers, artists or thinkers, should not be taken at face-value. In most instances, such harking back to the past arises from a pre-existent desire to find some earlier authority whose support could help validate thematic or stylistic innovations prompted by immediately contemporary concerns. One needs in each instance to enquire what elements within the creative artist's own time led him or her to select that specific historical model above all others, and one needs also to discern in what ways that precedent was, in the process of its adoption, subtly adapted to new needs. George Eliot, rejecting the heroic romanticism of Walter Scott and attracted to a more realistic form of portrayal – her preference for writing 'of commonplace people whose conversation might not be brilliant but who harboured within their dim and narrow existence joys and sorrows worthy of regard' – in a well-known passage cited the naturalistic domestic interiors of the Dutch school of painters as the impetus and model for her choice; but it is surely more relevant that, quite independently and at precisely the same time, Courbet was, across the Channel, proclaiming his 'Realist Manifesto' in defiance of contemporary modes, and depicting such similarly unheroic scenes as the simple village burial at Ornans.[20] The desire for a movement towards realism was thus already emerging in her time, and Eliot, searching for an established precedent that would help her to counter opposition, seized upon that earlier mode as a means of validating her own. So in this instance, Sartre and Camus may have seen in the work of the nineteenth-century theologian Søren Kierkegaard philosophical elements useful to their own immediate needs, but the gap between Kierkegaard's motivation and theirs makes any fundamental indebtedness dubious.

Kierkegaard's philosophical approach had resulted from intensely personal causes. Engaged to, by all accounts, a charming young lady, Regine, with whom he had been in love for some years, Kierkegaard found himself, as their relationship matured around 1840, unable to face the restriction of freedom intrinsic to matrimony, seeing such contractual undertaking as a fettering of his intellectual and emotional liberty. After an agonising inner struggle at the conclusion of which he broke off the engagement, he devoted the rest of his life in effect to justifying his action retrospectively, formulating both for himself and for others the principle of antinomianism, a rejection of all social or religious bonds that might hamper the independence of the individual. His motivation was not an attempt to reinstate the value of the individual in a world that had nullified its significance but, as in his attack on the established Danish church, to resist the institutionalising of religion and morality, of which matrimony formed a part. But in the terms he employed and in the instances he adduced to reassert the principle of personal responsibility there were elements that seemed adaptable to the needs of the twentieth-century thinker, concepts that they could usefully employ both to buttress and to lend authority to their own emergent ideas. Especially germane was his interpretation of Abraham's readiness to sacrifice his son Isaac in defiance of conventional ethics:

> The solitary man ascends Mount Moriah, which with its peak rises heaven-high above the plain of Aulis; he is not a somnambulist who walks securely above the abyss, while he who is stationed at the foot of the mountain and is looking on trembles with fear and out of reverence and dread dare not even call to him ... How then did Abraham exist? He believed. This is the paradox which keeps him upon the sheer edge and which he cannot make clear to any other man, for the paradox is that he, as the individual, puts himself in an absolute relation to the absolute. Is he justified in doing this? His justification is once more the paradox; for if he is justified, it is not by virtue of anything universal, but by virtue of being the particular individual.[21]

Abraham, Kierkegaard explains, is aware that high above there winds a solitary path, narrow and steep; that although it is terrible to be born outside the universal, to walk without meeting a single traveller, yet only in such lonely and individual choice can one find an authentic self.

Kierkegaard's stance won little respect during his lifetime, even within his native Denmark. It was, significantly, only in the twentieth century that he came to be known to the wider public, no doubt because by then the adaptability of his ideas to changing contemporary needs had begun to be perceived. The similarity between the above passage and Camus's use of the Sisyphus figure as a prototype for his own age highlights the attraction that Kierkegaard's version of Abraham provided, both characters resolute in their determination to ascend the mountain despite the seeming cruelty or absurdity of the assigned task, and refusing to submit to the accepted norms of society. The existentialists, however, in using the authority provided by the theologian, tended to underplay the fundamental difference between the two symbolic scenes – Abraham making his choice through unswerving faith in his Creator, while Camus's existentialist does so in flagrant defiance of the gods. What did seem relevant as a common denominator was their insistence on personal choice, Camus imagining, in his Sisyphus,

> the whole effort of a body straining to raise the huge stone, to roll it and push it up a slope a hundred times over; one sees the face screwed up, the cheek tight against the stone, the shoulder bracing the clay-covered mass, the foot wedging it, the fresh start with arms outstretched, the wholly human security of two earth-clotted hands. At the very end of his long effort measured by sky-less space and time without depth, the purpose is achieved. Then Sisyphus watches the stone rush down in a few moments toward that lower world whence he will have to push it up again toward the summit. He goes back down to the plain.
>
> It is during that return, that pause, that Sisyphus interests me. A face that toils so close to stones is already stone itself! ... At each of those moments when he leaves the heights and gradually sinks toward the lairs of the gods, he is superior to his fate. He is stronger than his rock.[22]

Sisyphus's recognition (in contrast to Abraham) of the absurdity of his human condition, coupled with his resolution to undertake the task nonetheless, leads him, by that act, to prove his 'existence' in a manner similar to that which Heidegger had defined. Men and women, Heidegger had maintained, thrown into this inexplicably harsh world, for the most part passively resign themselves to their lot, taking refuge in norms, routines and rituals, thereby transforming their lives into wearisome banality. To *exist* in any real sense – *Dasein*, as he called it – demands the individual's determination to live up to the highest ideals, a determination to achieve full human stature by effectuating acts of personal choice, choices fraught with a full awareness of the heavy responsibility involved.[23] Sartre, positing a similar distinction between *en-soi*, existence related merely to the world of objects, and *pour-soi*, the exertion of will within the self in order to attain to an awesome freedom, brought that concept into the public domain in his *Being and Nothingness* of 1943. In all such doctrines, the empirically provable and rationally defensible are cast aside as irrelevant, to be replaced by a subjective leap of faith by which alone life can be justified in any real sense. In a generation for which selfhood seemed to have been nullified, the existentialist moved outside logic to an entirely emotional plane, claiming that the dignity of the individual could be reasserted only by positive acts of choice.

Existentialism came to comprise a broad and variegated range of philosophical positions, embracing the secular versions of Sartre and Camus, the Protestant theology of Paul Tillich, the Catholic credo of Gabriel Marcel, and the *I–Thou* concept of Martin Buber derived from Hasidism. But whatever the form, the basic shared element, without which no viewpoint can be termed existentialist (an element entirely missing in Kierkegaard's philosophy) was an initial recognition of the seeming meaninglessness of the universe and the urgent necessity for choice and commitment – whether to achieve selfhood in the secular world or, within the religious sphere, to bridge the intimidating gulf that had opened up between the human worshipper and the divine. The new demand was not for a single act of choice but for an ever-present awareness of the need to choose, to determine one's stance at every moment of one's life as though crossing some terrifying abyss by means of a narrow bridge or tightrope, where one false step could prove disastrous. To rely upon dogmas and rituals, to fall back upon socially approved moral standards, was to fail absolutely.

Central to this existentialist outlook and forming part of the desired commitment in almost all forms of the philosophy was an aspect permeating Osborne's play, the element defined by Buber as the *I–Thou* relationship. Buber, in his early years as a youth leader when approached for advice by a troubled youngster, had offered what he felt to be appropriate counsel, only to discover that the young man, shortly after that interview, committed suicide. Throughout his life Buber remained haunted by guilt, by the conviction that if only he had made a stronger effort of will and by more intense personal engagement achieved the kind of total commitment demanded by the new movement, he might have saved that man's life. The emotional bond created between one being and another would, he decided, not only serve to assist the other but also make one's own existence viable. Such authentic contact between humans, Buber wrote in 1947, is to be found 'only between real persons. It can be as strong as death, because it is stronger than solitude, because it ... throws a bridge from self-being to self-being across the abyss of dread of the universe.'[24] The concept of the abyss before each individual, the ever-present dread of the universe, was, of course, Buber's version of the twentieth-century crisis we have been examining, the dwarfing of the individual self in a vast, indifferent cosmos.

Within literature, the fictional writings of Sartre and Camus, in the form of both drama and novel, helped disseminate the new existentialist ideas. Camus's *L' Étranger* offered a vivid image of the failure to accept personal responsibility and commitment. Meursault, the central character, oppressed by what he terms the 'benign indifference of the universe' and unable to discover any means of validating his life, casually shoots dead an acquaintance he sees lying on the sand, not through animosity but because 'just then it crossed my mind that one might fire, or not fire – and it would come to absolutely the same thing.' Charged with murder, he responds with total indifference. In an absurd and illogical world, the court's search for a motive behind the murder, the concept of justice itself, even the assumption that death is a punishment are all to him empty notions. His only reaction throughout the story is a burst of laughter at the ludicrousness of his situation when he is led to execution – a chilling vision of the danger facing those unable to adopt the solution offered by existentialism.[25] These ideas came to permeate literature outside the narrower circle of the existentialists themselves, as in one of the works we examined earlier. One reason for the Vatican's disapproval of Graham Greene's novels despite their advocacy of Catholicism arose from his antinomian downplaying of the dogmas and doctrines of his church in favour of the more personal moral choice of the individual. The priest's omission of such rituals as fasting are dismissed by the author as venial sins, unimportant beside his unswerving commitment, his dedication to the spiritual needs of his parishioners and the *I–Thou* relationship he experiences with each. And in an even more obvious challenge to his adopted faith, Greene in *The Heart of the Matter* seemed to approve of Scobie's suicide, undertaken out of compassionate commitment to his estranged wife and to his young mistress, an act seen by the author as altruistic, meriting sainthood, a form of *imitatio Dei* as he sacrifices himself for the sake of others, even though that act defied the church's doctrinal condemnation of self-immolation as an unforgivable sin.[26] Outside fiction, in a manner contradicting the normal restriction of philosophical speculation to an intellectual élite, the message of existentialism produced the unprecedented public response to the Vietnam War, as thousands, often unaware of the source of their impulse, turned out day after day to participate in protest demonstrations in response to the new demand for personal commitment, the need to choose and act instead of, as in the past, leaving such decisions to the politicians.

Existentialism was thus at the height of public interest during the staging of Osborne's play, its principles and concepts permeating the 1950s even when such manifestations were not specifically identified with its philosophical stance. And it is there, I believe, that the clue to the theatrical impact of *Look Back in Anger* is to be found, those three basic concepts – acknowledgement of the absurdity of the universe, recognition of the utter loneliness of the individual, and acceptance of the urgent need to establish *I–Thou* commitments with others – providing the underlying motifs of the drama.

The anger and frustration from which Jimmy suffers is aimed not against the welfare state, nor against the views of the Bishop of Bromley. It arises from the anguish that lies at the heart of the twentieth century, his awareness of the inexplicable distress of human suffering. That knowledge, as the play informs us, had come to him early, long before the inauguration of the welfare state, in the traumatic experience of his childhood when, at the age of ten, for twelve months he watched his father slowly dying after returning wounded from the war in Spain. Even worse than the suffering was, for the child, the indifference he perceived in those around his father, the lack of commitment on the part of his mother and others as his father lay there ignored by friends and family, with only the sympathy of his young son to sustain him. As Jimmy recalls bitterly (the word he employs confirming its basic relevance to the play's title), 'I learnt at an early age what it was to be angry – angry and helpless. And I can never forget it. I knew more about – love ... betrayal ... and death, when I was ten years old than you will probably ever know all your life.' (p. 58)[27] Hence his belligerent trumpeting against the world, his burning contempt for the complacency of a middle class interested only in personal comfort and material well-being and so hopelessly blind to the tragedy of the human situation. At one point Alison, misunderstanding him completely as she does through most of the play, declares that her father is hurt because everything is changed, while Jimmy is hurt because everything is the same; but the truth is that, while Jimmy may momentarily scoff at the Edwardian era and at the Colonel's recollections of it as a golden era that is past, he can sympathise with such nostalgia, recognising the comfort such a time must have offered with its 'home-made cakes and croquet, bright ideas, bright uniforms. Always the same picture, high summer, the long days in the sun, slim volumes of verse' before the advent of the debilitating crisis of the twentieth century. As he adds thoughtfully, 'If you've no world of your own, it's rather pleasant to regret the passing of someone else's', a period when there were still causes to be fought and ideals to be attained. (p. 17)

It is their dim awareness of the depth of Jimmy's grief and anger that evokes in Cliff, Alison and the audience itself a respect for Jimmy, a sense of heroic stature however reprehensible and, at times, childish his expressions of frustration may be. He is spiritually cut off from his companions, totally isolated in his pessimistic perception of the human condition. In the incident with his father, he was the only one who cared, and coupled with this consciousness of the general indifference to suffering is his sense of the impossibility of finding any valid ideals to which he can dedicate himself. Like the Savage in Aldous Huxley's *Brave New World*, he longs for some noble aim, but all moral principles seem to have been disqualified in the sordid existence of the modern wasteland, moving, as science progresses, towards a cloning and standardising of humankind:

> There aren't any good, brave causes left. If the big bang does come, and we all get killed off, it won't be in aid of the old-fashioned, grand design. It'll just be for the Brave New-nothing-very-much-thank-you. About as pointless and inglorious as stepping in front of a bus. (pp. 84–5)

The natural antagonism between Jimmy and Helena is intimately connected with his existential awareness. She is, in effect, the anti-existentialist, the negative image or foil against which the play will assert its positive concepts. For her, the normative is the valid path. She attends church regularly – it is Jimmy's astonishment at Alison's joining her in attendance at church that precipitates the breach between them – she refuses to participate in suffering, she has, as Jimmy puts it, retired into a little cottage of the soul, cut off from the ugly problems of the modern world; and to round it all, she is, in the tradition of the Victorian era, totally blind to the contradiction between her religious principles and her readiness to replace Alison in Jimmy's bed. Above all, her friendship with Alison lacks, as that readiness reveals, the most elementary principle of personal commitment and responsibility. Jimmy's decision at a moment of high drama in the play to respond to her advances is prompted not by any genuine compatibility but rather by a desire to spite Alison, a somewhat immature means of wreaking vengeance. Her replacing of Alison is regarded with aversion by the choric figure, Cliff, who leaves the apartment in protest, unable to reconcile himself to so sordid a situation – sordid not on conventional moral grounds but in his sense of Helena's inferiority as a substitute for the Alison he deeply admires. All of which returns us to the central theme of the play, the relationship between Jimmy and Alison that has proved such an enigma to critics.

To argue, as many have done, that the conflict arises from class distinction, that Jimmy provokes her in order to revenge himself on the world from which she has come, is manifestly untenable. Alison has demonstrated as clearly as anyone can her readiness to desert her middle-class background and enlist in the ranks of Jimmy's cause by defying her family, by leaving the comforts of her home, and by joining him in a bohemian existence, actions that dissociate her entirely from her previous existence. Even such factors as Cliff's embracing her in the presence of Jimmy, or casually removing his trousers for her to repair isolates her from the puritanical attitudes of her previous class, so that any attempt on Jimmy's part to revenge himself through her would be patently misguided. The *ménage à trois* aspect with which the play seems to open turns out, of course, to be no more than an illusion, a false impression, Cliff's affection for her being entirely platonic, blessed with Jimmy's full trust and approval. But that hint of sexual licence and bohemian existence in the opening scene leaves no doubt that Alison has left her bourgeois origins behind her, disqualifying any suspicion that Jimmy's anger derives from class warfare.

It stems, in contrast, from one of those aspects that had been recognised as a disturbing contradiction in the various suggested readings of the play, from the deep love Jimmy has for her, revealed not least in the scene in which, in a moment of honesty, he admits to her how he is constantly watching and wanting her, the sweat breaking out when he sees her performing as ordinary an act as leaning over an ironing board. Her affection for him is no less, driven though she is to distraction by his unending and inexplicable provocations, insults and sarcastic gibes. The problem, therefore, can scarcely be sexual incompatibility; but it does arise from this love.

The problem for Jimmy is that Alison, the kindred spirit with whom he needs so urgently to establish a spiritual bond based upon mutual commitment, tenderness and love, and with whom he longs to construct an I–Thou relationship, suffers from one essential deficiency. She loves him deeply in return, she is ready to sacrifice all comforts in order to share his way of life, but she lacks the basic qualification for the existentialist – she has no conception of the absurdity of the human condition, of the cruelty of an indifferent universe, of the suffering of humankind within it. She cannot share with him the agony of such knowledge which is the *sine qua non* of existentialist awareness. As Jimmy recalls at one moment in the play, a major attraction she had held for him when they first met was her extraordinarily calm disposition, a peacefulness of soul which, he assumed, she had achieved despite or beyond her knowledge of the abysmal condition of mankind: 'You seemed to have a wonderful relaxation of spirit. I knew that was what I wanted. You've got to be really brawny to have that kind of strength.' (p. 94) Only after their marriage did he discover that the source of her spiritual tranquillity lay not in her strength but in her total obliviousness to the despair that obsessed the existentialist. Without such knowledge, there can never be the profound relationship between them that he yearns for. Hence his ceaseless goading and tormenting, his anger at her 'lethargy', his desperate attempts to shake her out of her monumental 'non-attachment', his jeering at her as Lady Pusillanimous:

> Here it is. I quote: Pusillanimous. Adjective. Wanting of firmness of mind, of small courage, having a little mind, mean spirited, cowardly, timid of mind. From the Latin pusillus, very little, and animus, the mind. (*Slams the book shut.*) That's my wife! That's *her* isn't it? Behold the Lady Pusillanimous. (p. 22)

Beneath that cruel goading, beneath the insults and the scorn, there remains, despite all appearances to the contrary, an unabated and profound love, Jimmy's longing for her to join with him in a deeper spiritual sense as the sole person with whom he can experience an authentic intimacy and commitment. Helena could never satisfy that need; but Alison, although a potential candidate for that role, will remain unqualified for it until she herself has undergone some powerful crisis that will open her eyes to the magnitude of human suffering. Her unsuitability to the role becomes evident in her refusal to attend the funeral of Hugh's mother, an incident marking a turning-point in their relationship. Jimmy had found in that lady a simple woman of gentle, generous spirit, offering the kind of love and commitment that Buber recommended – a relationship not as deep as that he yearns for with Alison but sufficient to evoke in him the compassionate, considerate side of his character, the warmly affectionate Jimmy of whom we catch glimpses in the play. But

Alison, in her decision not to attend the funeral, reveals once again her insensibility to that aspect of Jimmy's character and to the importance such I–Thou relationships hold for him. As Camus had claimed, it is essential not only to acknowledge the absurd in human existence but to confront that absurdity, to keep it constantly before one in order not to fall back into the passivity of the customary, into a mechanical acceptance of daily existence;[28] and that is a process of which Alison has no conception.

Only through the death of her child does Alison at last come to recognise the despair that must precede existentialist awareness: 'All I wanted was to die ... Don't you see! I'm in the mud at last! I'm grovelling! I'm crawling! Oh, God – ' Such new consciousness at last allows Jimmy to respond with tenderness and love, recognising in her now a fellow soul with whom to establish the relationship they so sorely need. With each other they will find warmth and comfort, like cuddly bears and squirrels embracing in the harsh, freezing wasteland of the existentialist world:

> We'll be together in our bear's cave, and our squirrel's drey, and we'll live on honey, and nuts – lots and lots of nuts. And we'll sing songs about ourselves –about warm trees and snug caves, and lying in the sun. And you'll keep those big eyes on my fur, and help me keep my claws in order, because I'm a bit of a soppy, scruffy sort of a bear. And I'll see that you keep that sleek, bushy tail glistening as it should; because you're a very beautiful squirrel, but you're none too bright either, so we've got to be careful. There are cruel steel traps lying about everywhere, just waiting for rather mad, slightly satanic, and very timid little animals ... (p. 96)

To describe Jimmy as 'a conscienceless sadist,' as suffering from an unresolved Oedipus complex, as a suppressed homosexual, or even to see the play in terms of a class struggle is to misconstrue the reasons for its profound theatrical impact. The audiences at those early performances may have been unable to identify consciously the deeper theme, to define precisely the nature of its appeal; but their awareness of existentialist ideas permeating the intellectual and emotional climate of that period led them to perceive through Jimmy's torturing of Alison the genuine love that motivated it, his longing to share with the one person ultimately capable of such mutual understanding a recognition of the harshness of the human condition and a determination to resist it by total commitment to each other.

If existentialism has constituted one of the major attempts in the century to reinstate the selfhood of the individual, to establish beyond the anguish of lost values the possibility of reasserting one's dignity and of making life meaningful, it was Osborne who brought that concept into the British theatre and changed the subsequent direction of its drama. He replaced the lighthearted accounts of country-house weekends and blithe spirits with a more solemn response to the sterility of the twentieth-century condition, a theme to be taken up in Pinter's plays and in such works as Stoppard's *Rosencranz and Guildenstern Are Dead*. In that regard, it marked in a very real sense the end of the British theatre's tendency to escape into the trivial and frivolous, directing it instead to grapple with the central concerns of its time.

* * * * *

The seemingly unstructured form of Samuel Beckett's *Waiting for Godot* (1952) – a drama in which, as Vivian Mercier has wryly noted, 'nothing happens, *twice*,'[29] – the digressive, circular, yet absorbing progression of its two acts, by breaking with the long-established requirement that drama must possess a clearly defined beginning, middle and end, was itself an expression of the new conditions of the time. The sense of an ending, the expectation of closure providing an aura of completion, is, Frank Kermode pointed out some years ago, intrinsic to the human personality, which even interprets the *tick* of a clock as an upbeat movement demanding a gratifyingly conclusive -*tock*.[30] The deliberate rejection of firm structural progression in this play, which in earlier eras had reflected belief in an ordered universe, by frustrating such expectations and discarding the established patterning of drama, conveyed the sense of the purposeless-ness of human existence in an inscrutably chaotic and directionless existence. Vladimir's mournful assertion, '*at this place, at this moment of time*, all mankind is us, whether we like it or not',[31] underscored the contemporaneity of the play's theme, Beckett's intention that it should function as a dramatic archetype for the twentieth-century crisis.

The layman who still associated the twentieth century with momen-tous advances in technology might have expected very different dramatic representatives of modern man – a physicist to exemplify the achieve-ments of scientific investigation, an astronaut to symbolise the conquest of space, a surgeon to signify the impressive applications of medical research. He was confronted instead by two pathetically lost souls evocative of clown and tramp, characters risible in their slapstick, their pratfalls, their vaudeville stage-play, yet at the same time evoking sympathy for the dreariness, insecurity and hopelessness of their condition. Their names, Vladimir and Estragon, by transcending national barriers, suggest the anguish of all human creatures subjected to the bleakness of this present age, compelling audiences to recognise their own features in these unprepossessing figures, simulacra of a shared spiritual plight.

Beckett was reluctant to discuss or answer questions about the play, but he did offer obliquely one relevant comment concerning the changed function of the artist, a remark ostensibly referring to Proust but reflecting his own sense of the altered conditions pertaining to the twentieth-century writer. In contrast to earlier periods, he claimed, the modern author 'is shadowed more and more darkly by a sense of invalidity, of inadequacy, of existence at the expense of all that it excludes.' Elsewhere, he stated even more specifically that the author was now, paradoxically, forced to undertake the function of recording vacuity, living as he does in a period in which 'there is nothing to express, no power to express, no desire to express', while at the same time recognising that there remained for him nonetheless the obligation to express. Beckett did not believe that art would henceforth lack structure because of the vacuity, but that an essentially new framework needed to be created, capable of representing the chaos of the contemporary condition: 'To find a form that accommodates the mess, that is the task of the artist.'[32]

One aspect of the dramatic form he created to express this sense of universal disorder was the play's continual undermining of spatial and temporal stability. Boots become transformed overnight from black to brown, doubt exists whether the tree forming the sole stage property is or is not the same as yesterday's, various characters, on a second meeting, deny that they have ever met before. Such protean fluidity, two acts repetitive yet non-identical, similar yet different, in which characters struggle to recall past events, reflected not only the contemporary doubts concerning the stability of human identity but also, and in a larger sense, the distrust of empiricism itself, the conviction that the tangible elements in this world are ultimately inconsequential, that they have shimmered away into insubstantiality as the individual searches for some overarching meaning beyond the merely tactile, beyond the terrestrial reality that has become so irrelevant to these fundamental concerns about the function of mankind in the universe and the ultimate purpose of living. The mutability of the factual applied even to the person searching for such metaphysical unity; for the self that existed yesterday is not the same as the self existing today, every cell of which the body is composed being, as we now know, replaced and renewed in the process of growth. Heraclitus long ago compared the flow of life to a river which, although it may seem constant in so far as it retains its name and locality, was in fact replacing at every moment the drops of water of which it was composed. But now that liquescence was seen equally relevant to the physical aspects of human existence, the loss of identity applying not only metaphorically but corporeally. To symbolise such fluidity of being, Estragon's name inexplicably metamorphoses into Catullus, Vladimir drifts into Mister Albert, while Pozzo, though retaining his name, is fundamentally transformed from the arrogantly brutal master of the opening act to the pathetic blind sufferer of the second, seemingly with no consciousness on his part that any change has occurred. The individual, forlornly yearning for selfhood, can find no secure foothold for the dislocated being he has found himself to be in the shifting, uncertain world around him, no stable ground from which even to begin his quest. Vladimir's cheery welcome, 'So there you are again,' elicits from Estragon the doubtful reply, 'Am I?'

With the weakening or disqualification of those moorings that had previously offered the individual a modicum of security – the concept of mankind as the centre of the universe, the confidence of belonging to a family unit within a clearly defined social hierarchy, and the belief in the firm measurability of time and space – the sense of self that had previously provided a feeling of permanence had become perilously impaired. The consciousness of biographical continuity linking past to present which, as R.D. Laing has shown, make yesterday's resolutions and commitments relevant to today's decisions could no longer exist in a character psychologically and physically splintered, as in Eliot's 'I can connect / Nothing with nothing.' Without such integrative awareness, as social structures and ethical values moved into a state of flux, confidence in a developing personal narrative was due to become radically disturbed, creating an impression of life as being a series of disconnected and hence meaningless fragments.[33] In such a setting, in a world devoid of guiding principles or moral tenets, lacking all stimulus to advance, time itself becomes a burden, the source of oppressive tedium only temporarily dispelled by the childish games indulged in between those monotonous stretches.

> *Long silence.*
> VLADIMIR: That passed the time.
> ESTRAGON: It would have passed in any case.
> VLADIMIR: Yes, but not so rapidly.
> *Pause.*
> ESTRAGON: What do we do now?
> VLADIMIR: I don't know.

Beckett, on attending a rehearsal of Peter Hall's production of the play, offered only one criticism, that the gaps in action, the pregnant lacunas in dialogue representing the weariness of existence, needed to be lengthened: 'you don't bore the audience enough', he urged. 'Make them wait longer. Make the pauses longer.'[34]

Since the only element in the wasteland setting of the play that offers even the faintest inducement to continue living is the dubious prospect of a visit by the elusive Godot, the identity of that mysterious figure becomes crucial to an understanding of the work; but the variety of interpretations proposed by critics has left that aspect inconclusive. He has been seen as an allegorical representative of Time Future, as a figure personifying Absence, as 'the promise that is always awaited and not fulfilled', even as a space that Beckett wishes us to fill with whatever we choose the character to mean at any particular moment.[35] The more obvious identification, based on the verbal association with God, has in general been rejected on two grounds. Hugh Kenner dismisses the possibility for what might appear to be a very cogent reason, that since the play was originally written and performed in French, the verbal association would have been entirely lost for audiences in a country where the word for God is *Dieu*.[36] But that argument is considerably weakened by the fact that the name Lucky also has no meaning in French and yet was clearly intended to carry its own verbal associations. Beckett had, in fact, originally assigned to Lucky the French name Lévy, but by the end of the first act had, while still composing the French version, altered it, retaining the name Lucky for all subsequent editions. That decision suggests that Beckett, fluent in both languages, assumed that such bilingual allusions would be caught by the intelligent, cosmopolitan audience at which the play was aimed. Asked in a later interview (conducted in English) whether he considered himself an English writer, Beckett replied ambiguously, '*Au contraire!*', a reply that wittily underscored the bidirectional aspect of the French and English versions. It would appear invalid, therefore, to exclude on linguistic grounds the deic allusion in the name Godot. [37]

The second reason for rejecting that identification derives from the author's repeated disparagement of the biblical deity both in his writings at large and within the play itself, his reiterated rejection of the concept of a divine power controlling the universe. There is, his characters suggest, no order to be perceived in their world, no benevolent providence, no retribution for sin, only senseless cruelty, the oppression of the poor, and the crushing of the victimised. On what basis, therefore, could Beckett be imagined to implant in his characters a yearning for the return of a Supreme Being who permits such grievous suffering for humankind, who could, as Pozzo derisively remarks, create in his own image such contemptible creatures as those now occupying the stage? Lucky's bitter parody of theological apologetics, his ridiculing of the claims for the existence of divine justice in the face of the patent inequities of this world, and his vision of hellfire and brimstone destined to consume indiscriminately the innocent as well as the guilty leave little room for assuming in Beckett any residual trust in the traditional God.

> LUCKY: Given the existence as uttered forth in the public works of Puncher and Wattmann of a personal God quaquaquaqua with white beard quaquaquaqua outside time without extension Who from the heights of divine apathia divine athambia divine aphasia loves us dearly with some exceptions for reasons unknown and suffers with those who for reasons unknown but time will tell are plunged in torment plunged in fire ...

Despite these attacks, there were those who, at the time of the play's original appearance, attempted to attribute Christian principles to Beckett, to deduce, for example, from the few leaves that sprout from the tree in the second act a suggestion of the immanence of the divine in a world too blind to perceive it, or to describe the drama (as did an anonymous reviewer in the *Times Literary Supplement*) as constituting a 'modern morality play on permanent Christian themes'; but George Wellwarth has justifiably rebuffed those attempts on the grounds that such critics cite passages out of context, reading into the play ideas clearly contradicted by the text.[38] Lucky's forthright and incisive ridiculing of the traditional God carries far more force than any symbolism imagined to exist in the reappearance of leaves.

On the other hand, scriptural and Christian references are so pervasive in the play that their centrality cannot be summarily dismissed, the main characters recalling almost obsessively such scenes as the thieves hanging beside Christ of whom one at least was saved, or discussing the arbitrary distinction between the sheep and the goats in the story of Cain and Abel. Moreover, despite their seeming rejection of religion, Vladimir's and Estragon's own engagement with Christian belief repeatedly enters the dialogue, however incongruously:

> VLADIMIR: But you can't go barefoot!
> ESTRAGON: Christ did.
> VLADIMIR: Christ! What's Christ got to do with it? You're not going to compare yourself to Christ!

ESTRAGON: All my life I've compared myself to him.
VLADIMIR: But where he was it was warm, it was dry!
ESTRAGON: Yes. And they crucified quick.

Their response to Christianity is ambivalent. Belief in a Divine Being is, as implied in the last line, scornfully to be rejected; yet the rejection is tinged with regret, both responses emanating from the same individual, from Estragon. There is, indeed, a reflection throughout their dialogue of the ambivalence characterising the twentieth-century disengagement from Christianity, an intellectual repudiation coupled with an emotional yearning. On the one hand, Beckett himself, it is clear from his writings, has accepted the standpoint that God is dead, has concluded that the revelations by Wellhausen, Darwin, Frazer and others have, for the thinking person, negated all possibility of continued belief in a deity. Yet there exists, together with that rejection, a sense that something enormously important to humankind has been lost in the process of such enlightenment. The clown-like characters bemoaning their lot, mourning the absurdity of their condition, represent on Beckett's part a lament for a forfeiture of human self-respect directly related to that change, an acknowledgement that the dignity of the individual has evaporated somewhere en route together with the abrogation of religious belief. The result, it would seem, is a longing not for the reinstatement of the biblical God – an eventuality Beckett sees as no longer viable – but for the arrival of someone or something, an undefined God/Godot, that might somehow restore meaning to life without demanding belief in the supernatural, without requiring from the thinking individual a denial of the powerful evidence adduced by the scientists and anthropologists. Hence the nostalgia for a lost past when such belief had been a source of comfort, when the world was warm and dry:

VLADIMIR: Do you remember the Gospels?
ESTRAGON: I remember the maps of the Holy Land. Coloured they were. Very pretty. The Dead Sea was pale blue. The very look of it made me thirsty. There's where we'll go, I used to say, there's where we'll go for our honeymoon. We'll swim. We'll be happy.

And at the nadir of their despair, discarding all intellectual reservations, they spontaneously utter the cry:

ESTRAGON: God have pity on me!
VLADIMIR: And me?
ESTRAGON: On me! On me! Pity! On me!

– prayers that, despite the irony and egocentricity, scarcely indicate a total abrogation of religious faith.

As Lawrence Graver has noted, the suffix in the name *Godot* evoked for the Frenchman numerous subtle associations which an English audience, even if competent in French, would probably miss but which indicate, at the very least, the thoughts passing through the mind of the author as he composed the work, sparking off connections with objects or concepts prominent in the play. *Godillot* is French for a hob-nailed boot or shapeless old shoe, *godet* for the kind of pipe Pozzo smokes, while the appending of *-ot* to a word or name is both diminutive and endearing.[39] The result we may deduce from that latter association is, in his choice of the name for the absent visitor, the substitution of the awesome Supreme Being of the Old Testament by a figure more personal, closer to the human condition, and hence less intimidating, a figure such as could provide the kind of comfort that the characters seek, while being to some extent detached from the traditional and no longer acceptable deity.

One element implicit in the loss of Christian belief and instrumental in creating the nostalgia was clearly the cancellation of hope in an afterlife, the trust that had, throughout the generations, offered the soothing prospect of some eventual recompense for the suffering experienced in this world. Without it, there is left only a depressing recognition that life is no more than a brief interval between crib and tomb, as in Vladimir's grim summary telescoping mortal existence into a passing moment: 'Astride of a grave and a difficult birth. Down in the hole, lingeringly, the grave-digger puts on the forceps.'

Despite the mournful note pervading the play, the subtitle defines the drama not as tragedy but as 'a tragicomedy in two acts', that insertion suggesting the author's desire to draw attention to an aspect that might otherwise be overlooked, namely, that the play marked the inception of an essentially new variety of that hybrid genre, a form that was to become characteristic of the mid-century stage.[40] As Marvin Herrick has pointed out in his classic study of the genre, the term 'tragicomedy' has, since its first appearance at the time of Plautus's *Amphitryon*, defied definition, being applied somewhat vaguely to any drama that mingles elements from the two dramatic forms.[41] What does emerge from his study, however, is that, in most instances throughout the ages, those contrasting elements have remained separate even when coexistent within a play. In such hybrid plays during the earlier years of the Renaissance, comedy was confined to the low-born characters, who performed in scenes segregated from the main plot, and was inserted as relief from the more sombre main theme. Even as those subordinate scenes became more closely intertwined with the main plot, they did not produce an integrated genre. The Fool may evoke laughter by jibes very pertinent to the play's theme, but Lear, even in such exchanges, retains his tragic dignity, never involved in slapstick. In contrast, within the form of tragicomedy initiated by Beckett, the distinction disappears, not fortuitously but as the expression of an essentially new concept. For the tragic condition of humankind, the exploration of earthly suffering, now merges with an awareness of the ludicrous ineffectuality of all mortals, stripped as they are of their potential for grandeur or majesty, their every attempt at achievement inevitably ending in a pratfall. Tragedy in its established sense could not, it has been noted, exist in the modern world with its lack of belief in some supernal power or fate directing the affairs of the universe, a controlling force that the hero or heroine must confront and become in some way reconciled to at the conclusion of the drama. As a basis for such confrontation, the individual challenging or wrestling with the divine must be of significant worth. Without that overarching presence and individual dignity, the human is lost in a void, robbed of the divine image, reduced to clumsy, pointless games, a figure tragicomic in a new and unprecedented sense of the term, with silence as the only real means of communication and that silence too wearisome to bear:

> VLADIMIR: Say something!
> ESTRAGON: I'm trying.
> *Long silence.*
> VLADIMIR: (*in anguish*) Say anything at all!
> ESTRAGON: What do we do now?
> VLADIMIR: Wait for Godot?
> ESTRAGON: Ah!
> *Silence.*

Deprived of any hope not only of tragic stature but even of basic self-respect, Beckett's figures have no recourse in the bleak world of their wasteland but to wait for the coming of Godot, however remote the possibility of that visit may be – to wait for an unidentified figure or idea able in some way to compensate for the absence of the divine, capable of restoring some meaning to their dreary lives. In response to Estragon's puzzled enquiry, 'What exactly did we ask him to do for us?' Vladimir replies:

> VLADIMIR: Oh ... nothing very definite.
> ESTRAGON: A kind of prayer.

> VLADIMIR: Precisely.
> ESTRAGON: A vague supplication.
> VLADIMIR: Exactly.
> ESTRAGON: And what did he reply?
> VLADIMIR: That he'd see.
> ESTRAGON: That he couldn't promise anything.
> VLADIMIR: That he'd have to think it over.

The terminology they employ is the terminology of religious invocation, prayer and supplication; and failing to obtain any satisfactory reply, they will, they know, be left with only one alternative, the alternative that Camus had defined as the central concern of his time, in contemplation of which they had begun the play and to which they return in the final scene:

> VLADIMIR: We'll hang ourselves tomorrow. (*Pause.*) Unless Godot comes.
> ESTRAGON: And if he comes?
> VLADIMIR: We'll be saved.

There still remains hope within the morass of twentieth-century despair, a hope very faint, unlikely ever to be fulfilled, but representing, Beckett suggests, the last resort for an age that has been liberated from the superstitions and taboos of the past but exposed, by the process of that liberation, to the sterility of a futile existence.

That same awareness of diminished selfhood motivated Tom Stoppard's impressive experiment in intertextuality, *Rosencranz and Guildenstern Are Dead*, first performed at the Edinburgh festival in 1966 and, as he readily admitted, indebted in many ways to Beckett, apart, of course, from its more patent indebtedness to Shakespeare.[42] The originality of the angle from which *Hamlet* is viewed there, the transfer of focus from the central figure to two minor, negligible, virtually interchangeable characters carried a weightier symbolic meaning than the mere dramatic ingenuity to which it has most often been relegated. It reflected the contemporary displacement of humanity from centre-stage to the periphery, the audience no longer identifying with the hero but with these two inconsequential figures. The members of the audience too see themselves as incapable of having any serious impact on the development of the plot into which they are born and, indeed, as preordained to fulfil their prescribed roles as they are driven helplessly to their doom.

The play's seemingly frivolous opening, Ros's spinning of a coin which inexplicably lands 'heads' eighty-five times in succession and continues to do so in defiance of actuality in fact explores one of the major problems of the period we are examining, an offshoot of the larger dilemma that had so reduced the significance of humankind. It represented the new awareness that there existed somewhere in the universe mathematical formulae mysteriously dictating the events of this world. As far back as the governmental fact-finding committees that had begun to be established in the 1850s (caustically satirised in Dickens's *Hard Times* as the universal worship of 'hard facts'), there had been a growing realisation, reaching its acme in the mid-twentieth century, that in medical, social and economic research it was now possible to determine with precision the proportion of the population due to contract a disease, likely to survive into old age or fated to fall below the poverty line. Insurance companies could now reliably gauge such percentages by means of actuarial tables. The result suggested the replacement of a supernal fate meting out rewards or punishments in accordance with the meritorious or evil actions of the individual, and its substitution by impersonal statistical tables arbitrarily placing this or that individual within the percentile of those marked out for poverty, illness, prosperity or death. It suggested that the liberation of humankind from a superstitious belief in providence had transferred it to the jurisdiction of an even less discriminating destiny, that of predetermined numeration.

That disturbing sense of a statistically ordained fate Stoppard represents here by the uninterrupted succession of 'heads', symbolising the fact that their destiny has already been apportioned. Their place in a drama, written long ago and hence unalterable, underscores their predicament and that of humanity at large as helpless puppets in an impersonal universe. Guil, the more intelligent of the two, initially finds comfort in his syllogistic proof that they are safely outside the laws of probability, a conclusion which, he suddenly realises, is ominously contradicted by the unvaried results of the coin-spinning:

> If we postulate, and we just have, that within un-, sub- or supernatural forces *the probability is* that the law of probability will not operate as a factor … And since it obviously hasn't been doing so, we can take it that we are not held within un-, sub- or supernatural forces after all; in all probability, that is. Which is a great relief to me personally. (*Small pause.*) Which is all very well, except that – (*He continues with tight hysteria, under control.*) We have been spinning coins together since I don't know when, and in all that time (if it *is* all that time) ninety-two coins spun consecutively have come down heads … ninety-two consecutive times …[43]

Contemporary man, no longer a Renaissance figure of splendid potential determining his own fate, has been dislodged here from the role of admired cynosure to that of a pathetically impotent spectator located on the sidelines in a predetermined existence.

The vaudeville slapstick and verbal misunderstandings that Stoppard had learnt from Beckett are here carefully geared to undermine and indeed ridicule the seriousness of Shakespeare's play. Polonius's suspicions concerning the origin of Hamlet's madness become, in this modern version, material for comic music-hall dialogue hinting at the kind of sexual perversion revealed by twentieth-century psychology, in the process of which the grandeur of the original drama evaporates:

> PLAYER: The old man thinks he's in love with his daughter.
> ROS (*appalled*): Good God! We're out of our depth here.
> PLAYER: No, no, no – *he* hasn't got a daughter. The old man thinks he's in love with *his* daughter.
> ROS: The old man is?
> PLAYER: Hamlet, in love with the old man's daughter, the old man thinks.
> ROS: Ha! It's beginning to make sense ...

Not only Polonius – who is, after all, burlesqued to some extent in Shakespeare's play – but Hamlet himself is cunningly divested of his dignity by the mordant commentary of these lesser characters, as they parody his remarks, diminishing their import, as though Stoppard can no longer tolerate in the new dispensation the very idea of human nobility or splendour:

> ROS: Denmark's a prison and he'd rather live in a nutshell; some shadow-play about the nature of ambition which never got down to cases, and finally one direct question which might have led somewhere, and led in fact to his illuminating claim to tell a hawk from a handsaw.
> *Pause.*
> GUIL: When the wind is southerly.
> ROS: And the weather's clear.

Hamlet is accordingly drawn into the farcical stage-action itself, dragged down by the end of the play to a level of clownish behaviour not very different from their own condition, thereby substantiating Beckett's new conception of tragicomedy whereby the tragic figures are now themselves undifferentiated from the clowns:

HAMLET, *in the lead, leaps into the left barrel.* PLAYER *leaps into the right barrel.* ROS *and* GUIL *leap into the middle barrel. All closing the lids after them. The lights dim to nothing while the sound of fighting continues. The sound fades to nothing. The lights come up. The middle barrel (ROS's and GUIL's) is missing. The lid of the right-hand barrel is raised cautiously, the heads of* ROS *and* GUIL *appear. The lid of the other barrel (HAMLET'S) is raised. The head of the* PLAYER *appears.*[44]

Together with the comic aspect, however, there remains throughout the play a profound sense of the grim condition of mankind, as these pathetic figures wander aimlessly in a totally incomprehensible and uncaring world, unable to control their fate and doomed to a meaningless death.

Stoppard has been attacked as 'a clever author manipulating rather than exploring, a parasite feeding off Shakespeare, Pirandello and Beckett'[45]; but he was surely doing far more than that. Shakespeare's own drama had reflected a major change in the setting of his time. As the Bottom scene in *A Midsummer's Night's Dream* had suggested with humour and the chorus's speech at the opening of *Henry V* had pleaded more seriously, the movement from medieval to Renaissance concepts demanded a transition from the traditional concern with the eternal and apocalyptic – as in the plays of the mystery cycles – to a more actualised setting with humans of heroic stature located firmly in the reality of this world. Hence the chorus's apology for the physical limitations of the theatre, the narrowness of the 'wooden O' in which such impressive scenes as the battle of Agincourt must needs be performed, and Bottom's suggestion, now laughably anachronistic, that even the wall needed to be 'signified' by allegorical representation. But if Shakespeare needed to adjust the drama to the new assumptions of his time, so did Stoppard for his own age. Unlike Beckett and Pirandello, he chose to represent the metamorphosis in the human condition by offering a powerful contrast between the contemporary situation and that of the past, employing Shakespeare not for parasitic purposes but to reveal the diminished selfhood of his peers, the bewildering shrinking of human life, now seen as devoid of heroic potential and subject to the inscrutable laws of a universe oblivious to the good or evil actions of its inhabitants.

* * * * *

On the European continent, exploration of the absurdity of the human condition had found expression in the experimental drama of Ionesco, Genet, Adamor and others, whose works were soon taken up on the British scene where Harold Pinter was creating a similar, no less haunting depiction of the plight of modern man. His debt to Beckett he fully acknowledged, admitting he admired the latter's work so much 'that something of its texture might appear in my own.'[46] Where Beckett had maintained that 'the attempt to communicate where no communication is possible is merely a simian vulgarity',[47] Pinter extended the technique by adopting into his plays ponderous silences that deconstruct speech, the seemingly trivial dialogue between the pauses suggesting, together with those silences, the collapse of verbal intercourse:

> *Bill*: What time did you get in?
> *Harry:* Four.
> *Bill:* Good party?
>   *Pause.*
> *Harry:* You didn't make any toast this morning.

The brief stage instruction *Pause* takes on increased significance when presented in prolonged form upon the stage. Such silences, Pinter remarked, are technically of two kinds, the first being cessation of speech, the second a torrent of language, but they function in essentially the same way, both versions serving on the stage as smoke screens for the inner poverty of the speakers, a pathetic stratagem to cover nakedness.[48] That new technique reflected a change that occurred in the visual arts during the 1950s, when Andy Warhol's simple depiction of a can of Campbell's soup consigned to the reader the task of commentary previously regarded as the responsibility of the artist. Parodying the venerated objectivity of science, Warhol presents the object without authorial commentary, transferring to the viewer the role of interpreter. He himself remains silent, saying in effect, 'Make of this whatever you wish – I have no assistance to offer.' It expressed in visual form Wittgenstein's contemporary assertion that absence of speech may indicate the avoidance of the unmentionable and the unthinkable: 'What we cannot speak about we must pass over in silence'.[49] So here, the silences in the plays of Beckett and Pinter represent the spiritual paralysis of the speaker and, by extension, of the dramatist himself, impotent to offer any cogent explanation of the human predicament. Having been stripped of the accoutrements that had previously accorded the individual a sense of personal value, such characters as Stanley, the central figure in *The Birthday Party* (1960), become intensely vulnerable, pursued by vague, menacing, intangible forces impossible to resist, impossible even to identify.

In plays such as *The Dumb Waiter*, as in Beckett's *Godot*, tragedy and farce are not merely intertwined, but their fusion symbolises the disappearance of any framework or meaningful order within which the paradoxes of existence can be questioned, within which the seeming injustices can be confronted and some semblance of harmonious pattern re-established. All that remains is a conviction of universal mayhem, a world devoid of design. There is, Pinter explained in connection with that lack of design, 'a kind of horror about and I think that this horror and absurdity go together.'[50] In the dialogue quoted above, there appears an additional dimension, that characters when they do attempt to communicate, really give expression to their own inner dialogue, remaining concerned only with their personal needs and desires. Harry, asked about the party, replies inconsequentially about the toast. The revelations of psychology posit individuals as essentially isolated, absorbed in their personal thoughts, frustrations and fears, and only nominally responsive to or aware of others.

* * * * *

In the United States, there appeared at this time an innovative play of a very different kind, not indebted to Beckett and, in fact, resisting the symbolic or allegorical depictions of the human lot that had come to dominate the avant-garde stage. Edward Albee's *Who's Afraid of Virginia Woolf?* (1961) adopted instead a dramatic realism outwardly conventional, a vividly actualised depiction of a young couple who have just joined a university faculty invited for drinks in the early hours of the morning, after a staff cocktail party, to the home of a somewhat older history professor and his wife. Riveting as it is dramatically, the play has, partly because of that realism, been disappointingly docketed by critics as little more than the representation of a sado-masochistic marriage, the conflict between a small-town university professor and his earthy wife, the latter flaunting her sexual promiscuity before her husband but eventually subjected in her turn to his vengeful shattering of her illusions. A leading reviewer at the time of the play's first performance described it with remarkable myopia as a 'frighteningly well-observed picture of a matrimonial *corrida*, with the scarred and bloody husband at last taking the cow by the horns after a long, liquor-logged evening' – a comment that has, as with a play mentioned above, appeared on the cover of the Penguin edition for the past thirty years, presumably on the assumption that it offers a valid summary of the work. A distinguished historian of drama similarly dismissed it as no more than the dissection of an extremely sick marriage; while another critic defined it as depicting two people's 'harrowing battle to destroy each other'. That this reading has continued to hold its place in criticism is evidenced by the fact that the only article on the play selected for inclusion in a recently-published collection of essays on Albee, a piece written by John Galbraith, while admitting its dramatic power, similarly discounted its importance as being merely the portrayal of a matrimonial sex-duel.[51]

The impact of the play on audiences has, I believe, a more profound source, the effect it produced emanating from the fact that it touched upon a sensitive nerve in contemporary audiences, a recognition (for many only subliminal) that it addressed an urgent problem of the time to which they too were subject. For all its apparent naturalism – the accuracy of the academic stage-setting and the conventional time-progression – there is a dream-effect throughout, produced by a number of factors. The placing of the action in the hallucinatory early hours between two and four in the morning contributes to that effect; there is the heavy drinking, with its consequent blurring of speech and action, and, not least, there is the feeling that the young couple are being held hostage throughout the long night. They repeatedly try to leave, but are restrained, persuaded, almost bullied to remain. The result is, as Albee calls it, a *Walpurgisnacht*. He himself carefully dissociated his work from the 'realistic' drama occupying much of the contemporary stage, claiming that it belonged, despite the fidelity of the *mise-en-scène,* within the same genre as Beckett's and Pinter's. In an article contributed to the *New York Times Magazine* in 1962, he argued that the terms, as they were generally employed, needed to be reversed:

> The Theater of the Absurd . . . facing as it does man's condition as it is, is the Realistic Theater of our time; and the supposed Realistic Theater pander[ing] to the public need for self-congratulation and reassurance and present[ing] a false picture of ourselves to ourselves, is really and truly The Theater of the Absurd.[52]

His play belongs within that latter group not by discarding realistic settings but in its shared sense of the misery, tribulation and absurdity of the human lot.

The reviews quoted earlier, describing the play as merely depicting the sado-masochism of a sick marriage, overlook a contradiction of that reading evidenced within the play, the deep affection existing between the older couple, their tender mutual concern emerging at various moments, their warm, shared sense of humour bubbling up into spontaneous laughter as a verbal thrust from one of them is parried with amusing effectiveness. Their affection is confirmed in their frequent hugs and kisses when they are alone. If their marriage were one of mutual viciousness and cruelty, the *corrida* of an ill-assorted couple, what is one to make of Martha's admission to an incredulous Nick of her deep, abiding love for her husband, a love underlying all the pain of their relationship, her confession that the only person she really cares for is

> George who is out somewhere there in the dark . . . George who is good to me, and whom I revile; who understands me, and whom I push off; who can make me laugh, and I choke it back in my throat; who can hold me, at night, so that it's warm, and whom I will bite so there's blood; who keeps learning the games we play as quickly as I can change the rules; who can make me happy, and I do not wish to be happy, and yes I do wish to be happy . . . (p. 113)[53]

Their relationship may be far from conventional, barbed as it is with the desire to wound and torment; but to describe it simply as sado-masochism is to miss the subtlety and complexity of their troubled lives and the more universal relevance to their times that created its impact on contemporary audiences. Nor, one may add, do such reviews explain why Albee should have chosen such a strange and seemingly inept title for the play.

Nick and Honey, as dramatic foils to the main characters, provide an initial pointer to the deeper theme. On their entry, a fresh young couple still near the threshold of marriage, polite, eager to please, they seem to typify the norms of good behaviour in American society. Momentarily shocked by the expletive hurled at George that greets them as the front door is opened, uncomfortable at the often raucous bickering between host and hostess, they attempt to extricate themselves, to leave pleading the late hour, in much the same way as would most members of the audience were they in their situation. There is, accordingly, an initial sense of identification with them. On being pressured to stay, Nick tries to calm the atmosphere, to change the subject when it threatens to become personal and incriminatory, even to stand up rather heroically to George's demeaning comments. Yet by the end of the play, they have been so totally discredited as to swing audience sympathy away from them to George and Martha, however strange the latters' behaviour may first seem. Nick, under the influence of drink, has by then been led to admit that the ill-gotten wealth his bride was due to inherit from her father played a significant part in his initial interest in her and has confessed his plan to 'insinuate himself' into the biology department by gradually taking over the courses of older professors, as well as to 'plough' a few pertinent faculty wives likely to ensure his advancement; while Honey, seemingly the sweet, wholesome, loyal wife, emerges as a neurotic terrified of the responsibilities of motherhood and deceiving her husband by the clandestine use of contraceptives. Above all, the bad faith involved in such covert plans, the façade they present of being clean-cut American youngsters and their refusal (except when influenced by liquor) to confront their true selves not only highlight by contrast the extraordinary unconventionality of their hosts but prepare the audience to evaluate the latter more positively, a tendency notably aided by the excellent sense of humour both George and Martha evince.

To comprehend the real theme of the play one needs to recognise a change that had occurred in the general pattern of mid-century thought. By the period of the sixties, the shock provided by Freudian theory had abated. A new generation had arisen, born into a society acknowledging as indisputable the existence in each person of childhood traumas, hidden fears, and repressed desires churning below the level of consciousness and endangering the functioning of the individual in society. The only method of coping effectively with those unknown impulses was to plunge into the murky depths of the psyche, to uncover and to confront the truths that lay there. Psychiatric counselling had by then become endemic in leading Western countries, an integral part of the lifestyle of the middle and upper classes, the principle having now been accepted that the cloaking of such inner anxieties, pressures and fears, a failure to acknowledge the traumas of childhood, and, even more so, to admit to their repression when once recognised could prove severely damaging to mental health. Hence the sessions of communal therapy widely conducted at that time, in which participants were encouraged to disclose in open forum the most secret guilts and terrors of their inner world, as well as the most intimate details of their sexual experience. Everything hidden was now to be exposed, not only to oneself and to one's psychiatrist but, more effectively, by public divulgence, the presence of others at those communal confessionals ensuring that the individual could not retract, becloud or minimise the revelations and admissions. It is for that reason, it would seem, that George and Martha require the presence of Nick and Honey as an audience before which they can conduct their painful explorations, blocking every attempt of the younger couple to leave, insisting that they remain present to the end of the 'exorcisms', and demanding their participation in the ritual.

There is, however, a more personal aspect to such exorcism which, although arising out of the new concept of communal therapy, is specific to the relationship between George and Martha – their conviction that self-analysis is insufficient, that because of the human tendency to conceal one's repressions and either to justify or to deny them, the aid of another is requisite for fulfilment of the process. Hence the unspoken agreement between them, the mutual acceptance of certain 'rules' derived from the principle that, no matter how agonising the task, how painful the operation, each must assist the other in stripping away all illusions, in tearing out hidden fears and secret longings, and in learning to live in total honesty with themselves. Martha thus exposes, in the presence of the young couple, George's covert sense of academic failure, his frustration at the censoring of his novel, and his repressed guilt towards his parents. As both George and Martha repeatedly inform the youngsters, neither they nor we are ever to know whether the stories they relate are true, whether George was indeed responsible for his parents' deaths, whether Martha did seduce the gardener in her youth. As everyone had learnt by now under the direction of Freud, facts become distorted in dreams, repressions enter the consciousness in disguised form, incidents arousing fear or hatred are transformed into substitutes or become sublimated as part of an infinitely complex psychological process. But it is painfully evident that those stories of parents and gardener are in some way related to hidden traumas or repressions that need to be rooted out, to be confronted, and to be publicly paraded if the healing process is to begin.

Such acts of exposure are not only agonising but infuriating, at times driving the victims into frenzy, their anger often directed at the partner who has exposed the secret fear, especially during the process of exposure. Yet ultimately there comes the recognition that the operation needed to be performed, that only a relentless cutting out or cauterising of the covert guilt can produce the necessary healing. As George explains to a totally uncomprehending Honey, tipsily engaged in peeling off the label from a brandy bottle, the disclosure of hidden psychoses allows for no clemency:

George: We all peel labels, sweetie; and when you get through the skin, all three layers, through the muscle, slosh aside the organs . . . them which is still sloshable – and get down to bone . . . you know what you do then?
Honey: [*terribly interested*]: No!
George: When you get down to bone, you haven't got all the way yet. There's something inside the bone . . . the marrow . . . and that's what you gotta get at [*a strange smile at Martha.*]
Honey: Oh! I see.
George: The marrow. But bones are pretty resilient, especially in the young. Now take our son . . .
Honey: [*strangely*]: Who?
George: Our son . . . Martha's and my little joy! . . .

Their seemingly vicious probing of each other's weaknesses, Martha's constant jeering at George's failures and his own quieter, more cerebral, yet no less effective ripostes uncloaking her own problems, her alcoholism and her neurotic relationship with her father, lead them at times to teeter on the very edge of an acrimonious breakup, but never to cross that border, bound as they are to each other by their deep mutual affection. These are the 'rules' Martha referred to in the passage quoted earlier, the unformulated agreement between them that no quarter may be given in their relentless search for hidden traumas and guilts.[54] In response to George's protest at her repeated attempts to humiliate him, she had replied in self-justification that such undiluted honesty formed the very basis of their union: 'YOU CAN STAND IT! YOU MARRIED ME FOR IT!' And when it is Martha's turn to be enraged at George, incensed at his disclosures, his reply, meaningless as it is to the younger couple, carries for her a weighty significance, a reminder that the binding compact between them is two-directional – the comment again capitalised in the text to ensure due emphasis: 'YOU KNOW THE RULES, MARTHA! FOR CHRIST'S SAKE, YOU KNOW THE RULES!'

Nick and Honey will never, it is suggested, achieve that level of honesty; but even by their presence as witnesses of *Walpurgisnacht* they gain some degree of maturity, just as, no doubt, Albee hopes that the audience may. George's revelation of the innermost secrets of the younger couple – the application to her of the principle of confronting repressions – ultimately frees Honey of her terror of motherhood, evoking from her at the end of the play the announcement that she now wants a child; and Nick, to his own astonishment, begins to learn, begins to understand in the final scene something of the heartrending process being enacted before him. Throughout the play, except for occasional witticisms from George and the moments of demonstrative affection between them, Martha appears to be by far the stronger of the two, an Earth Mother confident of her sexual prowess, constantly brow-beating George, scorning his ability to outwit her, provocatively flirting with and then bedding Nick, and, although watching with some amusement her husband's gradual exposure of the younger couple, remaining somewhat aloof from that process. But in the final game, entitled 'Hump the Hostess', the truth emerges, that it is George who is the stronger of the two. The climax of the play, his shattering of Martha's pretence that she has a son, marks the breaking down of a final barrier. That pretence George had tenderly tolerated until now as the one exception to their unflinching confronting of facts. He had recognised it as a consoling recompense to her for their tragic inability to bear a child, a device permissible only as long as they both know that it is make-believe. But the moment Martha shares the pretence with the visitors, he perceives she has crossed the dangerous borderline into self-delusion. The fiction must be publicly cauterised, however harsh the pain. Hence the conclusion, where Martha asks George once they are alone whether the cauterising was really necessary, and George's gentle assurance that it was unavoidable, a reply eliciting her own gradual admission that his action was indeed justified. Such a reading would explain a further aspect of the play, the puzzling choice of their names, so obviously evocative of George Washington and his wife. But if one recalls the association of that past president with unhesitating truthfulness, his childhood admission that it was he who had cut down the cherry tree, the relevance is patent.[55] In that tradition, their namesakes here, however agonising the task, are similarly dedicated to revealing truths that others would be sorely tempted to conceal.

For the audience, the impact of the play is so powerful as to seem a one-time event, a rare nightmarish experience that we have been privileged to witness. But it becomes apparent after reflection that, for the two of them, such nights will occur again and again, as they persevere in the constant struggle to expose the inner world of repressed experience, to exorcise traumas and fears as they emerge anew from day to day. That necessity forms the justification for the title. Initially merely facetious, Martha's pun on the nursery-rhyme of the 'big bad wolf', intended by her to amuse the cocktail party, conceals, as the concluding words of the play confirm, Martha's grim fear of the confrontation with the hidden self, that exposure of secret anxieties and dreads represented in Virginia Woolf's writings, as in her depiction of the disquieting contrast between outer and inner self in her portrayal of Louis, the manager of a shipping line. 'I beg you', he muses,

> to notice my cane and my waistcoat. I have inherited a desk of solid mahogany in a room hung with maps. Our steamers have won an enviable reputation for their cabins replete with luxury. We supply swimming-baths and gymnasiums. I wear a white waistcoat now and consult a little book before I make an engagement.
>
> This is the arch and ironical manner in which I hope to distract you from my shivering, my tender, and infinitely young and unprotected soul. For I am always the youngest; the most naively surprised; the one who runs in advance in apprehension and sympathy with discomfort or ridicule – should there be a smut on a nose or a button undone. I suffer for all humiliations.[56]

As George in the final moments of the play attempts to soothe and comfort his wife, quietly singing 'Who's afraid of Virginia Woolf?' Martha, the erstwhile earth mother, brashly censorious of the weaknesses in those around her, brokenly replies: 'I ... am ... George ... I ... am ...'

In a very brief discussion of this play elsewhere, I noted a correspondence in the visual arts that may be of interest here. It was in the 1960s, just when the play was being first produced, that Richard Rogers of England and Renzo Piano of Italy were commissioned to design the Pompidou Cultural Centre in Paris, a structure that, like Albee's play, shocked the public by its abrupt break with previous tradition; for it provocatively placed on the outside of the building those elements that had, throughout the centuries, been so carefully concealed within. Water supply pipes coloured green criss-cross the outer walls of the structure, intersecting with giant ventilation ducts painted in bright blue to ensure that their presence should not be missed, while conduits for electric wiring marked in yellow cut across elevators in a reddish hue, to provide full external exposure of the 'bowels' of the building. While laying bare the sewage system to the visitor's gaze might not produce beauty in any traditional sense of that term, it expressed in architectural form the same contemporary desire for psychological honesty as motivated this play, the architects' refusal to suppress or conceal those subterranean utilities essential to the building's function, but formerly hidden away as distasteful to the sight. They were now, like George and Martha's repressions, traumas and guilt feelings, to be determinedly exposed to the public gaze.

So, far from being merely a matrimonial *corrida* between a badly matched pair, the play's exploration of the anguish and suffering of an affectionate couple's struggle to achieve an integrity devoid of lies and concealment expressed with subtlety and power the problem of a generation compelled, in a manner unparalleled in earlier eras, to confront the dark and infinitely complex world of the subliminal in an environment redolent of human suffering. The theatre, like the novel, was responding with remarkable effectiveness to the new dispensation.

5
Terminal

The counter-culture emerging during the period when *Look Back in Anger* was being produced in London, the hippie and beatnik movements in the United States and the Beatles-inspired movement in Great Britain that dominated art, music and literature for the next few years, represented a further stage in the crisis we have been following. The disquietude among the intellectual avant garde during the earlier decades of this century had by this time seeped down to the wider public, affecting the younger generation at large. While the sciences had begun to be viewed with some suspicion earlier in the century as the less palatable implications for humankind began to be perceived, at least the technological advances they offered in medical research, in media communication and in household labour-saving devices could not be faulted. But now, in the aftermath of Hiroshima, the threat they posed for the potential destruction of the human race cast doubt on the value of the entire scientific venture. In America, campus protests, frequently with the most brilliant university students at their head and often supported by members of the faculty, were directed against the physics buildings, demonstrators at times being urged by their leaders to burn down those structures.[1] Rationalism and empiricism, the two fundamentals of scientific research, were contemptuously discarded, to be replaced by a cult of mysticism, a search for *gurus* remote from Western tradition who might, by the use of mantras and mental concentration, lead the searcher to an inner serenity replacing the depleted sense of selfhood. Meditation, a withdrawal from the obnoxious world of reality, came into vogue. Having rejected the crew-cut, career-oriented lifestyle of their predecessors, hippies reverted to the primitive, wearing Indian beads, growing their hair long, spurning urban life and establishing rustic communes not through a deistic belief in the benevolence of Nature but in protest at the materialism motivating twentieth-century civilisation. And allied to those tendencies was a further aspect placing those movements firmly within the modes we have been examining – the widely accepted use of marijuana and LSD, drugs such as Aldous Huxley had experimented with during his own mystical phase in the late thirties.

The use of hallucinatory drugs arose from motives very different from those motivating members of the Romantic era and producing the exotic, dream-like effects of Coleridge's *Kubla Kahn* or the haunting visions of De Quincey's *The English Mail-Coach*.[2] Those two writers, like so many of their peers, had resorted to opium neither from a desire for pleasurable experience nor as a release from mental stress. They had become addicted through employing it medicinally, laudanum and morphine, derivatives of opium, being the only effective pain killers then available as palliatives for intolerable physical ailments. The opium derivative Godfrey's Cordial was among the most popular, widely used in the nineteenth century even to quiet fretful children. De Quincey, although he was to become fascinated by the visions induced by the drug, was unequivocal in his condemnation of the practice, indignantly rejecting any charge that he had indulged in it willingly and insisting that he had resorted to this 'insidious remedy', as he termed it, only as an anodyne for the physical distress from which he frequently suffered, including excruciatingly painful attacks of neuralgia.[3] In contrast, the twentieth-century addict took hallucinatory drugs voluntarily, as an anodyne not for bodily pain but for the pain of modern existence, as an escape from the debilitating madness of contemporary living, Allen Ginsberg recording in 'Howl':

> I saw the best minds of my generation destroyed by madness starving
>   hysterical naked,
> dragging themselves through the negro streets at dawn looking for an
>   angry fix,
> angelheaded hipsters burning for the ancient heavenly connection to
>   the starry dynamo in the machinery of night
> who poverty and tatters and hollow-eyed and high sat up smoking in
>   the supernatural darkness
> cold-water flats floating across the tops of cities . . .

Having lost the 'the ancient heavenly connection in the starry dynamo', they sought artificial means of re-establishing that celestial contact.

A primary attraction of such drugs was their effectiveness in combating one of the anxieties central to the twentieth-century crisis. For the solipsistic haven those drugs provided constituted a dreamworld in which the hallucinator was the undisputed arbiter of all experience. Isolated within that self-contained world and encapsulated from all outside intrusion, the dreamers were not only mercifully released from the pressures of social conformity and the materialist rat-race but protected also from the humiliating probings of psychological analysis, whether initiated by others or by their own cerebral promptings. The self soared there beyond the definitions and labels that hampered its activities, ceasing to be an entity subject to dissection. As Jack Kerouac described the experience, it provided respite from the burden of an ego oppressed by the outer world as well as from the pervasive sense of guilt, sin, or wrongdoing that had been imposed upon the individual:

> I'd got a little drowsy in the mind but was somehow physically wide awake sitting erect under my tree when suddenly I saw flowers, pink worlds of walls of them, salmon pink ... the vision, was devoid of any sensation of I being myself, it was pure egolessness, just simply wild ethereal activities devoid of any wrong predicates ... devoid of effort, devoid of mistake.[4]

A film such as *Yellow Submarine* vividly conjured up that sense of emancipation in a setting untrammelled even by the laws of physicality, where the mind could run free, without inhibition, empowered to mock at the scientific world, parodying its black holes by means of creatures amusingly sucking in everything within sight with no apparent enlargement of their bodies, and where the dreamer, enrolled among the 'lonely hearts' of Sergeant Pepper's Club, could feel restored to personal integrity, social acceptance and a lighthearted contempt for the establishment.[5] It was a tendency visible even beyond the popular use of drugs, writers at this time often drifting away from reality into an imaginary universe such as the time-warp entity of Kurt Vonnegut Jr's Tralfamodore or the chimerical world of Thomas Pynchon's *V*. And kinetic art, such as the paintings by Jeffrey Steele and Briget Riley, created a hypnotic, dizzying effect, seeming to draw the spectator out of the real world into some metaphysical entity beyond.

John Barth, in contrast, remained within the real world, at least during his early phase as a writer, brilliantly exploring in his fiction the quandary of the contemporary thinker. Deserting the two literary forms predominant in the mid-century novel, the genre of the anti-hero and the cult of existentialism, he presented in his first two books a refreshingly new type of character. Todd, the protagonist of *The Floating Opera* published in

1955, and Jake, the protagonist of *The End of the Road* completed a year later, differ invigoratingly from their fictional peers – highly intelligent, witty, ebullient, critically perceptive and, above all, no longer inferior to the society about them. By unabashedly adopting the principle of inconsistency both in their beliefs and in their behaviour, they are able to regard with amused disdain the deficiencies of a society circumscribed by the limits of the conventional. Logic, the cornerstone of twentieth-century thinking, they reject as outmoded, since the rational process restricts by its fixed rules or formulae the individual's freedom of choice. And together with that rejection of inhibiting rules, they eschew the proprieties of social intercourse, a process that repeatedly produces a lively reversal of reader expectation:

> I felt that the evening had been the pleasantest I'd spent in months; that in Joe I'd found an extremely interesting new acquaintance; and that I had no special wish to see this interesting, new acquaintance of mine again for at least a week.[6]

They are, moreover, as part of this inconsistency, continually play-acting, shifting from role to role with no attempt to reconcile or coordinate the variegated masks they have assumed. This aspect is rooted in the new configuration of the time, an echo of T.S. Eliot's 'To prepare a face to meet the faces that we meet.' It betokened a recognition of the twentieth-century revelation of the complex inner world of each individual, the divorce between the inner and the outer self. In the nineteenth-century novel outer appearance had been accepted as a reliable indication of inner personality, authorial descriptions of the external features of a character offering the reader the clues necessary for a grasp of his or her inner qualities; thus, of the unpleasant Mr Slope in Trollope's *Barchester Towers* we are informed that a 'cold, clammy perspiration always exudes from him', while the refined ascetic tendencies of Dorothea in George Eliot's *Middlemarch: A Story of Provincial Life* are made manifest in the delicacy of her body and the austerity of her apparel: 'Her hand and wrist were so finely formed that she could wear sleeves not less bare of style than those in which the Blessed Virgin appeared to Italian painters.' But the fragmentation of the individual, and especially the awareness of repressed elements undisclosed to others, often only partly grasped by the conscious self, created a concept of the inner human as an agitated, restless, protean personality concealed behind a façade defensively presented to the outside world.

Barth's innovation lies in his protagonists' conscious delight in the exchange or manipulation of those masks in accordance with their fluctuating moods, their adoption of the new concept of self as a means of watching the ludicrous effects upon others produced by the unpredict-ability of their words and actions, the confusion and incredulity their unanticipated comportment evokes. In *The End of The Road* Jake, invited to dinner by Rennie and her husband, surprises them by responding with reluctance, prompting the understandable rejoinder:

> 'We neither one want you to come if you don't feel like it, Jake. You have to be – '
> 'Now wait a minute. *Why* don't you want me to come even if I don't feel like it?'
> 'What?'
> 'I said why don't you want me to come even if I don't feel like it?'
> (p. 289)

That provocative question he follows with a lengthy disquisition on the probable reasons behind her casual statement, a disquisition concluding quixotically with the statement that he will, in fact, be coming to dinner at six o'clock, whether he wishes to or not. Time after time, his own accounts of viewpoints he holds, related with all the authority of a first-person narrator, are scuttled by a laconic addendum, 'In other senses, of course, I don't believe this at all.' (p. 367)

Such amusing tergiversations have led some to see Barth as primarily a humorist. But Barth clearly believed the contrary, remarking, 'If my writing were no more than an intellectual fun and games ... I wouldn't be interested in it myself.'[7] For beneath that seemingly lighthearted banter may be perceived a despair perhaps more profound than any we have yet witnessed, a sense of the utter futility of life, the impossibility of finding any valid reason for existence. The comic masks that his protagonists adopt form, it transpires, only temporary and ultimately unsatisfactory camouflages for this inner despondency, Jake admitting in a moment of harsh self-awareness

> that all my masks were half-conscious attempts to master the fact with which I had to live; that none had made me master of that fact; that where cynicism had failed, no future mask could succeed ... The impulse to raise my arms and eyes to heaven was almost overpowering – but there was no one for me to raise them to ... every motion pierced me with its own futility, every new feeling with its private hopelessness, until a battery of little agonies attacked from all sides, each drawing its strength from the great agony within me.

Religion, as he had informed us earlier, he had long ago rejected, but the impulse here to raise his arms and eyes to heaven remains strong, the abrogation of religious solace leaving him spiritually destitute, producing, as he confesses, '*despair*, utter despair, a despair beyond wailing.' (pp. 224–6)

The Floating Opera begins on the day that Todd (Barth solemnly assures us that the double-*d* is to deter readers from associating it with the German word for 'death') has cheerfully decided to fulfil a long-time decision:

> finally and miraculously, after no more than an hour's predawn sleep, I awoke, splashed cold water on my face, and realised that I had the real, the final, the unassailable answer; the last possible word; the stance to end all stances. If it hadn't been necessary to tiptoe and whisper, I'd have danced a *trepak* and sung a *come-all-ye*! Didn't I tell you I'd pull no punches? That my answers were yours? *Suicide*!' (p. 16)

As he comments (with patent echoes of *The Myth of Sisyphus*): 'the question of whether or not to commit suicide is the first question [a man] has to answer before he can work things out for himself.' (p. 168)

Like Tristram Shandy, the narrator idiosyncratically meanders back and forth in time, following up side-issues, doubling back to pick up an earlier reference, leaping forward to the present, yet gradually revealing in the course of those narrative peregrinations that he has been engaged for many years in drawing up an *Inquiry*, an investigation into the reasons that prompted his father's suicide. For all his surface flippancy, the shock of his discovery of the body hanging from a roof-beam and the horror involved in cutting it down is ever-present. By the end of the novel, Todd is, in fact, compelled to admit the failure of his enquiry, acknowledging the impossibility of knowing precisely why his father ended his life; but the reasons for his own planned suicide emerge with logical lucidity, presented as a series of syllogistic propositions developed cumulatively through the course of the novel and culminating in the depressing formulation of Proposition V:

> I. *Nothing has intrinsic value.*
> II. *The reasons for which people attribute value to things are always ultimately irrational.*
> III. *There is, therefore, no ultimate 'reason' for valuing anything.*
> IV. *Living is action. There's no final reason for action.*
> V. *There's no final reason for living.*

In the nineteenth-century novel, the statement that there are no values for living or that any existent values are merely irrational would have shocked readers, running counter to the accepted Christian standards of the time. Even a writer such as George Eliot, whose belief in Christianity had not survived her contact with Charles Hennell's circle of freethinkers, would never have adopted so radical an attitude, and in her writings she preserved a validation of the moral code of Christianity while rejecting the faith itself. But Barth here voices that sad conclusion unequivocally, expressing the twentieth-century belief that even such seemingly self-evident virtues as kindness to others were merely instinctive biological promptings for the preservation of the species, and that both the reasons for acknowledging values and the values themselves had proved depressingly hollow. He does, however, move a significant stage beyond that conclusion. For Todd, after some further thought, adds a brief but pregnant parenthesis to the last proposition:

V. *There's no final reason for living (or for suicide).*

To realise that nothing makes any real difference is, he perceives, overwhelming. But if one goes no further and becomes a saint, a cynic, or a suicide on principle, one has not, he argues, grasped the full implications. 'The truth is that nothing makes any difference.' To which he adds wryly, 'including that truth.' Hamlet's question concerning suicide, he now determines, is thus absolutely meaningless.[8] This is nihilism in its most advanced form, a rejection of values which nullifies even nihilism itself.

Barth's stance contains within it, in a manner made clear in the course of his fictional work, a perceptive undermining of the fundamental principle of existentialism that had come to dominate so much of the art and literature of his time. The only method of asserting selfhood in the nihilistic environment of our day, the proponents of existentialism had argued, was by determinedly undertaking acts of choice and commitment. But, Barth asks, if there are no absolute or authentic values (as all but the religious existentialist admitted), what value is there in the assertion of selfhood? The idea that willed action *proves* one's identity is, Barth deduces, itself a chimera.

The first novel, then, with its rejection of suicide, ends on a note of cautious optimism, even of contentment. Life may be empty of meaning and purpose but at least there is, in so vacuous an environment, no obligation to take any specific action, whether of commitment to some supposedly positive notion or, inversely, that of self-destruction. In the final scene, therefore, Todd's mild desire to see what tomorrow's mail may bring provides him with sufficient incentive for him to remain exuberantly alive. Barth, however, had not supplied his last word on the subject. Although *The End of the Road* contains an entirely new set of characters located in a different setting, it is clear that the novel functions as a sequel to *The Floating Opera*, a continuation of this exploration of the twentieth-century predicament, but now carried a stage further.[9] And it is there, in that continuation, that Barth's most penetrating examination of the contemporary problem is to be found, the earlier novel, as he described it some years later, functioning as a nihilistic comedy and its sequel as a nihilistic catastrophe, with the same melody reorchestrated there in a grimmer key.[10]

The primary focus of this second novel is not suicide but the loss of selfhood, the forfeiture of personal identity induced by the revelation of warring elements within, over which the individual has no conscious control, as well as by the absence of ethical or social imperatives providing a framework for meaningful existence. Those aspects are latently present in both novels. But the new angle from which Barth approaches the subject concerns the problematics of choice. A central enigma facing thinkers in the twenties had been the bewildering contradiction between seemingly valid yet mutually exclusive viewpoints. In literature, Aldous Huxley's *Point Counter Point* had, both in its title and in the text itself, contemplated the disturbing discovery that one could stand at Point A and annihilate Point B, and then stand at Point B to annihilate Point A in a manner leaving the thinker with no secure place on which to stand, and this in a context that had not existed in previous generations. The empirically provable solidity of a table is nullified by the physicist's evidence that it consists of molecules in continual motion; yet acceptance of the physicist's view in our daily lives would lead to chaos. Humanism seemed incompatible with biology:

> Six months from now her baby would be born. Something that had been a single cell, a cluster of cells, a little sac of tissue, a kind of worm, a potential fish with gills, stirred in her womb and would one day become a man – a grown man, suffering and enjoying, loving and hating, thinking, remembering, imagining. And what had been a blob of jelly within her body would invent a god and worship; what had been a kind of fish would create, and having created, would become the battle-ground of disputing good and evil; what had blindly lived in her as a parasitic worm would look at the stars, would listen to music, would read poetry.

As Delmore Schwarz described that dichotomy, there was for the lover the ever-present notion of the brute within that seemed to disqualify all gentleness and affection:

> That inescapable animal walks with me,
> Has followed me since the black womb held,
> Moves where I move, distorting my gesture,
> A caricature, a swollen shadow . . .
> Stretches to embrace the very dear
> With whom I would walk without him near,
> Touches her grossly, although a word
> Would bare my heart and make me clear,
> Stumbles, flounders, and strives to be fed
> Dragging me with him in his mouthing care,
> Amid the hundred million of his kind,
> The scrimmage of appetite everywhere.[11]

The resulting irresolvable contradiction is not a conflict between poet and scientist but between the emotional and intellectual elements within the mind of the same twentieth-century thinker. For the layman, there seemed nothing left on which to rely, a situation producing the abrogation of selfhood that prompts Jake mischievously to introduce himself in the opening line of the novel with the comment: 'In a sense, I am Jacob Horner.'

As that remark indicates, Jake, an extension of Todd, remains witty, self-confident, and pleasurably conscious of his superiority to those around him in so far as he has penetrated further into the philosophical dilemma of the time and reached a conclusion that places him in a formidably secure position. Having rejected the moral, social and rational imperatives that restrict others, he has achieved an enviable freedom of both action and comportment. Committed to the doctrine of inconsistency, he cannot be entrapped by rational arguments, a dialectical invulnerability that is a constant source of amusement to him. At one point Rennie, momentarily infuriated by that trait and its contradiction of the existentialist demand for commitment, evokes from him a response characteristic of his amused stance:

'You know what I've come to think, Jake? I think you don't exist at all. There's too many of you. It's more than just masks that you put on and take off – we all have masks. But you're different all the way through, every time. You cancel yourself out. You're more like somebody in a

    dream. You're not strong and you're not weak. You're nothing.'
I thought it appropriate to say nothing. (pp. 316–17)

His intellectual elusiveness, however, comes at a heavy price. If he is
entertainingly victorious in discussions with Joe and Rennie, he is, as the
reader soon learns, less self-assured outside the confines of Wicomico. Aware
of the disturbing plethora of valid yet contradictory viewpoints emergent in
the modern world, with no preference to be accorded to one over another, he
is incapacitated, frozen from action by a paralysing inability to choose. The
conflict of choices produces in him a catatonic state that Barth terms
cosmopsis, the vision of a universe where no criteria exist for justifying any
specific action, a world in which, like the sightless eyes of Greek statues fixed
on infinity, there is no reason to do anything, even to change the focus of
one's eyes. Having lost the sense of identity that provides continuity and
coherence to one's actions, alone in his room away from others, he finds his
life dominated by unpredictable moods, moods he projects onto the small
statue of Laocoön on his mantelpiece whose changing expression reflects his
inconstant mental states or, as he terms it, his variable 'weather'. He dreams
one night of a meteorological announcement that, on the following day,
there was, in fact, to be no weather. Impossible as that might be climatically,
the principle held true, he notes, for his own self, as on many days he is not
only without mood but also without identity. On those days he has ceased to
exist except in a meaningless, metabolistic sense. Like the microscopic
specimens that biologists must dye in order to make them visible, he needs to
be coloured with some sort of mood if he is to exist even minimally as a
recognisable self.

    Jake's personality is thus, by its vacuity, ready to adopt whatever
happens to be environmentally dominant at that moment, at other times
blanking out to nothing. It was in one of those catatonic attacks that he
had been found, shortly before the novel begins, by an unlicensed doctor-
psychologist specialising in such problems of immobility who, taking him
under his care, recommends that he take up a teaching post at Wicomico
to provide a temporary framework to replace the set of ethical and social
values of which his era had deprived him. Significantly, Jake chooses to
teach prescriptive grammar, based as it is upon a set of irrational and
totally arbitrary rules, a task that leads him (with tongue in cheek) to
declare to his attentive students that the greatest radical is not the rebel
advocating free love or provocatively growing his hair long. It is the
person who sees the arbitrariness of all rules and social conventions but
who has such a scorn or disregard for the society he lives in that he
embraces the whole waggonload of nonsense with a smile.

Such disdain may serve for his amusement in a class setting, but does not solve his personal problems. The advice the doctor offers for avoiding a recurrent paralysis while in Wicomico is the enchanting principle of Sinistry. Whenever faced with alternatives between which he has no basis for choice, he is always to select the item on the left. If the choice is chronological, he is to adopt the earlier. And if neither principle is applicable, he is to follow alphabetical priority. The advice is, of course, a *reductio ad absurdum* of the existentialist concept of significant choice; yet it is by no means ridiculous in its perception that existentialism had, in fact, provided no criteria upon which the momentous choice confirming one's existence was to be based. In the final analysis, existentialist choice was, as Barth has recognised, no less arbitrary than the Sinistry suggested by the doctor. Sartre had recognised the existence of that lacuna in existentialist philosophy and had suggested that one should adopt as a criterion the consideration of what would happen if everyone else made the same choice, a precept that would, he believed, lead one to prefer altruism over selfishness and place the good of the community above that of the individual. But one wonders how effective such a principle really is. It leads at times to absurdity – what would happen if all members of an audience at a cinema performance followed that advice and waited patiently till everyone had made their way out? [12] More seriously, there is no moral basis demanded for the choice and technically Hitler's commitment to conquering the world would suffice to make him exist in that philosophical system. The lacuna remained, echoed here in a conversation between Jake and the doctor, the latter employing the traditional terminology of the existentialist current at that time. He states firmly,

> Choosing is existence: to the extent that you don't choose, you don't exist. Now, everything we do must be oriented toward choice and action. It doesn't matter whether this action is more or less reasonable than inaction; the point is that it is its opposite,

a statement evoking from Jake the perspicacious query, 'But why should anyone prefer it?' (p. 331) On another occasion, urged to avoid choice by learning facts upon which he could rely in making choice, a practice that would enable him, for example, to answer unhesitatingly the query how many seats the Cleveland Municipal Stadium contains, Jake comments mordantly that he would still have to choose whether to answer the question or not, as well as, even if he did know the right number, whether to answer it correctly.

Jake Horner thus emerges in the novel as an intriguingly dualistic character. On his own or when in session with the doctor, he is a mental invalid, rendered cerebrally impotent by the mutually exclusive viewpoints fostered by twentieth-century thought. But when together with others, he is, by his happy adoption of the principle of inconsistency, a formidable personality. It was, as he remarks, easy for him to maintain simultaneously and with equal unenthusiasm contradictory or polarised views on any given subject. 'I don't have any opinion ... Or rather, I have both opinions at once', is an attitude that makes him well-nigh invincible in argument, secure in his superiority to the rationalists, hidebound as they are by their rigid rules of logical coherence. He is, accordingly, acknowledged by his brilliant dialectical opponent, Joe, as a philosophical adversary worthy of the deepest respect. The doctrinal conflict between the two, fought on the battlefield of Rennie's soul, is in effect a contest between the two most fundamental concepts of the twentieth century. Joe, on the one hand, represents the rationalist-empiricist stance that had activated scientific, anthropological and psychological research in its attempt to formulate theories based on consistently verifiable facts, while Jake, on the other, embodies the perception that such rationalism had lost its validity, having been, paradoxically, negated by the inherently contradictory principles to which it had led the thinkers of the time. Rationalism, by demonstrating that the human race was no more than another species of insect crawling over the surface of a spinning globe in a pointless competition for survival, had undercut its own significance. Reason in that setting could perhaps provide improved tools for survival but it revealed at the same time the ultimate futility of the rationalist exercise itself.

Both men are fully cognisant of the altered twentieth-century configuration. Joe, while acknowledging its disqualification of objective standards, ethical, social and religious, believes in the ability of the individual to create a substitute set of values by which to live, however subjective and restricted to the single self those values may be. For him, the aim of the thinker (in direct contrast to Jake's ideology of inconsistency) must be an internal and rationally defensible coherence, an ability to explain to oneself and to others the reasons prompting any action, even if those reasons are unacceptable to one's auditors, since all standards are now variable and individualistic. Moreover, as all actions are, by Joe's reasoning, the result of personal decision or preference whether conscious or unconscious (a typically Freudian position), the corollary of that doctrine is the principle that apologies are meaningless. They indicate an irrational desire to justify one's personal decisions by values other than one's own, and that at a time when everything is subjective and hence nothing ultimately defensible.

Such was Joe's original conflict with Rennie (his philosophical protégée as well as his wife, playing throughout this novel the role of Galatea to his Pygmalion),[13] who needed in the early days of their marriage to be weaned from her natural tendency to excuse her actions, and to be trained to stand firm in accepting personal accountability both for her behaviour and for the subjective standards upon which they were based. Implicit in Joe's philosophy is total responsibility for one's actions, the ability not only to identify one's motives both before and after the performance but to accept fully any consequences of such actions. Even if the motivation cannot be precisely identified, the fact that one has adopted a certain course of behaviour is retrospective proof, he argues, that knowingly or unknowingly such had been one's choice, however slight the preference: 'It's like combining plus one hundred and minus ninety-nine ... The answer is just barely plus, but it's completely plus', Joe insists.

From the larger viewpoint, therefore, the contest between the two males emerges as a twentieth-century morality play, not, as in the fifteenth-century *Everyman*, presenting a choice between established standards of Good and Evil but, in an age when the distinction between those standards appeared blurred or non-existent, exploring whether new values could be constructed, even in this restricted subjective sense, in order to fill in some way the vacuum created by contemporary theories; investigating whether, in fact, there was such an act as choice or whether, as Jake maintains, the plethora of mutually exclusive alternatives makes choice itself entirely inconsequential.

The novel presents two possibilities – that Jake, despite the spiritual paralysis from which he suffers, will learn eventually to overcome his disability and emerge with his superiority intact, qualified to function successfully and effectively in the new environment by his very discarding of meaningful choice, or that the positive solution to the quest will be found to reside in Joe's philosophical approach, his faith in rationalism and responsible choice in a manner approximating to the concepts espoused by existentialism.

The contest operates both on the intellectual and on the practical level, the theories to which the two men subscribe directing their behaviour. For Jake, the application to daily life is less complicated, since the principle of inconsistency allows him total free-play, including the right to act both irresponsibly and amorally, as in his deliberate exploitation of a middle-aged Peggy Rankin whom (in the tradition of his Restoration namesake[14]) he merrily seduces by means of knowingly specious arguments, with no

intention of reciprocating her declarations of affection, a scene constituting, in his supposed insistence on her reaching her own decisions, a
humorous parody of Joe's philosophy:

> I made a mental salute to Joseph Morgan, *il mio maestro,* and another to
> Dr. Freud, caller of the whole cosmic hoedown: up to Miss Peggy's flat
> we tripped. A *pas de deux,* an *entrechat* and that was that. I left on
> promises of greater things to come, which I had no special plans to
> keep. (p. 346)

For Joe, however, the implementation of the principles he has evolved
is infinitely more demanding, since he bears the full weight of personal
accountability not only for his conscious actions but even, with echoes
of psychological theory, for actions dictated by submerged impulses
which, he maintains, ultimately express the person's will. In his own
person, Joe is a model of commitment to those beliefs, rigorously
ensuring that his own conduct conform to his principles, unforgiving of
any personal deviation from them, and winning the admiration both of
Rennie and of Jake himself for his integrity in following the precepts he
has fashioned.

The triangular love affair that had served as a somewhat lighthearted
background to the suicidal theme of *The Floating Opera* here takes on a
more central function, serving as the testing-ground for the philosophical
combat. Rennie, by nature more spontaneous in her responses than Joe,
reliant upon her instinctual emotions but hampered by the rules of
behaviour she has adopted under the direction of a husband she reveres,
drifts into a totally unplanned sexual encounter with Jake. Bound by the
requirement to be totally honest with Joe, she at once informs him of the
fact. And with the originality that marks the entire novel, an unanticipated consequence ensues. Since, Joe maintains, her action must have
been instigated by desire on her part, whether conscious or not, she is, to
her consternation, advised by him to test out the precise nature of her
impulse by returning to Jake for a further sexual encounter. On the
principle that behaviour should be based upon entirely subjective values
for which one should never apologise, and that each person has a full
right to establish those personal values, Joe refuses to restrict her actions.

For Jake, the effect of his unpremeditated affair with Rennie is shock, at
least momentarily. His confident amorality is suddenly and startlingly
undercut by as conventional a sense of guilt as any moralist might
experience – providing the first suspicion that his principle of superior
non-involvement might not survive so easily the pressures of actuality:

the guilt poured in with a violent shock that slacked my jaw, dizzied me at the wheel, brought sweat to my forehead and palms, and slightly sickened me. What in heaven's name was I doing? What, for God's sake, had I done? I was appalled. Does Jacob Horner betray the only man he can think of as a friend, and then double the felony by concealing the betrayal?

But the attack of conscience does not last; the doctrine of non-involvement and deliberate inconsistency he has adopted reasserts itself, so that, when badgered by Joe's repeated and (in Jake's eyes) absurd demand to know the *reasons* for the totally unintended sexual encounter, he shrugs off the temporary feeling of guilt as the residue of outmoded concepts. Now amused and delighted by the new situation in which he finds himself, a situation granting him a pleasantly available mistress together with the consent, if not the approval, of her husband, he comes, upon reconsideration, to see it as a triumph of his own system of non-ethical non-commitment over that of the inflexible rationalist. Accordingly, he settles down contentedly to this variation on the *ménage à trois,* a situation seemingly destined to continue undisturbed in defiance of traditional values.

By this point, Rennie is not only the battleground for the philosophical contest. She has emerged in her own right as a very human, gentle creature, at home in the natural world of the horses she loves and sadly unsuited to the rigid, rule-enforcing system into which her respect for Joe has propelled her. She has come to represent humankind at large, a figure evoking sympathy, not least for the way Joe has exploited her as the guinea-pig for his philosophical experiments. The surprise of discovering that she is pregnant despite the careful precautions she has taken with both men and the consequent impossibility of determining the identity of the father not only abruptly ends the triangular affair but brings the clash between the two men to its climax. Since she expresses her unswerving decision, in the face of that paternal indeterminacy, either to end the pregnancy if an abortionist can be found (an unlikely eventuality in the deeply conservative town in which they live) or, failing that, to commit suicide, Rennie's condition is transformed from a somewhat conventional novelistic dilemma into a crucial test for the two philosophical systems.

Joe's response is not only simple; it is devastatingly cold and business-like. He may claim that he loves Rennie deeply (and no doubt does, in his own way) but, remaining firm in the principles he has formulated and by which he had determined to live, he insists that Rennie must make her decision entirely alone, pronouncing himself prepared, if necessary, to assist her in carrying out her suicidal purpose if that is her ultimate decision. When it seems that no abortion can be arranged, he solemnly hands her a loaded revolver to facilitate her choice. The existentialist must choose with total personal responsibility, unaided in reaching the decision. Neither rationalism nor existentialism allows for a sharing of such accountability and the frigidity of Joe's responses to all appeals for his opinion becomes unnerving in its inhumanity, as well as in the patent lack of any moral or other criteria by which he can aid her in determining the choice. The situation must, he maintains, be handled in a manner free from sentiment: 'We're not playing games, Jake! Forget all the movies you ever saw and all the novels you ever read. Forget everything except this problem. Everything else obscures and confuses it.'

For Jake, on the other hand, the situation is an unmitigated disaster. His policy of amused, uninvolved inconsistency crashes down about him, to be replaced by a frenzied desperation as he searches for an abortionist in order to save Rennie's life, being driven as a last resort to appeal for aid to his dubious doctor-psychologist mentor. The latter botches the affair, the horror of Rennie's death in Jake's presence leaving him not only emotionally devastated but also bereft of any possible direction for his future. Joe, still rational, cold and businesslike, leaves Wicomico to start life elsewhere; but for Jake the helpless longing to take responsibility for what has occurred, to surrender his principles of uninvolvement in a world that no longer recognises responsibility or guilt, impels him to the appalling conclusion that, in the modern reality in which he finds himself, science, learning and philosophical speculation lead only to catastrophe and destruction, that the serpents of Knowledge and Imagination represented in the Laocoön statue, 'grown great in the fullness of time, no longer tempt but annihilate.' He too leaves Wicomico, returning in effect to the catatonic state from which he had hoped to emerge, the final word of the novel being 'Terminal'. It is in a very real sense the fulfilment of the title – the end of the road.

What no doubt fails to emerge from the above analysis is the delightful humour, intelligence and originality distinguishing this novel, as well as the vivid characterisation of the central threesome who might so easily have become somewhat wooden representatives of the philosophical systems they represent. At the time of the novel's appearance, one might well have wondered in which direction Barth would continue as a writer after that crushingly negative ending. For Barth, it is clear, neither existentialism, the philosophical system favoured in intellectual circles in his day, nor the initially attractive policy of an amused, superior, uninvolved inconsistency can function as substitutes for the ethical systems of the past, systems that are no longer available to him. And in fact, that word 'Terminal' did mark an ending for him too. Barth continued to write prolifically, producing huge, sprawling works enlivened by his ever-present wit, including *The Sot-Weed Factor* (1960), a picaresque tale burlesquing the eighteenth-century English novel, and *Giles Goat-Boy* (1966) a bizarre tale of the career of a mythical hero in a vast, computer-run world. But after *The End of the Road,* he deserted any attempt to confront again the challenges of his time, admitting that, on completing it, he had turned away from realism to write 'high-energy extravagances'. In his widely read essay, 'The Literature of Exhaustion' (1967), he pronounced the traditional novel obsolescent. The contemporary writer, he declared, was now restricted to parodying earlier forms, and he wryly described his own burlesques with his characteristically circular reasoning, as 'novels which imitate the form of the novel, by an author who is "imitating" the role of Author.' Those later writings are, as Earl Rovit has rightly described them, a kind of prolonged academic joke.[15] They adopt, in fact, a postmodernist approach, conforming to Gerald Graff's comment that in our own day novelists, having lost confidence in the moral and interpretative authority of art, tend to adopt instead a refusal to take art seriously and a preference for displaying the vulnerability and tenuousness of art itself.[16]

In Barth's fiction subsequent to *The End of the Road,* therefore, he no longer employs the novel as a means of achieving a new vision, nor as an instrument for searching for meaning in the appalling quandary of the contemporary world. Henceforth, fiction becomes for him a theme for entertainment, the escape route for a gifted writer eager to use his many talents but powerless to exercise them more fruitfully – frustrated, indeed, by a depressing awareness of the philosophical cul-de-sac into which his attempts to find a solution to the modern crisis have led him. Like Jake, when Joe hangs up on him in their final telephone conversation, he finds himself 'left with a dead instrument in the dark.'

* * * * *

In contrast to Barth's fictional Todd, casuistically inventing at the last moment a reason for postponing suicide, the end of the road that Sylvia Plath chose for her brief but brilliant career was the self-inflicted death she had long courted. Attempted suicide is often a device for attracting attention in the hope of timely rescue, but for Plath it was no subterfuge. It was, after an earlier attempt, the awakening into life that she regretted. The act of dying is easy, she claimed. 'It's the theatrical / Come back in broad day / To the same place, the same face' that proves so depressing.[17]

For the public, unaware of that deep-seated desire, her death came as a profound shock, and the publication of the remarkable *Ariel* poems composed during the burst of creativity during her final months transformed her into a cult figure, eliciting a flood of critical studies. There is, however, an aspect of her writing and, indeed, of her life, that deserves further investigation, an aspect closely related to this present study.

By the mid-century, when the principles of psychological analysis had spread beyond the medical world to enter the public domain, its terminology becoming part of common parlance, there emerged a tendency, especially among intellectuals, to usurp the task of the analyst, to probe, like George and Martha, into the self in search of symptoms classifiable into the newly revealed behavioural patterns. That process had, in fact, helped earlier in the century to generate the Surrealist movement in painting. The ridiculing of art by their predecessors, the Dadaists, arose, it was suggested in an earlier chapter, from the frustration of artists at discovering that in the new dispensation they could no longer be regarded, nor even regard themselves, as gifted creators sensitive to and effecting cultural change but were now categorised in Freudian terms as neurotic transcribers of unconscious impulses implanted in them in their childhood. There was no quarrelling with such authoritative pronounce-ments as Freud's that incestuous or narcissistic impulses experienced during childhood were liable, if not directed into suitable channels during puberty, to transform them in adulthood 'into neurotics, perverts, artists, or madmen'. For the Dadaists themselves it seemed that the only valid forms of art available for them to engage in, apart from the parodying of their profession, were such forms as excluded the artist entirely. Arp's dropping of torn scraps of paper to form fortuitously a pattern on the floor was a process absolving him from any possible charge of unconscious sublimation. As Hans Richter recalled: 'Chance appeared to us a magical procedure by which one could transcend the barriers of causality and of conscious volition.'[18]

That however, was only an initial phase and was succeeded by an ingenious means of rebutting such reductive evaluation. Salvador Dali, originally a member of the Dadaist movement, began in the 1930s to develop a new form of art which he defined in his *Conquest of the Irrational* as 'paranoiac-critical' activity. The term *critical* in that definition indicated that, instead of seeing himself as a helpless victim of his repressions and paranoias, he planned to function henceforth as their interpreter and decoder. He chose to serve as his own analyst, exposing his hidden repressions, defining them in accordance with accepted psychological theory, and uninhibitedly displaying the results of his self-analysis upon his canvases. The process was not aimed at relieving symptoms (he became increasingly neurotic over the years), but it did restore to him the self-respect of being an artist and creator, no longer vulnerable to the charge of 'unconscious' sublimation, since the process was so deliberate and calculated. In commenting, for example, on his painting *William Tell*, he deflected potential criticism by forestalling it, appropriating to himself the mythic codes of the professional psychologists:

> What we have here is Saturn devouring his own children; God the Father sacrificing Jesus Christ; Abraham sacrificing Isaac; Guzmán the Good with a dagger in his hand ready to kill his son; and William Tell pointing his arrow at the apple on the head of his own son.

Moreover, as he confirmed with disarming frankness, the painting symbolised at the same time his own oedipal relationship with his father and consequent castration complex. Hence the depiction of himself in this painting turning away, protected only by a figleaf, from the virile figure of his father who threateningly wields a pair of scissors.[19]

There was, however, a danger inherent in this practice of self-analysis, namely the engendering of a fissure in personal identity, a split between the dual elements of self, one section functioning as the dissector or analyst, the other as patient or analysee, a dichotomy only too liable to encourage schizophrenic tendencies. Sylvia Plath, it would seem, conformed to that emerging pattern. Constantly probing into her inner being in search of the psychological complexes or hidden traumas she believed were there, she cherished and nurtured them as the creative forces of her writing. And the result was indeed a breach in personality, the splintered identity liable to result from such activity. Outwardly, she appeared the very antithesis of a potential suicide. Blessed in that portion of her being with a generally happy disposition, she delighted in her surroundings, engaged enthusiastically in student affairs, and developed a healthy ambition to achieve success as a writer. Her letters, published posthumously, although revealing the superior intelligence and felicity of expression that were to win her so many well-deserved awards, provide in themselves an unremarkable record of a young lady experiencing the joys and disappointments involved in the process of maturing into adulthood. There are the many relationships developed with boyfriends, the deep affection for her brother, the thrill at each prize or literary achievement and, perhaps above all, her rapturous joy at the challenges and opportunities offered by her Fulbright scholarship to Cambridge. From there she wrote soon after her arrival:

> I can't describe how lovely it is. I walked through countless green
> college courts where the lawns are elegantly groomed ... formal
> gardens, King's Chapel with the lace-like ceiling and intricate stained
> glass windows, the Bridge of Sighs, the Backs, where countless punts,
> canoes and scows were pushing up and down the narrow River Cam,
> and the shops on the narrowest streets imaginable where bikes and
> motorcycles tangled with the little cars ... I feel that after I put down
> roots here, I shall be happier than ever before, since a kind of golden
> promise hovers in the air along the Cam and in the quaint crooked
> streets.[20]

Dorothea Krook, the lecturer whom Plath idolised at Cambridge and
with whom she worked closely throughout the period of her studies, has
recorded the amazement with which she read years later of Sylvia's
suicide, how astonished she had been to discover from her own
subsequent reading of *The Bell Jar* and of the *Ariel* poems the dark,
death-enchanted side that had been so completely concealed from her.
During that period in Cambridge, Plath, despite their close relationship,
made no mention of her earlier suicide attempt and nervous breakdown.
Even more surprisingly, at no time did she offer even a hint to her mentor
of the poetry which at that time was absorbing so much of her creative
energy. Accordingly, she left Krook with the image of her as an eager,
intelligent, but fundamentally serene student: 'All that comes back to me
is a general vision, clear and pure like the golden light of the Platonic
world we appropriated, of an extraordinarily happy freedom of communication.' Christopher Levenson, a poet and editor who also knew her
well at Cambridge, was similarly oblivious to her darker side, summarising
her as being 'almost a golden girl, gifted and poised, energetic, serious and
intent.'[21] And Clarissa Roche, recalling the impression made upon her
shortly after this period when they became close friends at Smith College
to which Plath had returned as a teacher, describes her as an attractive,
essentially normal person: 'Sylvia was a wife and housewife and new
enough at the game to be enthusiastic. She was young, beautiful,
charming, successful, busy and happy.'[22]

Plath herself was fully conscious of the discrepancy between her two
selves, noting in her private journal how she needed to fight daily to
impress on the world the image of an integrated identity while inwardly
that image collapsed:

> I am feeling very sick. I have a heart in my stomach which throbs and
> mocks. Suddenly the simple rituals of the day balk like a stubborn

horse. It gets impossible to look people in the eye: corruption may break out again? Who knows. Small talk becomes desperate.

Hostility grows, too. That dangerous, deadly venom which comes from a sick heart. Sick mind, too. The image of identity we must daily fight to impress on the neutral, or hostile, world collapses inward: we feel crushed.[23]

The poem entitled *In Plaster*, inspired by the condition of a fellow patient lying beside her in hospital, depicted with a touch of humour her own sense of being a divided being, the white plaster cast, following the contours of the body, contrasted with the self that was encased within:

I shall never get out of this! There are two of me now:
This new absolutely white person and the old yellow one,
And the white person is certainly the superior one.
She doesn't need food, she is one of the real saints.
At the beginning I hated her, she had no personality
She lay in bed with me like a dead body
And I was scared, because she was shaped just the way I was ...

The tone of mild amusement in this poem may detract from its value as evidencing that split, but the antithesis between her external normalcy and her internal torment is vividly revealed elsewhere. A cheerful letter sent to her mother in 1956, for example, concluding, 'Love from a very happy Sivvy', had appended to it the harrowing poem, *Pursuit*, testifying to the terrors latent in her being:

There is a panther stalks me down:
    One day I'll have my death of him;
    His greed has set the woods aflame,
He prowls more lordly than the sun.
Most soft, most suavely glides that step,
Advancing always at my back ...

Insatiate, he ransacks the land
    Condemned by our ancestral fault,
    Crying: blood, let blood be spilt:
Meat must glut his mouth's raw wound.
Keen the rending teeth and sweet
    The singeing fury of his fur;
    His kisses parch, each paw's a briar,

> Doom consummates that appetite.
> In the wake of this fierce cat,
>   Kindled like torches for his joy,
>   Charred and ravened women lie,
> Become his starving body's bait ...

There are patent echoes here of Blake's *Tyger*, yet the two poems are worlds apart, the gap indicating not only the changed view of nature that had occurred over the years but also indicating a major source of Plath's disturbance. Blake's tiger had been for him a creature of awesome beauty and might, an image of the sublime, fearsome in its power yet of wondrous grace and symmetry. With the self-reflexive quality that was to characterise Romantic poetry, whereby the poet acknowledges the inspiration derived from some outside source yet at the same time appropriates it as emanating from within, the tiger also functions in that poem as a symbol of the burning inspiration of the prophet-poet himself, the bard who parallels on earth the creativity of the Being who made both tiger and lamb.[24] Plath's panther, in contrast, comes from the cruel, rapacious domain of nature as conceived in the post-Darwinian era, where insatiate beasts tear their prey apart, glutting their mouths with meat rent by their teeth. If the panther functions here as allegory, the corollary to that usage is even more disturbing as its presence imaginatively extends the cruelty and rapacity to the human realm, revealing the forces menacing the individual, especially the female, charred and ravened by them.

Plath was constantly analysing herself, sometimes adducing the aid of a professional therapist to help her delve into the hidden world of her inner being. Before embarking on one such series of therapeutic sessions, she records her intention of using them to further her own investigation: 'I am going to work like hell, question, probe, sludge & crap & allow myself to get the most out of it.'[25] There was, however, one major element in her psyche that she needed no help in uncovering, namely the trauma created when, at the age of eight, her father died, leaving her with the feeling that he had deserted her in an hour of need. The anger, intensity, and indeed venom of that resentment is conveyed with astonishing force in her poem 'Daddy', a rancour in startling contrast to the seeming serenity of her outer personality:

> Every woman adores a Fascist,
> The boot in the face, the brute
> Brute heart of a brute like you ...

If I've killed one man, I've killed two –
The vampire who said he was you
And drank my blood for a year,
Seven years, if you want to know.
Daddy, you can lie back now . . .

There's a stake in your fat black heart
And the villagers never liked you.
They are dancing and stamping on you.
They always knew it was you.
Daddy, daddy, you bastard, I'm through.

The hostility, frightening in its virulence, indicated some deep urge, to which we shall need to return.

Like Dali, Plath was sufficiently experienced in psychological theory to identify the behavioural pattern to which her condition belonged. In an introduction she wrote for a proposed reading of 'Daddy' on the BBC, she announced uninhibitedly that the poem is 'spoken by a girl with an Electra complex. Her father died while she thought he was God . . . she has to act out the awful little allegory once over before she is free of it.' There is in that statement a mild attempt at dissociation, a use of the third person discouraging identification of poet and speaker; but the frequency throughout her verse of thematic parallels to her own experience leaves no doubt of the personal applicability. She recognised, moreover, that in accordance with the definition of the Electra complex the fury felt towards her father's memory was a fury arising from frustrated love, producing a love-hate relationship. As she recorded in another poem, 'Electra on the Azalea Path', 'I brought my love to bear, and then you died . . . It was my love that did us both to death' – an aspect evidenced by her repeated attempts to contact her father's spirit through the Ouija board.

What are we to deduce from all this? The widely accepted explanation that her love-hate relationship was a natural outcome of the sense of deprivation experienced at her father's sudden death fails to explain one strange aspect of her reaction, the imaging of her father as a Fascist. Her father Otto, born long before the rise of Nazism and resident in the United States from his youth, had in fact been a pacifist. There was not the slightest foundation for picturing him in this and other poems as a brutal Nazi associated with the most savage and inhuman elements of that regime. The motive for that denigration of her father lay, it would seem, in the mirror image that her vilifying of him allowed her to construct for herself. For in the complex domain of psychological experience, the association of her father with Fascism meant that she, as the sufferer, could project herself into the role of the Jewish victim of Nazism even though she was not Jewish and had been spared any contact with the extermination camps, growing up in the distant security of Wellesley while those heinous acts were being perpetrated. But that interpretation leaves unexplained her reason for desiring to adopt that imagined role.

George Steiner, while lauding the contribution Plath's poems made in keeping alive the horrors of the holocaust for her generation, was disturbed, even resentful that she should have chosen that role. He regarded it as a kind of larceny for her to have borrowed images from a catastrophe in which she had no share, and assumed therefore that her conjuring up of such scenes with herself as the victim was simply an elaboration of her own personal problem, the translation of a private, obviously incurable hurt into a public framework.[26] But the intensity of her role-playing suggests that it has much deeper roots. She visualises herself with extraordinary immediacy as imprisoned in one of the boxcars carrying its passengers inexorably towards their death: 'An engine, an engine / Chuffing me off like a Jew. / A Jew to Dachau, Auschwitz, Belsen.' In the poem 'Getting There', she locates herself on that final railroad journey, experiencing vicariously the despair and terror of those destined to be exterminated:

> The gigantic gorilla interior
> Of the wheels move, they appall me –
> The terrible brains
> Of Krupp, black muzzles
> Revolving, the sound
> Punching out Absence! like cannon.

The crucial word here is 'Absence'. It is the *liquidation* of the individual, the transforming of the human being into a nothing that appalls. For her the holocaust represented (as it was in fact) the consummation, or rather the nadir of the progressive twentieth-century abrogation of individual sanctity, the embodiment of the loss of human significance that was proving so profoundly disturbing to her generation. In 'Lady Lazarus', she sees herself, like the victims of that despicable process, as totally eliminated, annihilated, her body reduced to a Nazi lampshade and a cake of soap, the sole relics of her existence being an anonymous wedding ring and a gold filling.

That is the horror that oppresses her, a horror from which her father, had he lived, might have saved her, protecting her as she emerged from the security of childhood into the devastating savagery of a newly defined world in which animals, like the panther of her poem, tear each other apart, and humans, no less viciously, murder and reduce to a wisp of smoke all creatures obstructing the advance of the master race. Hence her bitter resentment of her father's death for having failed to shield her from that discovery, and the retrospective clothing of his memory in the garb of the gauleiter:

> I was ten when they buried you.
> At twenty I tried to die
> And get back, back, back to you.
> I thought even the bones would do.
>
> But they pulled me out of the sack,
> And they stuck me together with glue.
> And then I knew what to do.
> I made a model of you,
> A man in black with a Meinkampf look.[27]

She was oppressed by a double loss of identity. Her participation in the contemporary trend towards self-analysis created a split between the outward calm of daily existence and her inner tormented self, depriving her of the sense of an integrated being. And the agony of that inner world derived from the broader problem of her time, the post-Darwinian belief that all humans, including herself, had lost their ultimate significance and sanctity, a loss symbolised for her by the wholesale exterminations of the holocaust. The result was a daunting, debilitating feeling of hollowness and despair from which only death could free her. The collapse of her marriage in the months before her demise did indeed severely exacerbate her sense of loneliness and alienation; but it was not the cause of her despair, as her periods of depression, her nervous breakdowns and her attempted suicide occurred before she ever met her husband, Ted Hughes.

Throughout her poetry evidence abounds to corroborate this reading. During their final year together, she and her husband became amateur beekeepers, in part, no doubt, through Plath's latent memories of her father's profession as an entomologist specialising in the bumblebee. Outwardly, once again, she displayed gleeful enthusiasm in undertaking the venture, recording how thrilled she was at the new avocation and the delight she experienced when, after hiving a swarm, she watched the bees settling into their new home, bringing to it their full pollen sacs.[28] But in her poetry, her view of their activities was sinister. In the verse she produced at the peak of her creativity during her final year there emerged a cluster of five poems – 'The Bee Meeting', 'The Arrival of the Bee Box', 'Stings', 'Swarm', and 'Wintering' – a theme obviously reflecting by its recurrence some central concern. We are no longer in the traditional universe of a benevolent nature infused with moral lessons for mankind, where the busy bee improves each shining hour. For her, nature is a battlefield where creatures compete fiercely in the struggle to proliferate, concerned only with the survival of the species, and callous towards the single being. The drones, she notes, are killed off, cast out of the hive to die once the task allotted to them has been fulfilled. The queen bee and her female peers 'have got rid of the men,/The blunt, clumsy stumblers, the boors.' In that world even the one drone who succeeds in impregnating the queen is doomed. At the moment of insemination, his abdomen slits open and his entrails fall out, the queen trailing them aloft in her flight like a flag of victory.[29] Cruelty and barbarity are everywhere, the queen bee herself not immune as the young females await the opportunity of destroying her, they themselves due eventually to succumb to that fate.

> ... in their fingerjoint cells the new virgins
> Dream of a duel they will win inevitably,
> A curtain of wax dividing them from the bride flight,
> The upflight of the murderess ...

The human species is, she realises, no different. In 'Swarm', the furious struggling of the hiving bees, heedless of those they injure, she sees in terms of the conflict between human armies in Poland, Russia, Germany or at Waterloo, where the mud squirms with throats that have become stepping stones for bootsoles. Sadly, Plath acknowledges that she, like the queen bee, is part of that lethal process. I too, she notes in 'Stings',

> Have a self to recover, a queen.
> Is she dead, is she sleeping?
> Where has she been,
> With her lion-red body, her wings of glass?
>
> Now she is flying
> More terrible than she ever was, red
> Scar in the sky, red comet
> Over the engine that killed her
> The mausoleum, the wax house.

In 'Wintering', with which Plath ended the *Ariel* collection,[30] she mused whether the royal lady of the hive, her body cold and herself too dumb to think, would live through the harsh, forbidding winter. Plath chose not to, dying by her own hand before the arrival of the spring.

The horror that motivated her inner angst was thus of much wider significance than has been acknowledged. Her nervous breakdowns, her attempt at suicide and her eventual self-immolation have been attributed to setbacks in her career and, during the final period, to the collapse of her marriage. But as the poems evidence, notably those composed during that final phase, the underlying cause lay not there – topics that are absent from her writings – but in her haunting conception of the brutality of nature and its callous disregard for the individual, a callousness of which the Nazi holocaust formed the human counterpart. In her intense identification with the victims of Nazism she revealed her own appalled response to the twentieth-century nightmare haunting the intellectuals of her day – her sense of the vacuity of her existence in a merciless world.

* * * * *

The novels of Richard Wright and Ralph Ellinson were, as was noted earlier, not included in this present study since their subject-matter, the plight of the black person in Western society, constitutes a problem reaching back to earlier generations, not specific to the twentieth-century crisis we are examining. James Baldwin's *Another Country* might appear to fall within the same category. It has been identified in almost all critical discussions as a novel of black protest, vividly castigating the hostility of the white sections of the population towards the black. In one of the most sympathetic contemporary reviews of the book, Granville Hicks remarked how magnificently it conveys the effects of that hostility and how fully it justifies the indignation of the black community. Although, Hicks maintains, not all blacks may feel hatred for whites as powerfully as Rufus, Ida and Baldwin himself do, 'if they do not, [Baldwin] convinces us, they ought to.'[31] I propose to argue that the theme of the novel is, in fact, almost exactly the reverse, and that its real distinction lies in the author's ability to transcend racial animosities and to confront instead, through the plight of a group of people caught up in that hostility, the broader tragedy of the human condition in the twentieth century – a reading that would place the novel firmly within the parameters of our present concerns.

By the time of its publication, Baldwin's writings had indeed won him a reputation as a fiery champion of black rights. His *Go Tell It On The Mountain* of 1953, although a semi-autobiographical account of his teenage discovery of a vocation as religious preacher, repeatedly displayed the author's indignation at the cruelty of racist persecution. A young Deborah is cruelly raped there by a gang of white men, a black soldier is found battered to death, his body mutilated, an innocent Richard, mercilessly beaten by the police solely because of his colour, commits suicide at the humiliation. And John, the central character, comes to learn how

> white people cheated them of their wages, and burned them, and shot them – and did worse things, said his father, which the tongue could not endure to utter. He had read about colored men being burned in the electric chair for things they had not done; how in riots they were beaten with clubs; how they were tortured in prisons ...[32]

For a time, especially during his stay in France, Baldwin tried to distance himself from the problems of the black American – an element suggesting how deeply involved he was even at that early time in the theme that was to occupy him in *Another Country* – but the Little Rock crisis in 1957 drew him forcefully back into involvement in the civil rights movement, an involvement leading to his passionately eloquent *The Fire Next Time,* originally published in the *New Yorker* magazine in 1962 and issued in book form the following year. His short story 'Going to Meet the Man' of 1965 provided what many have acknowledged as the most compelling description yet of the iniquitous cruelty of southern racist persecution, the appalling account, as seen through the eyes of a white boy taken there by his father, of the public castration and burning of a black man.

Shortly before the story's appearance, Leslie Fiedler's *Love and Death in the American Novel* had suggested that the American myth carried symbolic undertones in which the black man played a major role. In the pioneering days of American society, he pointed out, women such as Widow Douglas in *Huckleberry Finn* had served symbolically as the guardians of Protestant morality, frightening the male, who flees into the untamed world of nature, 'lighting out for the territory'. There the black man, representing the macho power he craves, functions as a counter-figure to the castrating female, Huck finding comfort in the friendship of Jim, as does Ishmael in comradeship with Queepeg.[33] Perhaps reliant to some extent on Fiedler's widely admired study, Baldwin in this story traces back the sadistic treatment of a young black boy by the white sheriff to the sheriff's traumatic witnessing as a child of the public castration and burning of a black man accused of raping a white woman. That act of castration Baldwin interprets as resulting from the white man's suppressed envy of the black's virility; and to the trauma of that childhood experience he attributes the sheriff's sexual impotence and sadism. With those two powerful indictments of racial persecution, one published before the appearance of *Another Country* and one shortly after, it was perhaps natural that the novel itself should have been seen as falling within the same category.

It too is permeated with civil rights protests, the opening section of the novel recounting in moving terms the deterioration of Rufus, an accomplished jazz musician, as he descends into desperation and suicide in a world in which he can find no haven from colour discrimination, from such brutal victimisation as is described in the scene of the vicious bar-brawl. For the negro, jazz had become a weapon of protest. As a specifically Afro-American art-form, it expressed in a manner to which no other genre compared a plea for the right to be oneself, a symbol of the struggle for emancipation and identity. Jazz musicians do not aim in their performances at blending into harmonious unity but strive in provocative contest, each solo flight or improvisation challenging the other players, daring them to respond, to affirm in their turn the singularity of their talent. Rufus, too, had striven to find in his art a means of ridding himself of his anguish, only to discover that jazz failed to achieve its purpose, that it had become merely a form of imprecation hurled at a crowd that did not listen, 'a malediction in which not even those who hated most deeply any longer believed.'[34] And throughout the novel the voice of Bessie Smith, the blues singer, is heard in the background bewailing the poverty, the suffering and the desperation of blacks, *Weeping and crying, tears falling on the ground ...*

To Baldwin's chagrin, the novel was greeted by a chorus of critical condemnation, censure being directed most frequently at the proliferation of explicitly described sexual incidents, and especially at the assumption within the novel that Eric's homosexuality could serve as a redemptive force, offering balm to each of its main characters. Robert A. Bone typified that response in his study of *The Negro Novel in America*, contemptuously dismissing the novel as 'drowned in the nonsense of five orgasms (two interracial and two homosexual), or approximately one per eighty pages' – a condemnation persisting in criticism through the following decade, as in Keneth Kinnamon's reference to 'the interracial and bisexual bedhopping' of the characters.[35] The changing attitude to homosexuality that has emerged in subsequent years leaves that criticism singularly dated today. Moreover, as regards the proliferation of orgasms, Bone seems not to have perceived that those scenes are never, as in pulp literature, introduced for purposes of pornographic titillation but function as part of the literary strategy, carefully differentiated to provide insights into the experience of each character within the framework of the larger theme, the sexual act serving as an instrument or symbol of their quest. Thus Vivaldo attempts to discover through their love-making the mystery of Ida's African heritage, a mystery that seems so persistently to divide them: 'She opened up before him, yet fell back before him, too, he felt that he was travelling up a savage, jungle river looking for the source which remained hidden just beyond the black, dangerous, dripping foliage' (p. 177); while in a very different scene, Rufus, exploiting Leona as the object of his pent-up racial hatred, feels at the climactic moment 'the venom shoot out of him.' (p. 31)

As the antagonistic chorus died down, two critics came to Baldwin's defence. Norman Podhoretz, in an article in *Show* magazine entitled 'In Defense of a Maltreated Best Seller', deplored the indignant attacks upon it, pointing out that the reviewers

> disliked the book not because it suffers from this or that literary failing, but because they were repelled by the militancy and cruelty of its vision of life ... [Baldwin] holds these attitudes with puritanical ferocity, and he spells them out in such brutal and naked detail that one scarcely recognises them any longer – and one is frightened by them, almost as though they implied a totally new, *totally revolutionary conception of the universe*. [His italics]

And Mike Thelwell condemned in his turn the strident middle-class indignation of the reviewers who had, he suggested, seen the book 'as the spearhead of some insidious homosexual conspiracy to subvert the sexual sensibilities and responses of the reading public.'[36] We may now, perhaps, approach the novel with the comparative objectivity of a later generation no longer threatened by its message, bearing in mind that, since that time, critical evaluation of the novel has changed, the book being gradually acknowledged in retrospect as a major work of its time, its merits winning grudging admiration, although with no reasons offered for the altered appraisal.

If the novel has been seen, even by its defendants, as a militantly aggressive instrument of the black power movement, conceived by an author who had already established himself as a writer of polemical essays on the negro question and presenting the white characters as the prime movers in all the evil,[37] a very different picture may be seen to emerge from a close reading of the text. There is, indeed, evidence within the novel indicating that Baldwin had originally intended it to be a novel of negro protest but that, in the actual course of writing, a broader concern with humanity took control, subverting his conscious intent. In a passage that should be seen as central to the entire work, Vivaldo – the novelist within the novel dedicated to the highest standards of his art and hence to some extent a projection of Baldwin himself – is struggling to make his characters come to life, but they resist him. They seem not to trust him. They are all named, their futures are more or less destined in a manner clear to him; but not, it seems, to them:

> He put words in their mouths which they uttered sullenly, uncon-vinced. With the same agony, or greater, with which he attempted to seduce a woman, he was trying to seduce his people: he begged them to surrender up to him their privacy. And they refused – without, for all their ugly intransigence, showing the faintest desire to leave him. They were waiting for him to find the key, press the nerve, tell the truth. *Then*, they seemed to be complaining, they would give him all he wished for and much more than he was now willing to imagine. (p. 130)

Earlier in the novel, Vivaldo has unconsciously revealed to the reader the reason for his writer's block. He mentions in a moment of weariness how tired he is of the troubles of real people, and his desire to return to the people he was inventing, 'whose troubles he could bear.' (p. 78) His fictional characters, therefore, are at that stage a form of escape, an alternative to confronting the truth of the human condition. Only when he is compelled to acknowledge the actuality of life, when he reaches the nadir of his suffering at the close of this novel, does something Vivaldo had been searching for 'fall neatly and vividly' into place. The novel Vivaldo will write after that revelation, after the close of the story, recounting with total integrity what he had been subconsciously trying to avoid, is, we may assume, *Another Country*, the novel about Brooklyn that, as he assured Ellis earlier, had never yet been written. Those hints within the novel suggest Baldwin's own transitional process, his gradual acceptance of the necessity, as artist, to be totally honest with himself, to confront his deepest convictions, whatever the cost to his overt political commitments. In that reading of the novel it becomes apparent that Baldwin had moved beyond the somewhat stereotyped elements of black power writing, valid as that protest may have been, into an engagement with the broader predicament of his time, the universal sense of futile suffering to which not only suppressed minorities but all humankind seemed condemned.

One aspect of the change that Vivaldo's dissatisfaction with his embryonic novel symbolises is Baldwin's discernment of a truth hovering beyond the traditional racial protests, a growing awareness that the blacks themselves are not free from guilt. The key needed to make his characters come to life is the recognition, however painful, that Baldwin's black peers have become warped and corrupted by their suffering, filled with a hatred that, however warranted in its origins, had destroyed their humanity. Should they fail to regain their humanity, they will, Baldwin prophesies, be doomed, as their animosity insidiously brutalises their personalities, blinding them to their moral responsibilities. Patent as that message is (*pace* the critics) in the opening chapter describing Rufus's downfall, were that section to stand alone the warping of his character could, perhaps, have been interpreted as specific to him, his personal experiences having distorted his values, filling him with an all-consuming desire for vengeance that drowns all ethical ideals and the promptings of compassion. But the message emerges as integral to the entire novel, extended through the remaining chapters in a manner leaving no doubt of Baldwin's intent.

It is surely significant that, in the opening section, Leona, a poor white girl from the South, conventionally depicted in such protest novels as bigoted 'white trash', is presented here with unvarying authorial sympathy and understanding. Having been repeatedly beaten by a brutal white husband and tragically deprived of her child, she has come north in search of a haven. Her freedom from racial prejudice is total, and her love for Rufus, transcending any distinction of colour, is confirmed repeatedly. His viciously taunting remarks, intended at moments of anger to force her to admit to the racial prejudice that he believes must lie concealed beneath her affection, are countered by her with such firm and simple declarations as to leave no doubt of her convictions, such ingenuous remarks as 'People's just people as far as I'm concerned' – comments that are never in any way undercut by the narrator. From the first, Baldwin underscores the dreadful disparity between her unaffected love for Rufus and his sadistic desire to wreak, through her, his vengeance on the whites he detests, making her into what Baldwin calls the 'unwitting heiress of generations of bitterness'. Even at the climax of their love-making, Rufus associates her with his persecutors: 'nothing could have stopped him, not the white God himself nor a lynch mob arriving on wings. Under his breath he cursed the milk-white bitch ...' As their relationship develops, that inborn hatred drives Rufus, with a roaring in the head and an intolerable pressure on the chest, to suppress his affection for her, to torture and beat her until, to the horror of Vivaldo and Cass, he drives her into a mental asylum. Despite the natural revulsion of his friends, including Vivaldo, their compassion prompts them to come to his aid, to attempt to comfort him in the despair that descends upon him; but there is no doubt in their minds of the unforgivable injustice with which he has treated Leona. They recognise the truth in her generous insistence at the height of his brutality towards her that something has 'got all twisted up in his mind and he can't help it', that this is not the real Rufus. His suicide is, indeed, a form of atonement, a belated acknowledgement on his part of the perverted misdirection of his wrath. But if he himself has recognised too late the evil to which such hatred may lead, the iniquity of his past actions is, Baldwin suggests, not his alone but one shared by his black peers.

For many readers the conclusion of that opening section, Rufus's leap from the bridge marking the demise of the character on whom our interest had been focused for so many pages, leaves a sense of puzzlement concerning the direction the novel can go from there. Vivaldo's burgeoning love for Ida becomes, of course, a major theme of the subsequent chapters; but were that all, the continuation would have seemed only tenuously connected, an independent story that could have been prefaced by a few lines recounting Rufus's death.

The underlying theme that links those subsequent chapters so integrally with the first is not the love of these two but Ida's only-too-willing adoption of Rufus's mantle, her undertaking in his place of the same perverted desire for reprisal that her brother had exemplified, a conscious decision to continue what he had only begun, namely revenge upon the white enemy. Her proud wearing of the ruby ring he gave her symbolises that continuity. Of the enemy she remarks bitterly in sweeping generalisation, 'How I hated them, the way they looked, and the things they'd say, all dressed up in their damn white skin.' She alone, one notes, of all those in the novel treats Leona with contempt, with a vicious, untempered racial prejudice, describing her as

> a terrible little whore of a nymphomaniac, from Georgia ... I swear, there's nothing like a Southern white person, especially a Southern *woman*, when she gets her hooks into a Negro man. And now she's still living, the filthy white slut, and Rufus is dead. (p. 261)

The blatant injustice of that description for readers who have witnessed Leona's touchingly gentle, unselfish love can only evoke disgust for Ida's callous misinterpretation of the relationship. Such remarks, quite apart from the ramifications of that theme in those chapters, offer little support for Granville Hicks's statement that the novel aims at *justifying* Rufus's, Ida's and Baldwin's own hatred of white people.[38]

Ida's adoption of Rufus's hatred becomes, then, the major connecting theme of the novel. In contrast to her, Baldwin, continuing his inversion of normal expectations, presents the white Vivaldo as, like Leona, entirely devoid of racial prejudice, unable to comprehend Ida's hostility. She, like her dead brother and despite her affection for Vivaldo, taunts him constantly and quite undeservedly with possessing a concealed contempt for all black women, regarding them as mere whores. She castigates him for having deserted her brother in his time of greatest need, for having proved useless as a friend because of his innate prejudice against her race. That charge is especially painful to Vivaldo as he suffers from his own, quite independent sense of guilt, a feeling of having failed Rufus on the final night and hence of bearing responsibility for his death. During the long night vigil beside the tormented Rufus, he had, he believes (perhaps with echoes of Buber) omitted to embrace and comfort him, actions that might have prevented the suicide. Only towards the end of the story do we learn retrospectively the reason for his failure to embrace him – his realisation, only too justified, that Rufus would, in that dark malignant mood, have misunderstood, would have interpreted the embrace as a homosexual advance, an attempt to take advantage of his vulnerability (in much the same way as Antolini had attempted to exploit Holden):

> I wondered, I guess I still wonder, what would have happened if I'd taken him in my arms, if I'd held him, if I hadn't been – afraid. I was afraid that he wouldn't understand that it was – only love. Only love. But, oh, Lord, when he died, I thought that maybe I could have saved him if I'd just reached out that quarter of an inch between us on that bed, and held him. (p. 336)

Baldwin's exoneration of Vivaldo in this passage confirms once again how incorrect it is to maintain, as do most critics, that 'everyone betrays everyone else in this novel.'[39] For Baldwin's main purpose here is to reveal how false was Ida's judgmental condemnation. Vivaldo's gradual perception of a further truth reaches its climax in the dream he experiences towards the end of the novel, the recognition of what he had until then perceived only at a submerged level, namely the malevolence that lay beneath Rufus's friendship, the latent hatred motivating even the black emotionally closest to him, who acknowledged the fact that Vivaldo was his only true friend (p. 77):

Go up! Rufus' hands pushed and pushed and soon Vivaldo stood, higher than Rufus had ever stood, on the wintry bridge, looking down on death. He knew that his death was what Rufus most desired. He tried to look down, to beg Rufus for mercy … From far away, far beyond this flood, he saw Ida, on a sloping green meadow, walking … alone she saw him, was aware of him standing on the cruel wall, and waited, in collusion with her brother, for his death. (p. 374)

Occasionally, Ida had admitted, a white man may prevail, may temporarily break through her animosity towards all whites and win her affection or regard; but such instances she sees as threatening the single-mindedness she cherishes. Assuming the whole world to be one huge whorehouse, she decides to play the whore that black women are supposed to be, betraying Vivaldo with a white man she despises, prostituting herself to Ellis in revenge for the humiliating treatment of her race. Only in the final pages of the novel does she recognise the iniquity in her misdirected craving for retaliation, acknowledging remorsefully, 'I'd got my revenge. Only, it wasn't *you* I was after. It wasn't *you* I was trying to beat.' The novel is, in that respect, an astonishing indictment by a black writer of the demoralising and corrupting effects of black hatred, a demand that, however warranted such animosity may be, it must be tempered by a readiness for rapprochement and reconciliation if the self-respect of black people is to be restored.

That theme, however, was not in itself any closer to the specific twentieth-century crisis than were the novels of Ralph Ellison or Richard Wright, nor could it validate the inclusion of the novel in this present study. What does authenticate its inclusion is the motive force behind Baldwin's castigation of his black peers – the sense of universal suffering that makes such reconciliation necessary; the recognition that, whatever evil may have been committed by one group or colour against another, in the final analysis *all* humanity is, in the bleak world of the twentieth century, subject to the same agony of living. If Baldwin informs us repeatedly and with extraordinary persuasiveness of the indefensible cruelty of black persecution, of the slums and ghettos in which they are condemned to live in the Western world, he is aware that their protests have no claim to exclusivity. Suffering, he acknowledges, has no colour, 'they were all equal in misery, confusion, and despair.' And here his choice of the white novelist to be contrasted with Rufus is especially significant.

Vivaldo is not, like Cass, a product of the middle-classes playing the bohemian in Greenwich Village. He is a white counterpart to the oppressed black, the son of a poor, struggling Italian immigrant family, sharing with them the prejudices, the poverty and the alienation from which they suffered. Visiting the slum area where Ida lives, Baldwin informs us how affected Vivaldo is by its familiarity, by the similarity of that depressing area to the squalid precinct in which he himself had grown up:

> there were the same kids on the block that used to be on my block – they were coloured but they were the same … really the same the hallways have the same stink, and everybody's, well, trying to make it but they know they haven't got much of a chance. The same old women, the same old men … I kept thinking, They're coloured and I'm white but the same things have happened, really the *same* things (p. 117)

The neighbourhood he grew up in was populated by a 'Wop' minority no less hounded by suspicious, sadistic police, a district in which most of the youngsters he had known were by now dead, in jail or junkies. His father had been a brutal alcoholic, beating him without reason. As Vivaldo remarks to Rufus elsewhere, theirs is ultimately a shared lot: 'We've all been up the same streets … There aren't a hell of a lot of streets.' Dickens in his day had also depicted the appalling conditions experienced by the poorer members of the community, but for him there is always in the background some benevolent figure such as Pickwick, Boffin or Brownlow living in comfort and able to relieve their suffering. In such nineteenth-century novels, as I noted earlier, it was assumed that the problem was temporary, that the evil conditions of workhouse and factory could be improved, perhaps even eradicated, were the wealthier members of the community to become aware of them – as in fact they were improved largely as a result of these protests. But here, as in almost all twentieth-century writing, the barrenness and frustration of living has come to be seen as both universal and irremediable.

Returning to New York from his haven in southern France, Eric is overwhelmed by the suffering and hopelessness affecting both rich and poor in this twentieth-century quagmire, as he rediscovers the dreadful morass that urban modernity has become:

> This note of despair, of buried despair, was insistently, constantly struck. It stalked all the New York avenues, roamed all the New York streets; was as present in Sutton Place, where the director of Eric's play lived and the great often gathered, as it was in Greenwich Village,

where he had rented an apartment and been appalled to see what time had done to people he had once known well. He could not escape the feeling that a kind of plague was raging, though it was officially and publicly and privately denied. Even the young seemed blighted ...'
(p. 228)

No-one in the novel can escape the trauma of human existence. Even Cass and Richard, who had seemed to embody the comforts of middle-class security and the stability of marital love, become devastated in the course of the story, reduced to the same inescapable anguish as those they had previously attempted to assist. The title of this novel is thus more profound and ironic than may appear. It does not offer, as one might expect, the depiction of 'another country' in the sense of the black ghetto contrasted with the suburban luxury enjoyed by most readers. When Cass blithely suggests that there are other countries to which one could go, countries free from such suffering, Ida throws back her head in derision. For it is life itself, the human predicament that is unbearable. (p. 343) As one learns from that incident, the novel depicts the twentieth century at large, an existence differing so radically from that of the past. It provides not the happy ending of nineteenth-century fiction but the unrelieved agony of modern experience independent of skin-colour, an anguish shared by rich and poor alike, with no benevolent patrons waiting in the wings to provide succour or refuge.

If that sense of purposeless human suffering places this novel centrally within the crisis we are examining, it reflects even more closely one aspect of the modern condition that has not been mentioned until now. Within the Victorian novel, even novels by Thomas Hardy whose sombre awareness of the tragedy of the human lot adumbrated the approaching change, love had been represented as an essentially wholesome emotion, a passion which, although it might undergo change in the course of time, was, during the period it was experienced, an essentially pure, unadulterated emotion. Jude's love for his cousin Sue, like Adam Bede's love for Hetty Sorrell, Pip's devotion to Estella and (for all Thackeray's sardonic reservations) even Dobbin's adoration of Amelia are firm and unwavering passions. But the rise of psychology, with its focus upon the dynamic complexity of the psyche, had introduced a totally new concept, a sense of the constantly warring factions within the human personality producing paradoxical and often self-contradictory emotions, such as the perpetual tension between the promptings of the life-instinct and of the death-wish. It was Freud who had introduced the term 'ambiguity' into popular usage to delineate the co existence of such contraries, a term especially relevant now that suppressed ideas were seen to emerge into the consciousness in disguised forms, images that required decoding by a specialist. [40] Such recognition of contrasting dyadic factors had prompted William Empson's seminal study, *Seven Types of Ambiguity*, appearing in 1930 shortly after the English publication of Freud's *Wit and Its Relation to the Unconscious,* that line of enquiry encouraging in its turn the New Critics' validation of the ambivalences and often inverse connotations of Metaphysical poetry. Instead of scorning, as had Samuel Johnson, the latter's violent yoking together of heterogeneous ideas, Cleanth Brooks could now admire unreservedly Donne's use of *die* to suggest simultaneously both decease and the life-giving act of sexual intercourse: 'Wee dye and rise the same, and prove / Mysterious by this love.'

One result of that new awareness of coexistent contraries was a recognition of love-hate relationships. Salvador Dali, acknowledging his indebtedness to psychological theory, proclaimed that his passionate affection for his mother coexisted with a vicious antipathy towards her, those conflicting attitudes vividly expressed in his paintings; while, within literature, such complexity of emotional experience emerged as a primary theme in D.H. Lawrence's novels – the alternating sensations of attraction and repulsion, of tenderness and cruelty, of an overpowering affection accompanied by a desire to maim or murder, as in Ursula Brangwen's feelings towards Skrebensky in *The Rainbow*:

> Stronger than life or death was her craving to be able to love him; and at such moments, when he was mad with her destroying him, when all his complacency was destroyed, all his everyday self was broken, and only the stripped, rudimentary, primal man remained, demented with torture, her passion to love him became love, she took him again, they came together in an overwhelming passion ... But it all contained a developing germ of death.[41]

In *Another Country*, that self-destructive element within human love constitutes a basic source of the anguish experienced by the characters, with their repeated, dissatisfied cry from the opening pages, '*Do you love me? Do you love me? And again, Do you love me? Do you love me ...?*' The tenderness and affection Rufus feels for Leona coexists with his detestation of her; Cass both loves and derides the Richard who has failed her; Ida admits that 'love and hate are very close together'. Even Vivaldo regards Ida at times with bitterness, as 'anger, pity, love, contempt and lust all raged together in him.'[42] In an era that seemed cut off from divine love, human love remained the sole refuge; but built in to that supposed refuge as part of the new dispensation was a destructive force that seemed to doom all lovers, black or white, wealthy or indigent, to eventual misery.

The one person within the novel who might seem to have achieved inner peace, not least in his ability to bestow a temporary calming influence upon others, is Eric. He has, accordingly, been identified by many as the central character of the novel, as the 'redeemer',[43] even though, as I noted earlier, Vivaldo's profession as a dedicated novelist, a projection of Baldwin himself, would seem to single him out for that role. But if Eric can arouse some degree of trust in those seeking his aid, his own condition reveals him to be no less agonised within, no less subject to the despair characteristic of his era. Baldwin relates at length the torment and agony experienced by Eric in his youth, in his gradual discovery of his homosexual tendencies in a Southern society contemptuously condemning such inclinations and especially infuriated when such affection was directed to 'nigger' boys. In maturer years, his relationship with Rufus proved, once again, an excruciatingly humiliating experience, as the latter deliberately treated him as a hideous sexual deformity. And if, with his male lover Yves ('Eve') in their garden of Eden located in France he appears to have achieved happiness, the ephemerality of that relationship is underscored throughout. Yves is presented as designedly seducing him, calculatedly exploiting him as a source of financial security while at the same time, as Eric knows, planning to leave him when the time is propitious. At that point Eric is aware that he will be cast into the dreadful world of the sexual outcast:

> On the day that Yves no longer needed him, Eric would drop back into chaos. He remembered that army of lonely men who had used him, who had wrestled with him, caressed him, and submitted to him, in a darkness deeper than the darkest night ... his infirmity had made him the receptacle of an anguish which he could scarcely believe was in the world. This anguish rendered him helpless, though it also lent him his weird, doomed grace and power, and it baffled him and set the dimensions of his trap. Perhaps he had sometimes dreamed of walking out of the drama in which he was entangled and playing some other role. But all the exits were barred ... (p. 209)

His charismatic attraction for others, therefore, was a power deriving not from inner peace but from the 'weird, doomed grace' of his sexual preference, a preference that he himself sees as an infirmity inevitably exposing him to humiliation and contempt, offering him little solace in the helpless agony of his own unenviable lot.

It is, perhaps, appropriate that we should close with this novel. For some mid-century writers, such as Greene and Bellow, a degree of human dignity could yet be rescued from the dreariness of the wasteland, a sense that, out of the nullification of human sacrosanctity in a mechanistic universe, a modicum of self-respect could yet be achieved, an ability to come to terms with the new configuration and to construct a basis for living, however tenuous. For others, like Beckett and Barth, humanity seemed to have reached a cul-de-sac, with only passing moments of warmth and humour relieving the bleakness of despair. Baldwin belongs to that latter category. The struggle for meaning continues, but for all his participants the conclusion is one of torment and foreboding in a world devoid of benevolence and trust. The final section of the novel he caustically entitles *Toward Bethlehem*, alluding to Yeats's sinister view of the Second Coming of the Messiah as conceived in the twentieth century: 'And what rough beast, its hour come round at last, / Slouches towards Bethlehem to be born?'

By elevating the novel from black protest to a more universal plea for mutual tenderness and forgiveness among humanity all of whom experience the sterility of the human condition, Baldwin provides a striking contrast between the modernist period and the more secure and comfortable world of past eras. Rufus's cursing of God as he leaps into the swirling dark current, '*all right, you motherfucking Godalmighty bastard, I'm coming to you*', sets the tone for the novel at large. It depicts a view of the cosmos as devoid of compassion, justice or order, as 'another country' where God, if he exists at all, can only be seen as merciless and blind. It is a country where love is mingled with hate. Vivaldo, alone in the novel, had struggled against those depressing concepts, attempting to be true to the older traditions of morality, humanism, loyalty and trust. But the struggle, he learns by the end, has been in vain; the new era can no longer sustain those principles. As he and Ida, shattered by her revelations, come wearily together at the end, embracing each other, like Osborne's Jimmy and Alison, in a childlike search for mutual solace amidst the devastation surrounding them, Vivaldo begins 'slowly, with a horrible strangling sound, to weep, for she was stroking his innocence out of him.' He will now be empowered to write his novel, but it will be a novel exposing to the full the anguish of contemporary living.

It is, perhaps in that regard that some comfort is to be found, the discovery that, despite the terrors and desolation that were intrinsic to the modern condition, the seeming loss of all meaning to individuals condemned to exist in a heedless and purposeless cosmos, the writer remained, like the tragedian of old, capable of transforming the pain and frustrations of human experience into deeply moving works of art.

Notes

Chapter 1: The Crisis of Identity

1   A. Alvarez, *The Savage God: a study of suicide* (London, 1971) examines examples from the past in an attempt to establish universal characteristics. For a fuller study of the phenomenon, see Émil Durkheim, *Suicide,* trans. J.A. Spaulding and G. Simpson (New York, 1951), and Louis A. Sass, *Madness and Modernism: insanity in the light of modern art, literature, and thought* (New York, 1992), which attempts to establish a connection between modern alienation and the symptoms of schizophrenia.

2   Cf. David Cecil's sensitive biography, *The Stricken Deer* (London, 1947), pp. 70 f. Michel Foucault, *Madness and Civilization: a history of insanity in the age of reason,* trans. Richard Howard (New York, 1965) pp. 244 and 256, and Roy Porter's valuable study, *Mind Forg'd Manacles: a history of madness in England from the Restoration to the Regency* (London, 1987), especially pp. 62–81, provide insights into the sources of suicidal trends in that period. Samuel Johnson was strongly opposed to suicide, but his fits of religious melancholia, his pervasive fear of death and his dismay at the prospect of the Day of Judgement recur throughout Boswell's account of his *Life.*

3   Sylvia Plath's *The Bell Jar*, published in 1960, was a thinly veiled fictionalisation of her earlier attempt at suicide in 1951, when she was aged nineteen. She died by her own hand in 1963. Whether that latter event was (as many have argued) prompted by the infidelity of her husband, Ted Hughes, is open to speculation; but the earlier attempt, occurring in the mid-century, the period under examination in this present study, arose from a more general sense of world-weariness. For Plath's description of that experience see the Bantam edition of *The Bell Jar* (New York, 1975), p. 208.

4   Malcolm Bradbury, *The Social Context of Modern English Literature* (New York, 1971), especially pp. 14f.

5   His funeral oration, recorded in Thucydides, *History of the Peloponnesian War,* book 2.

6   Thomas Sprat, *A History of the Royal Society*, ed. Jackson I. Cope and H.W. Jones (St. Louis, Mo., 1958), pp. 152–3.

7   In *The Roundabout Papers* (1860).

8   George Orwell, 'Inside the Whale' (1940), in *Collected Essays* (New York, 1957), p. 241. Wylie Sypher, *Loss of the Self in Modern Literature and Art* (New York, 1964) – the least effective of his series on art and literature – repeatedly refers to this period as 'anti-science' when in fact both media were reflecting with remarkable accuracy the new tendencies within science, including its movement away from empiricism towards more abstract concepts. As Eddington remarked in his Gifford Lectures of 1927, 'the physicist used to borrow the raw material of his world from the familiar world, but he does so no longer. His raw materials are aether, electrons, quanta, potentials, Hamiltonian functions ... Science aims at constructing a world which shall

be symbolic of the world of commonplace experience ... The external world of physics has thus become a world of shadows.' Other studies of the period which, while valuable in themselves, devote insufficient space to analysing the causes of the crisis are Malcolm Bradbury, *The Social Context of Modern English Literature* (New York, 1971), Ricardo J. Quinones, *Mapping Literary Modernism* (Princeton, 1985), Dennis Brown, *The Modernist Self in Twentieth-Century English Literature: a study in self-fragmentation* (London, 1989), Daniel R. Schwarz, *The Transformation of the English Novel, 1890–1930* (London, 1989), Michael Gorra, *The English Novel at Mid-Century* (London, 1990), Peter Nicholls, *Modernisms: a literary guide* (Berkeley, 1995) Philip Thody, *Twentieth-Century Literature: critical issues and themes* (London, 1996), Michael Levenson, ed., *The Cambridge Companion to Modernism* (Cambridge, 1999), in addition to works quoted elsewhere in the notes. Dennis Brown, for example, begins his study by attributing the change to 'the general diffusion of social alienation, the rise of the psychoanalytic movement, the disorientation brought about by the Great War, and the increasing experimentalism of almost all the contemporary artistic movements.' The collection of essays edited by George Levine, *Constructions of the Self* (New Brunswick, N.J., 1992), although occasionally touching upon earlier aspects, concentrates, as Levine notes in his introduction, primarily on the postmodern situation.

  9 Roy F. Baumeister, *Identity: cultural change and the struggle for self* (Oxford, 1986), pp. 76–8, who attributes the loss of identity to the years of Depression in the 1920s and the advent of mass media. Herbert Marcuse's influential *One-Dimensional Man: the ideology of industrial society* (London, 1968) argued that the healthy conflict between the 'higher culture' restricted to the wealthy classes on the one hand and the social reality of the working classes on the other had been ended by the advertisements, commercialisation and mass appeal of the technological age, a process he saw as negative – although he did admit in a comment tucked away in a footnote (p. 64) that the advent of paperbacks, general education and long-playing records gave the working class access to that higher culture in a manner unparalleled in previous generations.

10 Cf., for example, the collection of essays with the promising title, *Spiritual Problems in Contemporary Literature*, ed. Stanley R. Hopper (New York, 1957), containing contributions by such leading scholars of the day as Cleanth Brooks, David Daiches and William Barrett. Essays there are devoted to 'The Problem of Moral Isolation' or 'Man's Spiritual Situation in Modern Drama' but one searches in vain for any analysis of the causes of that moral isolation other than vague references to 'the long-standing feud between morals and aesthetics' (p. 153). Sanford Schwarz, *The Matrix of Modernism* (Princeton, N.J., 1985), provides a more persuasive approach in connecting some of the changes to altered philosophical concepts, such as Bergson's concern with time.

11 Frederick R. Karl, *A Reader's Guide to the Contemporary Novel* (New York, 1973), p. 12.

12 Colin Wilson, *The Outsider: an enquiry into the sickness of mankind in the twentieth century* (London, 1967), p. 49. Robert Langbaum's learned study, *The Mysteries of Identity: a theme in modern literature* (Chicago, 1977), aimed at establishing a connection between the twentieth-century crisis and the solipsism of the Romantics, a connection which, with all its interesting insights, was bound to underplay the revolutionary changes in science,

psychology and anthropology manifesting themselves during the intervening hundred years. That aspect is even more marked in Matei Calinescu's attempt in *Five Forms of Modernity* (Durham, 1987) to trace modernity back to the Renaissance.

13 Paul Fussell, *The Great War and Modern Memory* (Oxford, 1977), pp. 8 and 21. Other examinations of the loss of identity characterising this approach include John A. Lester, Jr, *Journey Through Despair, 1880–1914: transformations in British literature and culture* (Princeton, 1968), although he writes well on Darwinism; Christopher Lasch, *The Minimal Self: psychic survival in troubled times* (New York, 1984); Charles Taylor, *Sources of the Self: the making of the modern identity* (Cambridge, Mass., 1989) which admits that its purpose is really to reassert theism; and Anthony Giddens, *Modernity and Self-Identity: self and society in the late modern age* (Stanford, 1991). Valentine Cunningham, *British Writers of the Thirties* (Oxford, 1988), places a heavy emphasis on the homosexual tendencies of the writers of that time. Gertrude Himmelfarb, *The De-moralization of Society: from Victorian virtues to modern values* (New York, 1995), focuses, despite its subtitle, on the Victorian era with only a glance at elements in the twentieth century, such as the rise in crime-rate and in the number of illegitimate births.

14 Eliot's poem, published in 1917, was in fact completed in 1911. See Hugh Kenner, *The Invisible Poet: T.S. Eliot* (London, 1965), p. 31.

15 Wilfred Owen, 'Anthem for Doomed Youth'.

16 A further factor often cited as relevant is the breakup of class distinctions, especially in Britain. But those familiar with the British scene will know (as evidenced in such novels as John Braine's *Room at the Top*) how strong that emphasis on the subtleties of class remained on the British scene until the end of the Second World War, long after the emergence of the crisis we are examining here.

17 *Hard Times*, chapter 5.

18 In an article in the *Examiner* concerning the orphanage at Tooting where 1400 children, crowded together in unhygienic conditions, suffered from a deadly outbreak of cholera. Details in Humphry House, *The Dickens World* (London, 1960), p. 100.

19 Carl G. Jung, *Modern Man in Search of a Soul,* trans. W.S. Dell and Cary F. Baynes (New York, 1933), p. 197.

20 A.O. Lovejoy, *The Great Chain of Being: a study of the history of an idea* (London, 1936) remains the classic treatment of that concept. Thomas Burnet's *The Sacred Theory of the Earth* of 1681 had suggested the reservation concerning the Deluge.

21 Darwin, *The Origin of Species* (New York, 1963), pp. 462 and 469.

22 Thomas H. Huxley, 'On the Relations of Man to the Lower Animals', in his *Evidence as to Man's Place in Nature* (New York, 1897), p. 155.

23 Thomas H. Huxley, 'Science and Morals'', published in *The Fortnightly*, December 1886. There is a helpful discussion of this subject in Peter Morton, *The Vital Science: biology and the literary imagination, 1860–1900* (London, 1984), as well as in Gertrude Himmelfarb's earlier study, *Darwin and the Darwinian Revolution* (London, 1959). For the impact on the nineteenth century, see George Levine, *Darwin and the Novelists: patterns of science in Victorian fiction* (Cambridge, Mass., 1988).

24 From a letter by Huxley reprinted in *Life and Letters*, ed. Leonard Huxley (New York, 1901), 2:324.

25 The centrality of this fear in the nineteenth century is examined in Michael Wheeler, *Heaven, Hell and the Victorian* (Cambridge, 1994).

26 Gottfried Semper, *Der Stil in den technischen und taktonischen Kuensten* (1861), and Alfred Haddon, *Evolution in Art* (1895). On the misleading assumption behind E.K. Chambers's *The Medieval Stage*, see O.B. Hardison, Jr, *Christian Rite and Christian Drama in the Middle Ages: essays in the origins and early history of modern drama* (Baltimore, 1965) and Stanley J. Kahrl, *Traditions of Medieval English Drama* (Pittsburgh, 1975). On the superiority of the Europeans, see the presidential address by James Hunt at the opening of the British Anthropological Society in 1863, propagating the offensive theory that the negro was closer to the ape and therefore incapable of being civilised.

27 Although in the classical era the debate might be thought to have been between polytheism and atheism, it is clear that fifth-century Greece, despite its worship of certain aspects of the divine in the form of personified deities, was moving close to monotheism. Compare the chorus's hymn in Aeschylus's *Agamemnon*, 'Zeus, whoever he may be ... ', as well as the idea of the Beautiful-and-Good at the summit of Plato's ideal world, a concept that was, in Marsilio Ficino's day, smoothly incorporated into Renaissance Christianity.

28 Browning, 'Paracelsus', 2:393–5, in *Poems*, ed. J. Woolford and D. Karlin (London, 1991).

29 *Origin of Species*, pp. 191–2.

30 In a letter by Ruskin dated 24 May 1851 in *Works* (London, 1903–12) 26:115.

31 Harriet Martineau, *Autobiography* (London, 1877, originally published in 1857) 2:355–6.

32 Somerset Maugham, *Of Human Bondage* (Harmondsworth, 1963), p. 118.

33 These aspects are discussed in my *The Soul of Wit: a study of John Donne* (Oxford, 1976) and *Milton and the Baroque* (London, 1980).

34 Wellhausen's work was not, as he readily acknowledged, an original thesis but an attempt to confirm a theory promulgated a decade earlier by Karl Graf.

35 Mrs. Humphry Ward, *Robert Elsmere* (Lincoln, Nebraska, 1967, orig. 1888), p. 581, and Matthew Arnold's preface to his *God and the Bible* (1875).

36 There were important predecessors in cultural anthropology, such as Edward B. Tylor in England and Lewis Henry Morgann in the United States; but there is a qualitative difference that marks Frazer as the initiator of a more fundamentally scientific approach to the subject.

37 The impact of Frazer's work upon Christian belief has been seriously underestimated. The numerous references to him in the 1997 *Encyclopedia Britannica*, for example, make no mention of those implications of his theory, even though they became so central, not least as a result of T.S. Eliot's poem.

38 James G. Frazer, *The Golden Bough: a study in magic and religion* (New York, 1960; originally published in a series of separate volumes from 1890 onwards). I have here quoted from the more accessible one-volume edition, p. 407. The worship of Cybele, reaching back to much earlier times, was adopted and celebrated by the Romans some two hundred years before the Christian era.

39 The winter solstice in fact occurs on 21 or 22 December, but was believed at that time to occur on the 25th.

40 Frazer, pp. 416 and 419.

41   D.H. Lawrence, *The Man Who Died* (New York, 1960, orig. 1922), pp. 188 and 124. The quoted passages are not contiguous in the story, but their juxtaposition is in full accord with the story's theme and message, a conflation dictated here by the need for brevity. The story was originally entitled 'The Escaped Cock'. Surprisingly, there is only one minor reference to it in Robert Fraser (ed.), *Sir James Frazer and the Literary Imagination: essays in affinity and influence* (London, 1990).

42   From 'Totem and Taboo' in *The Basic Writings of Sigmund Freud*, ed. A.A. Brill (New York, 1938), p. 860.

43   Friedrich Nietzsche, *The Genealogy of Morals*, trans. Francis Golffing (New York, 1956), pp. 225–6.

44   *The Future of an Illusion*, trans. W.D. Robson-Scott (New York, n.d.; orig. 1927), pp. 88–9.

45   In Marxist terminology, 'socialism' refers to the period of the revolution when the proletariat will establish a society based on communal ownership of wealth. Marx reserved the word 'communism' for the subsequent phase, when society will have finally transcended class division and eliminated the coercive state. The Fabian society, insisting on its peaceful purposes, took its name from the Roman general, Fabius Cunctator, famed for avoiding pitched battles and achieving victory by patient and elusive tactics.

46   M.H. Abrams, *Natural Supernaturalism: tradition and revolution in Romantic literature* (New York, 1973).

47   Jonathan Rose, *The Edwardian Temperament, 1895–1919* (London, 1986), pp. 21 f., notes how frequently members of the Fabian movement had moved across from Anglican Evangelicanism, seeing in socialism a substitute for the lost faith, to be embraced with equal fervour.

48   Nietzsche, *The Gay Science*. Cf. J.B. Foster, Jr, *Heirs to Dionysus: a Nietzschean current in literary modernism* (Princeton, 1981).

49   Quoted in Eva Metman, 'Reflections on Samuel Beckett's Plays,' in *Samuel Beckett: a collection of essays*, ed. Martin Esslin (Englewood Cliffs, NJ, 1965), p. 117.

50   Arthur Koestler's essay in Richard Crossman, ed., *The God that Failed* (New York, 1965), pp. 16–17.

51   Preface to Shaw's *Major Barbara*.

52   In his *Luck or Cunning* (1887).

53   *Origin*, p. 470. Later in life, Darwin began to change, declaring in a letter to a student in 1879: 'The mystery of the beginning of all things is insoluble by us; and I for one must be content to remain an Agnostic.' *Life and Letters*, ed. Francis Darwin (New York, 1988), 1:282.

54   *Samuel Butler's Notebooks*, sel. and ed. by Geoffrey Keynes and Brian Hill (London, 1951), p. 167.

55   Gertrude Himmelfarb, *Darwin and the Darwinian Revolution* (New York, 1962).

56   G.J. Romanes, *A Candid Examination of Theism* (London, 1892).

57   Romanes recorded his return to orthodox Christianity and the reasons that impelled him in his *Thoughts on Religion* (London, 1895), pp. 102–3 and 155–7. John Lester's *Journey* discusses perceptively the growing disillusionment with the implications of evolutionist theory at that time.

58   Quotations are from Thomas Huxley's essay, 'Science and Morals' (1886), and from *Evolution and Ethics* (1893).

59   Charles Kingsley, 'The Meteor Shower', a sermon preached in 1866, in *Works* (London, 1880–5) 26:179–80. Leslie Stephen's article appeared in the *Fortnightly Review*, new series 19 (1876), 857.

60   Philip Rahv's introduction to *Selected Short Stories of Franz Kafka* (New York, 1952), p. xii. The translation, by Willa and Edwin Muir, is from the Penguin version (Harmondsworth, 1970).

61   Tennyson, *In Memoriam*, section 56. It was published in 1850, at a time when Lyell's *Principles of Geology* (1830–3), with its theory of the gradual evolution of the earth's surface over millions of years, was preparing the way for Darwin's *Origin of Species* and evoking similar concern,.

62   Yeats, 'Sailing to Byzantium' (1927).

63   Nietzsche, *The Genealogy of Morals,* op. cit., pp. 179–80.

64   There is a discussion of fascism's connection with modernism, if from a somewhat different angle, in Art Berman, *Preface to Modernism* (Urbana, 1994), pp. 233f.

65   The implications of the indeterminacy principle for that generation were enumerated by P.W. Bridgman in *Harper's Magazine*, 158 (1929), where he warned that, although 'the existence of such a domain will be made the basis of an orgy of rationalising …' in fact, it was a two-handled argument providing justification for both sides of the debate, and hence ultimately irrelevant.

66   One need only note how psychiatrists called as witnesses in legal cases generally differ radically in their assessments of a patient's mental state, while determination of a patient's physical condition can usually be based on such incontrovertible evidence as X-rays or blood tests.

67   S. Freud, *Introductory Lectures on Psycho-analysis* (1917), trans. Joan Riviere (London, 1923), p. 314.

68   Roger Fry, in a lecture delivered to the British Psychological Society and subsequently published under the title, *The Artist and Psycho-Analysis*; and Clive Bell, 'Dr. Freud on Art', in *The Nation and Athenaeum*, 6 September, 1924.

69   Albert Modell, *The Erotic Motive in Literature,* (New York, 1919), pp. 11, 123 and 146. For studies of the effect of psychology on art and its theory of the evolution of the artist in society, see Ernst Kris, *Psychoanalytic Explorations in Art* (London, 1953) and Frederick J. Hoffman, *Freudianism and the Literary Mind* (Baton Rouge, 1957).

70   Some of the ideas mentioned here were contained in my recent book on modernist art and literature but I have felt it necessary to summarise them briefly here as they will serve as a basis for subsequent chapters.

71   A comment by Mark Rampion, a fictional representation of D.H. Lawrence and the most admired character in Aldous Huxley's *Point Counter Point* (New York, 1928), p. 474.

72   Arthur Koestler's 'Postcript' to his 1943 *Arrival and Departure* (New York, 1967).

73   Steven Marcus, *The Other Victorians: a study of sexuality and pornography in mid-nineteenth-century England* (New York, 1966). The diaries of both Pepys and Boswell were intended as private records, not for publication, the former even being inscribed in code, so they may be accepted as believable records of their time.

74   *Origin of Species,* p. 71

75   The Oxford Dictionary records no usage of the term 'sex' as a substitute for 'sexual intercourse' earlier than the present century.

76 See Huxley, *Point Counter Point*, especially the end of chapter vi.
77 Cf. Eduardo Ortega y Gasset's famous essay on *The Dehumanization of Art*, first published in Madrid in 1925, and Joseph Frank's subsequent discussion of that theme in *The Widening Gyre: crisis and mastery in modern literature* (New Brunswick, 1963).
78 Virginia Woolf, *The Waves* (Harmondsworth, 1975, orig. 1931), p. 64.
79 J.W. Krutch, *The Modern Temper: a study and a confession* (New York, 1956, orig. 1929), pp. 52 and 93. George Steiner, *The Death of Tragedy* (London, 1956), aroused considerable interest on its appearance, but its central theme, that tragedy 'is that form of art which requires the intolerable burden of God's presence. It is now dead because His shadow no longer falls upon us as it fell on Agamemnon or Macbeth or Atalie' (p. 353) had been stated much earlier by Krutch.
80 Cf. R.D. Laing, *The Divided Self* (New York, 1960), Giddens, *Modernity*, and Wylie Sypher, *Loss of the Self in Modern Literature and Art* (New York, 1964).
81 Alan Wilde, *Horizons of Assent: modernism, postmodernism, and the ironic imagination* (Baltimore, 1981), especially pp. 10 f.
82 Janet Rainwater, *Self-Therapy* (London, 1989), p. 194, her comment quoted with full approval in Giddens, *Modernity and Self-Identity*.
83 Ionesco, in an essay on Kafka in *Cahiers de la Compagnie Madeleine Renaud–Jean-Louis Barrault*, 20 October, 1957.
84 Tony Tanner, *City of Words: American fiction 1950–1970* (London, 1971), pp. 33 and 203, the latter quoting an interview with Hawkes in *Wisconsin Studies in Contemporary Literature*, summer 1965.
85 Elaine Showalter, *A Literature of Their Own* (Princeton, 1977). Doris Lessing did not move into science fiction until the late seventies.
86 Virginia Woolf, *The Waves* (Harmondsworth, 1975, orig. 1931), pp. 162–3. James Strachey recalled, after dining with the Woolfs in 1924, that Virginia had made 'a more than usually ferocious onslaught upon psychoanalysis and psychoanalysts, more particularly the latter.' Elsewhere, Virginia remarked that 'these Germans' reveal in their theories only their own gull-like imbecility. She became less antagonistic to those theories in her later years.

Chapter 2: Commissar and Priest

1 From Richard Crossman's introduction to *The God that Failed*. (New York, 1950)
2 John Atkins, *Arthur Koestler* (London, 1956), pp. 177 f. The views of Malcolm Cowley, George Orwell and others are reprinted in Murray Sperber (ed.), *Arthur Koestler: a collection of critical essays* (Englewood Cliffs, 1977).
3 Arthur Koestler, *Darkness at Noon* (Harmondsworth, 1947), p. 183. The 'numbered heads' refers to a numbered photograph of the original leaders of the Russian revolution that had been mentioned earlier in the novel.
4 Koestler had actually faced poverty in his youth, but by the time he joined the Communist Party he had already achieved a degree of financial security.
5 There is a detailed account of the theories preceding *The Origin of Species* and the widespread interest in them in William Irvine, *Apes, Angels, and Victorians: Darwin, Huxley, and evolution* (New York, n.d.).
6 Koestler, *The Invisible Writing: an autobiography* (London, 1969), p. 356–7, originally published in 1954.

7 John Stuart Mill, *Utilitarianism* (1863), chapter 3.

8 *Invisible Writing*, p. 479.

9 *The Yogi and the Commissar and other essays* (New York, 1945), p. 3.

10 Koestler, whose parents were secular Jews opposed to religious belief, had been drawn to assert his Jewish identity on exclusively nationalistic grounds, joining a Zionist youth movement with which he came into contact during his student days when he perceived the need to provide a homeland to rescue his people from pogroms and persecution. Details of that experience are recorded in Iain Hamilton, *Koestler: a biography* (London, 1982), pp. 6f.

11 Sidney A. Pearson, Jr, *Arthur Koestler* (Boston, 1978), p. 67.

12 Goronwy Rees, '"*Darkness at Noon*" and the "Grammatical Fiction', in Harold Harris, ed., *Astride the Two Cultures: Arthur Koestler at 70* (New York, 1975), p. 116.

13 *Critical Essays by George Orwell* (London, 1960), pp. 154–6.

14 Ihab Hassan, *Radical Innocence: studies in the contemporary American novel* (Princeton, 1971), p. 21. Compare also David Galloway, *The Absurd Hero in American Fiction* (Austin, 1981).

15 The one exception to the demise of the traditional hero in respected literary works, the central figures in Hemingway's novels, who retain the qualities of courage, skill and dedication to a defined aim, was achieved by a technique unique to his novels, a technique that I have discussed at some length in *Modernist Patterns* – the creation of an enclave isolated from the contemporary world, such as the bull-ring with its ceremonially determined values, whose standards are, by means of the *afficionado*, made to eddy out into the real world. Hemingway's innovation testified to the need to circumvent the contemporary collapse of heroic values.

16 To Gerald Brenan, in *Letters* 2:598, dated 25 December 1922. In contrast, Ricardo J. Quinones, *Mapping Literary Modernism: time and development* (Princeton, 1985), sees the new view of time as constituting the essence of the modernist movement.

17 Stuart Gilbert, *James Joyce's Ulysses* (New York, 1955).

18 Hans Robert Jauss, *Toward an Aesthetic of Reception*, trans. Timothy Bahti (Minneapolis, 1982).

19 Graham Greene, *Ways of Escape* (Toronto, 1980), pp. 67–8. Quotations from *The Power and the Glory* are from the 1991 Penguin edition.

20 His admiration for T.S. Eliot expresses itself frequently in his work, one instance being his choice of the title for *The Third Man*, an allusion to *The Waste Land*'s, 'Who is the third who walks always beside you?' Raymond M. Olderman discusses the dominance on the American scene of Eliot's metaphor in his *Beyond the Waste Land: a study of the American novel in the 1960s* (New Haven, 1972).

21 Roger Sharrock, *Saints, Sinners, and Comedians: the novels of Graham Greene* (Notre Dame, 1984), p. 123; Francis L. Kunkel, *The Labyrinthine Ways of Graham Greene* (New York, 1959), p. 114; Michael W. Higgins, 'Greene's Priest', in *Essays in Graham Greene* 3 (1992), 10; R.W.B. Lewis, *The Picaresque Saint: representative figures in contemporary fiction* (Philadelphia, 1958), p. 249; and K.C.J. Kurismmootil, S.J., *Heaven and Hell on Earth: an appreciation of five novels of Graham Greene* (Chicago, Ill., 1982), p. 64. For a more extreme instance of this view, cf. Gwenn R. Boardman, *Graham Greene: the aesthetics of*

exploration (Gainesville, 1971), p. 65, who summarises his progressive corruption: 'The whisky priest yields readily to the world's demands: he gives up the wine that should have been preserved for the sacrament and, in doing so, loses all – wine, brandy, and freedom. The steps of his fall are carefully recorded …'

22 M.M. Bakhtin, *The Dialogic Imagination*, ed. and trans. Michael Holquist (Austin, 1988), especially pp. 76 and 272.

23 Michael Shelden, *Graham Greene: the enemy within* (New York, 1994), p. 221.

24 Theodore P. Fraser, *The Modern Catholic Novel in Europe* (New York, 1994), p. 100.

25 Daphne Erdinast-Vulcan, *Graham Greene's Childless Fathers* (London, 1988), has noted interestingly how, in all Greene's Catholic novels, 'Father' denotes not only the title conferred upon priests by virtue of their office but also the priest's need to undertake paternal responsibility towards some child within the novel.

26 This further instance is from Georg M.A. Gaston, *The Pursuit of Salvation: a critical guide to the novels of Graham Greene* (New York, 1986), p. 29.

27 Quoted in Marie-Françoise Allain, *The Other Man: conversations with Graham Greene*, trans. Guido Waldman (London, 1983), p. 136.

28 Discussions of framing were stimulated in the sixties by Rudolf Arnheim's *Art and Visual Perception: a psychology of the creative eye* (Berkeley, 1966) and Aaron Scharf's *Art and Photography* (New York, 1968), especially pp. 201–2, and have come to attract increasing interest in recent years .

29 Hemingway, *Death in the Afternoon*, pp. 191–2. Cf. Susan Beegel, *Hemingway's Craft of Omission* (Ann Arbor, 1988). Note, also, Hemingway's further comment in *A Moveable Feast* on his 'new theory that you could omit anything if you knew that you omitted and the omitted part would strengthen the story.' (p. 75)

30 Cf. Kurismmootil, p. 61.

31 The priest's statement at one point that he chose the priesthood because it offered a rise in social status and an improvement in his living standards forms, of course, part of his negative evaluation of his own actions.

32 Quoted in Michael Shelden's biography listed above, p. 227. Waugh, a friend and admirer of Greene, reproached him for his unorthodox doctrines in his review of *The Heart of the Matter*. For details, see Donald Greene, 'Greene and Waugh, "Catholic Novelists"', in Jeffrey Meyers, ed., *Graham Greene: a revaluation* (London, 1990); and on his Gnosticism, David H. Hesla, 'Theological Ambiguity in the Catholic Novels', in Robert O.Evans, ed., *Graham Greene: some critical considerations* (Lexington, 1963).

33 Dickens, *Nicholas Nickleby* (Harmondsworth,1986), p. 222.

34 Karl, *A Reader's Guide,* p. 93.

35 Marie B. Mesnet, *Graham Greene and the Heart of the Matter* (Westport, 1954), p. 60.

36 Karl, *A Reader's Guide,* p. 16.

37 G. Greene, *The Comedians* (Harmondsworth, 1976), p. 31. Subsequent quotations are from this edition.

38 'Perhaps you are a *prêtre manqué.*' 'Me? You are laughing at me. Put your hand here. This has no theology.' I mocked myself while I made love. (p. 225) The previous references are to pp. 49 and 182. Some aspects of this residual

priesthood quality in Brown have been noted in Michael Larson, 'Laughing Till the Tears Come: Greene's failed comedian', in *Renascence*, 41 (1989), 177.

39 Paul O'Prey, *A Reader's Guide to Graham Greene* (London, 1988), p. 118.

40 Cf. Dorothea L.L. Barrett, 'Communism and Catholicism in *The Comedians*', in P. Erlebach and Y.M. Stein (eds), *Graham Greene in Perspective: a critical symposium* (Frankfurt, 1991), pp. 119 f.

41 A.A. DeVitis, *Graham Greene* (Boston, 1986), pp. 10–122, Grahame Smith, *The Achievement of Graham Greene* (Brighton, 1986), pp. 159–60, and Michael Gorra, *The English Novel at Mid-Century* (London, 1990), p. 152, the latter referring to p. 279 in the novel. Gaston, *The Pursuit of Salvation*, pp. 88 f., provides a far more sensitive reading of the novel, perceiving its priestly sub-theme and the relationship to Jones, but assuming that the change occurs in Brown rather than in the reader.

Chapter 3: The Adolescent Rebel

1 William Golding, *Lord of the Flies* (London, 1967), p. 248.

2 The strange story of the nature of that conversion – originally undertaken merely to satisfy the demands of the girl he loved, who had refused to consider marriage unless he converted – and his gradual conviction of the validity of his adopted faith, a conviction retained long after his marriage collapsed, has been frequently told, most effectively in Norman Sherry's biography.

3 The conclusion to Evelyn Waugh, *Brideshead Revisited* (Boston, 1945).

4 He insisted on absolute secrecy for the act of conversion itself, the doors of Finstock church being firmly locked against spectators, as recorded in Lyndall Gordon, *Eliot's Early Years* (Oxford, 1977), pp. 130–1. The appearance of his *Four Quartets,* with its dominant religious theme, in 1943 was a literary event not to be ignored.

5 Blake had, of course, originally used the term as a nickname for Urizen in his poem, *To Nobodaddy.*

6 The Broadway production coincided with a national newspaper strike and hence its immediate impact there is not recorded in print. In Hanover, however, a local critic reported that 'hours after the curtain had fallen, cafés in the vicinity of the theatre remained full of groups of people discussing untiringly the problems thrown up by MacLeish.' Details of the play's reception are recorded in an article by Robert Downing in *Theatre Arts,* February 1960, p. 29.

7 Archibald MacLeish, *J.B.* (Cambridge, Mass., 1958), p. 120–3.

8 J.D. Salinger, *Franny and Zooey* (Boston, 1961, orig. 1955), pp. 201–2.

9 Erwin Panofsky, *Gothic Architecture and Scholasticism* (New York, 1957).

10 J.D. Salinger, *The Catcher in the Rye* (Penguin, 1958), p. 205.

11 Details of the ban appear in Donald P.Costello, 'The Language of *The Catcher in the Rye*', *American Speech* 34 (1959), 132.

12 Christopher Parker, 'Why the Hell *Not* Smash All the Windows', in *Salinger: a critical and personal portrait,* ed. H.A. Grunwald (New York, 1963), p. 282, Albert Fowler in *J.D. Salinger and the Critics,* ed. W.F. Belcher and J.W. Lee (Belmont, Calif., 1964), p. 34, Hugh MacLean in the same volume, p. 11, Ihab Hassan, *Radical Innocence: studies in the contemporary novel* (Princeton, 1961),

p. 275, and Maxwell Geismar, 'The Wise Child and the New Yorker School of Fiction', in *American Moderns* (New York, 1958). See also, John W. Aldridge, *In Search of Heresy: American literature in an age of conformity* (New York, 1956), pp. 126 f., for a similar view that Holden can find no concrete embodiment for the ideal by which he judges and accordingly has 'no objects other than his sister for his love'.

13 Gerald Graff, *Literature Against Itself: literary ideas in modern society* (Chicago, 1979), p. 222.

14 Duane Edwards, 'Don't Ever Tell Anybody Anything', *Journal of English Literary History (ELH)* 44 (1977), 556, and Ernest Jones, *The Nation*, September 1951, 176.

15 Peter Shaw, 'Love and Death in *The Catcher in the Rye*', in Jack Salzman, ed., *New Essays on the Catcher in the Rye* (Cambridge, 1991), p. 97.

16 Pp. 47–8. I have shortened the passage for the sake of brevity, but nothing of significance has been omitted.

17 Cf. Albert Fowler and others, cited in note 12.

18 Cf. the incident with Saul whose fit of madness is interpreted by bystanders as echoing that of the prophets: 'And he stripped off his clothes also and prophesied before Samuel in like manner, and lay down naked all that day and all that night. Wherefore they say, Is Saul also among the prophets.' (I Samuel 19:24).

19 For a study of earlier and essentially different forms, see Lillian Feder, *Madness in Literature* (Princeton, 1980).

20 Cf. the valid comment of Arthur Heiserman and James E. Miller, Jr, 'J.D. Salinger: Some Crazy Cliff', *Western Humanities* Review 10 (1956), 129: 'It is not Holden who should be examined for a sickness of the mind, but the world in which he has sojourned and found himself an alien.' There is a parallel to this theme of society's placing of misfits in an asylum in Stanley Elkin's *A Bad Man* (1967), where the free spirit, Feldman, is incarcerated in a gaol whose corrupt and cruel system reflects the debased values of the contemporary world.

21 Inevitably, this brief reference fails to do justice to the play. Many have seen in it a profound pessimism, quoting Gloucester's terrible line, 'As flies to wanton boys, are we to the gods.' But one should recall that such is not Gloucester's final view. It is countered by his later determination to abide patiently by the decisions of heaven, a determination praised by the choric figure, Edgar.

22 Warren French, *J.D. Salinger Revisited* (Boston, 1988), p. 41, and Duane Edwards, op.cit. Patrick Costello, 'Salinger and "Honest Iago"', *Renascence* 16, 171–4, argues that Holden sees evil where none exists, and Howard Harper, *Desperate Faith: a study of Bellow, Salinger, Mailer, Baldwin, and Updike* (Chapel Hill, 1967), p. 67, sees the scene as ambiguous and Holden's response an over-reaction.

23 John Seelye, 'Holden in the Museum', in Salzman, *New Essays*, 23.

24 Seelye, op.cit., and Aldridge, *In Search of Heresy*, p. 130. Cf. also David Galloway, *The Absurd Hero in American Fiction: Updike, Styron, Bellow, Salinger* (Austin, 1981), p. 208.

25 Malcolm Bradbury, *The Social Context of Modern English Literature* (New York, 1971), pp. 16 f.

26 Edwin T. Bowden, *The Dungeon of the Heart* (London, 1961), pp. 55 f., Charles Kaplan, 'Holden and Huck: the Odysseys of Youth', *College English* 18 (1956),

76, Edgar Branch, 'Mark Twain and J.D. Salinger: a study in continuity', *American Quarterly* 9 (1957), 144, and Arvin R. Wells, 'Huck Finn and Holden Caulfield: the situation of the hero', *Ohio University Review* 2 (1960), 31. See also Harold Bloom, ed., *Holden Caulfield* (New York, 1990).

27   Bellow was, of course, Canadian by birth, but took up residence in Chicago. In his writings he made no distinction between Canada and the United States as centres of twentieth-century Western civilisation with all its achievements and problems.

28   Cf. Sanford Pinsker, *The Schlemiel as Metaphor: studies in the Yiddish and American Jewish novel* (Carbondale, 1971), and Ruthe R.Wisse, *The Schlemiel as Modern Hero* (Chicago, 1971).

29   Saul Bellow, *Herzog* (Harmondsworth, 1965), pp. 162–3, 2, 202, 22 and 128. For further discussions, see John J. Clayton, *Saul Bellow: in defense of man* (Bloomington, 1979), *Saul Bellow: a collection of essays*, ed. Earl Rovit (Englewood Cliffs, 1970), and *Saul Bellow's Herzog*, ed. Harold Bloom (New York, 1988).

30   Bernard Malamud, *The Fixer* (New York, 1966), p. 270. The quotation from 'The Lady of the Lake' is from his collection of stories *The Magic Barrel* (Harmondsworth, 1968), p. 119.

31   Philip Roth, *Portnoy's Complaint* (New York, 1994), p. 76. All subsequent quotations are from this edition.

32   Roth, *Reading Myself and Others* (New York, 1975), p. 218.

33   Scholem's article, which appeared in the Hebrew newspaper *Haaretz*, is quoted in Alan Cooper, *Philip Roth and the Jews* (Albany, 1966), p. 110. Marie Syrkin's review appeared in *Midstream* (April 1969), while Shaw's comment is cited by Roth in his attempt to rebut such attacks, *Reading Myself and Others* (New York, 1975), p. 243.

34   All quotations from the New York edition of 1987. In view of the brevity of the story, page references are not provided.

35   As so often, Eli's 'madness' has been interpreted literalistically by certain critics who miss the positive implications of the nervous breakdown in the anti-hero genre. Allen Guttmann, in *Critical Essays on Philip Roth*, ed. Sanford Pinsker (Boston, 1982), p. 172, concludes that Eli's final act is pathetic. 'He has been driven to insanity, at least for the moment, by the hardness of the zealots who have treated him as a fanatic.'

36   His father's attitude is recorded in Jay. L.Halio, *Philip Roth Revisited* (New York, 1992), p. xv. The source of the fictional family is mentioned in *Reading Myself*, p. 38, based on a neighbouring family with whom he often stayed.

37   Mary Allen, *The Necessary Blackness: women in major American fiction of the sixties* (n.p., 1996), ignores the specifically Jewish setting of this novel, stating simply that Sophie Portnoy represents Roth's obsession with women's power.

38   Bernard F. Rodgers, Jr, *Philip Roth* (Boston, 1978), p. 94.

39   Reprinted in *Reading Myself*, p. 19.

40   *Reading Myself*, pp. 82–3.

41   Cf. M.M. Bakhtin, *The Dialogical Imagination*, ed. Michael Holquist (Austin, 1981), and Jacques Derrida, *Positions* (Chicago, 1981), especially pp. 38 f. Bakhtin's work was, of course, conceived and written much earlier, but only came to be known widely in the west during the sixties.

42   Cf. Michael Levenson, *Modernism and the Fate of Individuality* (Cambridge, 1991), especially the opening chapter; Michel Foucault, *Discipline and*

Punishment: the birth of the prison, trans. Alan Sheridan (London,1977); and Jacques Lacan, *Écrits: a selection* (London,1977), as well as his *The Four Fundamental Concepts of Psycho-Analysis* (London,1977). For a general account of the phenomenon through the generations, see Karl Miller, *Doubles: studies in literary history* (Oxford, 1985).
43   *Reading Myself,* p. 21.
44   J.W. Krutch, *The Modern Temper: a study and a confession* (New York, 1956, orig. 1929), pp. 9–10.

Chapter 4: Innovative Drama

1   Richard Aldington, 'Modern Poetry and the Imagists', *The Egoist* (1 June 1914), p. 19.
2   See Blake Morrison's fine study, *The Movement: English poetry and fiction of the 1950s* (Oxford, 1980), to which I am indebted for a number of references.
3   In *The London Magazine* (June 1957).
4   In *Scrutiny* 2 (1942), 78–9.
5   Wain, 'Oxford and After', in *Outposts* 13 (1949), 21.
6   'Autobiographical Fragment', in *Collected Poems, 1944–79* (London, 1979), pp. 67–68.
7   Kingsley Amis, *Lucky Jim* (Harmondsworth, 1965), pp. 14–15.
8   *Sunday Times*, 23 December 1955.
9   For the widespread use of the term, cf. Kenneth Allsop's classic study, *The Angry Decade: a survey of the cultural revolt of the nineteen-fifties* (London, 1964). He suggested there that the term might be usefully modified to read 'dissentient,' but he continued to employ it in its original form throughout the book, primarily in relation to these three writers.
10   Quoted without source in Allsop, p. 52.
11   The report was in fact commissioned by the coalition government under Churchill, but it was associated in the public mind with the socialist principles of the Labour Party that implemented most of its suggestions.
12   John Osborne, *Look Back in Anger* (Harmondsworth, 1957), p. 20, the stage direction appearing on p. 14 and repeated in various forms throughout the scene. Subsequent quotations are from this edition.
13   Excerpts of these reviews appear in John Russell Taylor, ed., *Look Back in Anger: a casebook* (London, 1968), pp. 35–56.
14   Roy Huss in *Modern Drama* 6 (1963), 63, Arthur Schlesinger in *New Republic* (December 1957) 19, M.D. Faber in *Modern Drama* 13 (1970), 67, and M.C. Bradbrook, *English Dramatic Form* (London, 1965), p. 186.
15   On the theory that his motivation is the class struggle, see Arnold P. Hinchliffe, *John Osborne* (Boston, 1984), p. 16; and on the view that Jimmy's anger has no particular target, vaguely resulting from sexual frustrations, see Austin E. Quigley, 'The Personal, the Political, and the Postmodern in Osborne's *Look Back in Anger*' in Patricia D. Denison, ed., *John Osborne: a casebook* (New York, 1977), 35.
16   A.E. Dyson in J.R. Taylor, ed., *A Casebook*, pp. 22–3. Some of the sociological aspects of that impact are interestingly discussed in Alan Sinfield, 'The Theatre and its Audiences', in his edition of a collection of essays entitled *Society and Literature 1945–1970* (London, 1983), pp. 173f.

17   Cf. Simon Trussler, *The Plays of John Osborne: an assessment* (London, 1969), pp. 44–5. Similarly, Austin E. Quigley notes the puzzling discrepancy between the faults he perceives in the play and 'its remarkable historical impact'.

18   The comment appeared regularly on the cover of the Faber edition of the play. For the responses cited here, see Allsop, *The Angry Decade*, p. 119, John Russell Taylor, *Anger and After: a guide to the new British drama* (London, 1962), p. 44, and A.E. Dyson's essay in John Russell Brown, ed., *Modern British Dramatists: a collection of critical essays* (Englewood Cliffs, 1968), pp. 53–4.

19   Virginia Woolf, *To the Lighthouse* (London, 1938, orig. 1927), p. 79.

20   She claimed the Dutch painters as precedents for her non-heroic scenes in chapter 17 of *Adam Bede.*

21   Søren Kierkegaard, *Fear and Trembling* (1843) trans. Walter Lowrie (New York, 1954), pp. 72 and 86.

22   Albert Camus, *The Myth of Sisyphus* trans. Justin O'Brien (New York, 1955), p. 89.

23   The impact of existentialism on fiction is examined in Richard E. Baker, *The Dynamics of the Absurd in the Existential Novel* (New York, 1993) and useful accounts of the concept are to be found in William Barrett, *Irrational Man: a study in existentialist philosophy* (New York, 1958), Ernst Breisach, *An Introduction to Existentialism* (New York, 1962), and Nathan A. Scott, Jr, *Mirrors of Man in Existentialism* (Abingdon, 1978).

24   Martin Buber, 'The Education of Character', the English translation published in the same year as the German original, in the collection of essays, *Between Man and Man* trans. Ronald Gregor Smith (London, 1947), p. 116. Buber's concept of an I–It relationship with tactile objects is presented in his work as a stepping-stone to an I–Thou relationship with the divine. See his *I and Thou,* trans. Ronald Gregor Smith (New York, 1958), pp. 107 f. On the incident with the young man, see Maurice S. Friedman, *Martin Buber: the life of dialogue* (New York, 1960), p. 50.

25   Albert Camus, *The Stranger,* trans. Stuart Gilbert (New York, 1960, French original 1942), p. 72.

26   Greene's approval of Scobie's act is revealed in the lines immediately following upon the suicide, his reference to the medallion in honour of 'the saint whose name nobody could remember'.

27   The lacunas are in the original.

28   Cf. Baker, *The Dynamics of the Absurd,* pp. 2–3.

29   Vivian Mercier, 'The Mathematical Limit,' *The Nation* 188 (14 February 1959), 144–5. On this point, see also Steven Connor, *Samuel Beckett: repetition, theory, and text* (Oxford, 1988), especially pp. 118 f.

30   Frank Kermode, *The Sense of an Ending: studies in the theory of fiction* (Oxford, 1967), a principle examined also in Barbara Herrnstein Smith, *Poetic Closure: a study of how poems end* (Chicago, 1968).

31   My italics. All quotations are from the Faber edition (London, 1969).

32   The first quotation is from his *Proust and Three Dialogues* (London, 1965, orig. 1957), p. 125, the second from an interview with Georges Duthuit reported in *Transition V* (1949), 97; the third recorded by Tom F. Driver in 'Beckett by the Madeleine', *Columbia University Forum* 4, 3 (1961), 23, and reprinted in John Pilling, ed., *The Cambridge Companion to Beckett* (Cambridge, 1995). There is a stimulating discussion of this play in David H. Hesla, *The Shape of Chaos: an*

interpretation of the art of Samuel Beckett (Minneapolis, 1971), but it suffers, to my mind, from one failing. He examines there the implied disjunction of mind and body, but does so in universal terms valid for all generations, whereas, as these comments by Beckett confirm, it is the contrast between the concerns of the twentieth century and those of previous generations that actuate the play.

33 Cf. R.D. Laing, *The Divided Self* (London, 1960), and Anthony Giddens, *Modernity and Self-Identity: self and society in the late modern age* (Stanford, 1991).

34 Quoted in Ruby Cohn, ed., *Samuel Beckett's 'Waiting for Godot': a casebook* (London, 1987), p. 31.

35 Hesla, p. 134, Ruby Cohn, *Back to Beckett* (Princeton, 1976), p. 132, and Michael Warton, '*Waiting for Godot* and *Endgame:* theatre as text', in *The Cambridge Companion*, p. 67.

36 Hugh Kenner, *A Reader's Guide to Samuel Beckett* (London, 1973), p. 120.

37 Quoted in David J.Gordon, ' "*Au contraire*": the question of Beckett's bilingual text', in *Beckett On and On*, L. Oppenheim and M. Buning (eds) (Madison, 1996), p. 164. The alteration of Lucky's name is recorded in the essay by Colin Duckworth in the Ruby Cohn collection.

38 George E. Wellwarth, *The Theater of Protest and Paradox: developments in the avant-garde drama* (New York, 1964), pp. 39–40, referring to Charles S. McCoy, '*Waiting for Godot:* a Biblical Appraisal', *Religion in Life* 28 (1959), 595. The anonymous review of the play appeared in the *Times Literary Supplement*, 10 February 1956.

39 Lawrence Graver, *Samuel Beckett: 'Waiting for Godot'* (Cambridge, 1989), pp. 44–5.

40 The characteristic aspect is noted in John Fletcher and James MacFarlane, 'Modernist Drama: origins and patterns', in Malcolm Bradbury and James McFarlane eds, *Modernism: 1890–1930* (Harmondsworth, 1991), p. 506 – a book which, despite its title, covers a period reaching much further into the century but they make no comment on the fundamental change introduced into the genre.

41 Marvin Herrick, *Tragicomedy: its origin and development in Italy, France, and England* (Urbana, 1962).

42 Although highly acclaimed by audiences, the intertextual use of Shakespeare's play has been frowned upon by certain critics. Charles Marowitz, *Confessions of a Counterfeit Critic* (London, 1973), p. 173, described the result as 'academic twaddle', while Robert Burstein, *The Third Theatre* (New York, 1969), p. 123, objected to the ease of writing offered by such 'prefabrication'. On the intertextuality of the play, see Kinereth Meyer, ' "It is Written": Tom Stoppard and the drama of the intertext', *Comparative Drama* 23 (1989), 105.

43 Tom Stoppard, *Rosencranz and Guildenstern Are Dead* (New York, 1967), pp. 17–18.

44 Pp. 68–9, 57 and 118.

45 Arnold P. Hinchliffe, *British Theatre 1950–70* (Oxford, 1974), p. 142, quoted in the course of an interesting analysis of the play by Tim Brassell, *Tom Stoppard: an assessment* (London, 1985), pp. 35 f.

46 In a BBC interview in 1963, quoted by Graver, p. 94.

47 Beckett, *Proust* (New York, 1957).

48   Pinter, in a speech delivered in 1962, at the National Student Drama Festival in Bristol, reported in the *Sunday Times* of 4 March.
49   Ludwig Wittgenstein, *Tractatus logico-philosophicus*, trans. D.F. Pears and B.F. McGuiness (London, 1961), p. 151. For further discussion of this point, see Leslie Kane, *The Language of Silence: on the unspoken and the unspeakable in modern drama* (Rutherford, 1984).
50   BBC interview with Hallam Tennyson, 7 August 1960. The idea that Pinter cleverly succeeded in 'fusing' tragedy and farce is mentioned in Martin Esslin's early and deservedly influential study, *The Theatre of the Absurd* (New York, 1961), p. 202.
51   The jacket quotation is from Alan Brien's review in the Sunday Telegraph, the second reference to Wellwarth, *Theater of Protest and Paradox*, p. 284, and the third to Allan Lewis, *American Plays and Playwrights of the Contemporary Theater* (New York, 1970), p. 8. John Galbraith's essay is reprinted in Philip C. Kolin and J. Madison David (eds), *Critical Essays on Edward Albee* (Boston, 1986).
52   Edward Albee, 'Which Theater is the Absurd One?', *New York Times Magazine* (25 February 1962), pp. 30–1.
53   Penguin edition (Harmondsworth, 1986), p. 113, the edition also for all subsequent quotations.
54   In the introduction to my *Modernist Patterns in Literature and the Visual Arts* (New York and London, 1999).
55   The story of the cherry tree, almost certainly apocryphal, first appeared some six years after the publication of Mason Locke Weems, *The Life and Memorable Actions of George Washington* (1800), inserted in the fifth edition of that work.
56   Virginia Woolf, *The Waves* (Harmondsworth, 1973), p. 188.

Chapter 5: Terminal

1   At Stanford University in California, for example, David Harris, who led the student revolt, offered as part of that rebellion a new programme of studies for the university which many faculty members thought brilliantly innovative. It was at the same university that a professor of English, Bruce Franklin, was eventually dismissed from his post, charged with having urged students during one of the demonstrations to set fire to the physics building.
2   For contrasting views on the indebtedness of *Kubla Kahn* to opium-inspired dreams, see M.H. Abrams, *The Milk of Paradise* (Boston, 1934), and Elizabeth Schneider, *Coleridge, Opium, and 'Kubla Kahn'* (Chicago, 1953). The classic study of the influence of the drug on writers of that period, a study that takes a middle course between the two works, is Alethea Hayter, *Opium and the Romantic Imagination* (London, 1971).
3   Thomas DeQuincey opens his *Confessions of an English Opium-Eater*: 'I have often been asked – how it was, and through what series of steps, that I became an opium-eater . . . I answer before the question is finished, was it on a sudden, overmastering impulse from bodily anguish? Loudly I repeat, Yes; loudly and indignantly – as in answer to a willful calumny. Simply as an anodyne it was, under the mere coercion of pain the severest, that I first resorted to opium; and precisely that same torment it is, or some variety of that torment, which drives

most people to make acquaintance with that same insidious remedy.' In *Works* (Edinburgh, 1863) 1:2.

4   Jack Kerouac, *The Dharma Bums* (London, 1972, orig. 1959), p. 107.

5   As was well known at the time, the song 'Lucy in the Sky with Diamonds' was a covert acrostic for the prohibited drug LSD.

6   John Barth, *The Floating Opera and The End of the Road* (New York, 1988), p. 285. In 1967, the two novels were, with the author's approval, published in this combined edition, the page numbering running sequentially through both novels to suggest they form part of a single work. Quotations are from this edition.

7   Beverly Gross, 'The Anti-Novels of John Barth', in Joseph J. Waldmeir, ed., *Critical Essays on John Barth* (Boston, 1980), 30, states that he is 'most immediately a humorist … The suicide issue of *The Floating* Opera is an existentialist put-on; all issues in Barth's novels come down to some sort of game.' Barth's comment is recorded in Alan Prince, 'An Interview with John Barth', *Prism* (1968), 42, cited in Charles B. Harris, *Passionate Virtuosity: the fiction of John Barth* (Urbana, 1983).

8   In the 1956 edition of the novel, his publishers insisted upon certain changes, and there the statement was less pithy: 'If nothing makes any final difference, that fact makes no final difference either, and there is no more reason to commit suicide, say, than not to, in the last analysis.' For detailed discussion of the alterations that Barth was compelled to introduce into the original edition of the novel, see David Morrell, *John Barth: an introduction* (London, 1976), and Enoch P. Jordan, '*The Floating Opera* Restored', *Critique* 18 (1976), 5.

9   While the connection between the novels is self-evident to any reader, there is confirmation from the author himself. Gregory Bluestone, 'John Wain and John Barth: the Angry and the Accurate', *Massachusetts Review* 1 (1959), 586, quotes Barth's comment: 'I deliberately had [Todd] end up with that brave ethical subjectivism in order that Jake Horner might undo that position in #2 and carry all non-mystical value-thinking to the end of the road.' See also the note above on his sequential numbering of the two texts within a single volume.

10   Barth's 'Foreword' to the 1967 edition, p. vii.

11   From the collection of poems by Delmore Schwarz entitled, *In Dreams Begin Responsibilities,* published by New Directions in 1938. The quotation from *Point Counter Point* is from p. 2.

12   Sartre suggests this justification of choice in his *Existentialism and Humanism* trans. Philip Mairet (London, 1948).

13   The metaphor is from Robert A. Hipkiss, *The American Absurd: Pynchon, Vonnegut, and Barth* (Port Washington, 1984), p. 84.

14   The name Jake Horner is, of course, twofold in reference, suggesting the boy who sat in a corner eating a plum, uninvolved in the affairs around him and also the central figure, Horner, in Wycherley's Restoration comedy, *The Country Wife,* whose aim was to place a cuckold's horns on the heads of all husbands in his society.

15   Barth's 'Foreword,' p. viii; and Earl Rovit, 'The Novel as Parody', *Critique* 6 (1963), 77. In his lengthy rambling novel *Letters* (1979), Barth continued the stories both of Todd Andrews and of Jake Horner, providing reworkings of the themes, including Jake's mental rehearsal of the events in a kind of

psychodrama in which (employing different names) he marries Rennie, and Joe Morgan commits suicide. But the purpose here, as in all his later novels, is literary ingenuity rather than a serious exploration of the human condition, an aspect summarised on the jacket of the American paperback edition, a summary presumably approved by Barth, describing the novel as a 'romp through a dazzling comic epic', Jac Tharpe, *John Barth: the comic sublimity of paradox* (Carbondale, 1974), also takes the view that the comedy is intended to conceal the author-observer's lack of moral or other position.

16   Gerald Graff, *Literature Against Itself: literary ideas in modern society* (Chicago, 1979), pp. 186 f. See also, John Aldridge's excellent analysis of this aspect in, *The American Novel and the Way We Live Now* (Oxford, 1983), pp. 121 f. Also, the opening chapter of Patricia Tobin's, *John Barth and the Anxiety of Continuance* (Philadelphia, 1992).

17   From *Lady Lazarus*. All quotations are from *The Collected Poems*, ed., Ted Hughes (New York, 1981).

18   Hans Richter, in his recollections of the Dadaist movement, *Dada, Art, and Anti-art* (Oxford, 1978), p. 57.

19   There is a fuller discussion of this point in my *Modernist Patterns*, chapter 5.

20   Sylvia Plath, *Letters Home*, selected and edited with commentary by her mother, Aurelia Schober Plath (New York, 1975), pp. 183–4.

21   Quoted in Linda Wagner-Martin, *Sylvia Plath: a biography* (London, 1987), p. 124.

22   Dorothea Krook, 'Recollections of Sylvia Plath', and Clarissa Roche, 'Sylvia Plath: Vignettes from England', both essays in *Sylvia Plath: the woman and the work*, ed. Edward Butscher (New York, 1985).

23   *The Journals of Sylvia Plath*, ed. Frances McCullough (New York, 1982), entry for 20 February 1956.

24   Discussed in my essay 'The Contemplative Mode' in *The Romantic Imagination: literature and art in England and Germany*, eds. Frederick Burwick and Jürgen Klein (Atlanta, 1996), pp. 377 f.

25   *Journals*, entry for 12 December 1958.

26   George Steiner, 'Dying is an Art', in *The Art of Sylvia Plath: a symposium*, ed. Charles Newman (Bloomington, 1970), p. 218.

27   From *'Daddy'*. She was, in fact, eight years old when he died, the change no doubt intended to fictionalise the speaker.

28   Anne Stevenson, *Bitter Fame: a life of Sylvia Plath* (London, 1989), p. 246.

29   See the interesting essay by Mary Lynn Broe, 'Enigmatical, Shifting My Clarities', in *Ariel Ascending: writings about Sylvia Plath*, ed. Paul Alexander (New York, 1985).

30   Stevenson, p. 263. Hughes altered the order in his edition of *The Collected Poems*.

31   Granville Hicks, 'Outcasts in a Caldron of Hate', *Saturday Review* 43 (1962), 21, reprinted in F.L. Standley and N.V. Burt eds, *Critical Essays on James Baldwin* (Boston, 1988), 149. In the essay, 'Everybody's Native Novel', included in *Notes of a Native Son* (Boston, 1955), Baldwin had attacked the protest novels of the black movement, but was seen by most critics as having continued, paradoxically, to write in that tradition. See, for example, Therman B. O'Daniel's editorial introduction to *James Baldwin: a critical evaluation* (Washington, DC, 1977).

32   Baldwin, *Go Tell It On The Mountain* (London, 1971), p. 41.

33 Leslie A. Fiedler, *Love and Death in the American Novel* (New York, 1967), especially pp. 370 and 461 f.

34 Pp. 14–15. All quotations are from the 1963 Penguin edition. Cf. Ralph Ellison's excellent description in 'The Charlie Christian Story,' *Saturday Review of Literature* (17 May 1958), p. 42: 'For true jazz is an art of individual assertion within and against the group. Each true jazz moment (as distinct from the uninspired commercial performance) springs from a contest in which each artist challenges all the rest each solo flight on improvisation represents a definition of his identity as member of the collectivity'

35 Robert A. Bone, *The Negro Novel in America* (New Haven, 1965), p. 230, and Keneth Kinnamon's introduction to *James Baldwin: a collection of critical essays* (Englewood Cliffs, 1974).

36 Norman Podhoretz, 'In Defense of a Maltreated Best Seller', *Show* magazine, quoted in Mike Thelwell's essay, which is itself reprinted in C.W.E. Bigsby, ed., *The Black American Writer* (Baltimore, 1979) 1:181. At the time of Baldwin's death in 1987, *The Times* stated in its obituary tribute that the novel 'stands comparison with any of its period to come out of the United States.'

37 F.W. Dupee, in 'James Baldwin and the "Man"', *New York Review of Books* 1:1 (1963), p. 1, remarked that Baldwin, as 'a writer of polemical essays on the negro question wears his color, as Hester Prynne did her scarlet letter, proudly.'

38 See note above.

39 Roger Rosenblatt, *Black Fiction* (Cambridge, Mass., 1976), p. 153, who also argues that in this novel the white characters are the prime movers in all the evil.

40 'In a line of associations ambiguous words (or, as we may call them, 'switch-words') act like points at a junction. If the points are switched across from the position in which they appear to lie in the dream, then we find ourselves upon another set of rails; and along this second track run the thoughts which we are in search of and which still lie concealed behind the dream.' Freud, *The Interpretation of Dreams*, reprinted in *The Basic Writings of Sigmund Freud*, ed. A.A. Brill (New York, 1938), p. 331.

41 D.H. Lawrence, *The Rainbow* (Harmondsworth, 1958, orig. 1915), pp. 462–3.

42 Pp. 343 and 420.

43 Cf. Brian Lee, 'James Baldwin: Caliban to Prospero', in C.W.E. Bigsby, ed., *The Black American Writer* (Baltimore, 1979) 1:169. So too, Edward Margolies, *Native Sons: a critical study of twentieth-century Negro American writers* (Philadelphia, 1968), p. 118.

Select Bibliography

Aldridge, John W., *In Search of Heresy: American literature in an age of conformity*, New York, 1956.

Alexander, Paul (ed.), *Ariel Ascending: writings about Sylvia Plath*, New York, 1985.

Allain, Marie-Françoise, *The Other Man: conversations with Graham Greene*, trans. Guido Waldman, London, 1983.

Allen, Mary, *The Necessary Blackness: women in major American fiction of the sixties*, n.p., 1996.

Allsop, Kenneth, *The Angry Decade: a survey of the cultural revolt of the nineteen-fifties*, London, 1964.

Alvarez, A., *The Savage God: a study of suicide*, London, 1971.

Atkins, John, *Arthur Koestler*, London, 1956.

Atkins, John, *The Art of Graham Greene*, London, 1966.

Baker, Richard E., *The Dynamics of the Absurd in the Existential Novel*, New York, 1993.

Bakhtin, M.M., *The Dialogic Imagination*, ed. and trans. Michael Holquist, Austin, 1988.

Barrett, William, *Irrational Man: a study in existentialist philosophy*, New York, 1958.

Baumeister, Roy F., *Identity: cultural change and the struggle for self*, Oxford, 1986.

Beegel, Susan, *Hemingway's Craft of Omission*, Ann Arbor, 1988.

Belcher, W.F. and Lee, J.W. (eds), *J.D. Salinger and the Critics*, Belmont, 1964.

Bergonzi, Bernard, *The Situation of the Novel*, London, 1979.

Berman, Art, *Preface to Modernism*, Urbana, 1994.

Bigsby, C.W.E. (ed.), *The Black American Writer*, Baltimore, 1979.

Bloom, Harold (ed.), *Saul Bellow's Herzog*, New York, 1988.

Bloom, Harold (ed.), *Holden Caulfield*, New York, 1990.

Boardman, Gwenn R., *Graham Greene: the aesthetics of exploration*, Gainesville, 1971.

Bone, Robert A., *The Negro Novel in America*, New Haven, 1965.

Bowden, Edwin T., *The Dungeon of the Heart*, London, 1961.

Bradbrook, M.C., *English Dramatic Form* London, 1965.

Bradbury, Malcolm, *The Social Context of Modern English Literature*, New York, 1971.

Bradbury, Malcolm and McFarlane, James (eds.), *Modernism: 1890–1930*, Harmondsworth, 1991.

Brassell, Tim, *Tom Stoppard: an assessment*, London, 1985.

Breisach, Ernst, *An Introduction to Existentialism*, New York, 1962.

Brown, Dennis, *The Modernist Self in Twentieth-Century English Literature: a study in self-fragmentation*, London, 1989.

Brown, John Russell (ed.), *Modern British Dramatists: a collection of critical essays*, Englewood Cliffs, 1968.

Buber, Martin, *Between Man and Man*, trans. Ronald Gregor Smith, London, 1947.

Buber, Martin, *I and Thou*, trans. Ronald Gregor Smith, New York, 1958.

Butscher, Edward (ed.), *Sylvia Plath: the woman and the work*, New York, 1985.

Calinescu, Matei, *Five Forms of Modernity*, Durham, 1987.

Clayton, John J., *Saul Bellow: in defense of man*, Bloomington, 1979.

Cohn, Ruby (ed.), *Samuel Beckett's 'Waiting for Godot': a casebook*, London, 1987.

Cohn, Ruby, *Back to Beckett*, Princeton, 1976.

Cooper, Alan, *Philip Roth and the Jews*, Albany, 1966.

Crossman, Richard (ed.), *The God that Failed*, New York, 1965.

Cunningham, Valentine, *British Writers of the Thirties*, Oxford, 1988.

Denison, Patricia D. (ed.), *John Osborne: a casebook*, New York, 1977.

DeVitis, A.A., *Graham Greene*, Boston, 1986.

Durkheim, Émil, *Suicide*, trans. J.A. Spaulding and G. Simpson, New York, 1951.

Erdinast-Vulcan, Daphne, *Graham Greene's Childless Fathers*, London, 1988.

Erlebach, P. Stein, Y.M. (eds), *Graham Greene in Perspective: a critical symposium*, Frankfurt, 1991.

Esslin, Martin, *The Theatre of the Absurd*, New York, 1961.

Esslin, Martin (ed.), *Samuel Beckett: a collection of essays*, Englewood Cliffs, 1965.

Evans, Robert O. (ed.), *Graham Greene: some critical considerations*, Lexington, 1963.

Feder, Lillian, *Madness in Literature*, Princeton, 1980.

Fiedler, Leslie A., *Love and Death in the American Novel*, New York, 1967.

Foster, J.B., Jr, *Heirs to Dionysus: a Nietzschean current in literary modernism*, Princeton, 1981.

Foucault, Michel, *Madness and Civilization*, trans. Richard Howard, New York, 1965.

Foucault, Michel, *Discipline and Punishment: the birt of the prison*, trans. Alan Sheridan, London, 1977.

Frank, Joseph, *The Widening Gyre: crisis and mastery in modern literature*, New Brunswick, 1963.

Fraser, Theodore P., *The Modern Catholic Novel in Europe*, New York, 1994.

Frazer, James G., *The Golden Bough: a study in magic and religion*, New York, 1960.

French, Warren, *J.D. Salinger Revisited*, Boston, 1988.

Friedman, Maurice S., *Martin Buber: the life of dialogue*, New York, 1960.

Fussell, Paul, *The Great War and Modern Memory*, Oxford, 1977.

Galloway, David, *The Absurd Hero in American Fiction: Updike, Styron, Bellow, Salinger*, Austin, 1981.

Gaston, Georg A.M., *The Pursuit of Salvation: a critical guide to the novels of Graham Greene*, New York, 1986.

Giddens, Anthony, *Modernity and Self-Identity: self and society in the late modern age*, Stanford, 1991.

Gordon, Lyndall, *Eliot's Early Years*, Oxford, 1977.

Gorra, Michael, *The English Novel at Mid-Century*, London, 1990.

Graff, Gerald, *Literature Against Itself: literary ideas in modern society*, Chicago, 1979.

Graver, Lawrence, *Samuel Beckett: 'Waiting for Godot'*, Cambridge, 1989.

Greenwald, H.A. (ed.), *Salinger: a critical and personal portrait*, New York, 1962.

Haddon, Alfred, *Evolution in Art*, London,1895.

Halio, Jay L., *Philip Roth Revisited*, New York, 1992.

Hamilton, Iain, *Koestler: a biography*, London, 1982.

Harper, Howard, *Desperate Faith: a study of Bellow, Salinger, Mailer, Baldwin, and Updike*, Chapel Hill, 1967.

Harris, Charles B., *Passionate Virtuosity: the fiction of John Barth*, Urbana, 1983.

Hassan, Ihab, *Radical Innocence: studies in the contemporary American novel*, Princeton, 1971.

Hauck, R.B., *A Cheerful Nihilism*, Bloomington, 1971.

Herrick, Marvin, *Tragicomedy: its origin and development in Italy, France, and England*, Urbana, 1962.

Hesla, David H., *The Shape of Chaos: an interpretation of the art of Samuel Beckett*, Minneapolis, 1971.

Himmelfarb, Gertrude, *Darwin and the Darwinian Revolution*, London, 1959.

Himmelfarb, Gertrude, *The De-moralization of Society: from Victorian virtues to modern values*, New York, 1995.

Hinchliffe, Arnold P., *British Theatre 1950–70*, Oxford, 1974.

Hinchliffe, Arnold P., *John Osborne*, Boston, 1984.

Hipkiss, Robert A., *The American Absurd: Pynchon, Vonnegut, and Barth*, Port Washington, 1984.

Hoffman, Frederick J., *Freudianism and the Literary Mind*, Baton Rouge, 1957.

Hopper, Stanley R. (ed.), *Spiritual Problems in Contemporary Literature*, New York, 1957.

Irvine, William, *Apes, Angels, and Victorians: Darwin, Huxley, and evolution*, New York, n.d.

Jauss, Hans Robert, *Toward an Aesthetic of Reception*, trans. Timothy Bahti, Minneapolis, 1982.

Jung, Carl, *Modern Man in Search of a Soul*, trans. W.S. Dell and C.F. Baynes, New York, 1933.

Kane, Leslie, *The Language of Silence: on the unspoken and the unspeakable in modern drama*, Rutherford, 1984.

Karl, Frederick, *A Reader's Guide to the Contemporary Novel*, New York, 1973.

Kenner, Hugh, *A Reader's Guide to Samuel Beckett*, London, 1973.

Kenner, Hugh, *The Invisible Poet: T.S. Eliot*, London, 1965.

Kermode, Frank, *The Sense of an Ending: studies in the theory of fiction*, Oxford, 1967.

Kinnamon, Keneth (ed.), *James Baldwin: a collection of critical essays*, Englewood Cliffs, 1974.

Klein, Marcus, *After Alienation*, Cleveland, 1964.

Kolin, P.C. and David, J.M. (eds), *Critical Essays on Edward Albee*, Boston, 1986.

Kris, Ernst, *Psychoanalytic Explorations in Art*, London, 1953.

Krutch, J.W., *The Modern Temper: a study and a confession*, New York, 1956.

Kunkel, Francis L., *The Labyrinthine Ways of Graham Greene*, New York, 1959.

Kurismmootil, K.C.J., SJ, *Heaven and Hell on Earth: an appreciation of five novels of Graham Greene*, Chicago, 1982.

Lacan, Jacques, *Écrits: a selection*, London, 1977.

Lacan, Jacques, *The Four Fundamental Concepts of Psycho-Analysis*, London, 1977.

Laing, R.D., *The Divided Self*, New York, 1960.

Langbaum, Robert, *The Mysteries of Identity: a theme in modern literature*, Chicago, 1977.

Lasch, Christopher, *The Minimal Self: psychic survival in troubled times*, New York, 1984.

Lester, John. A., Jr, *Journey Through Despair, 1880–1914*, Princeton, 1968.

Levenson, Michael, *Modernism and the Fate of Individuality*, Cambridge, 1991.

Levenson, Michael (ed.), *The Cambridge Companion to Modernism*, Cambridge, 1999.

Levine, George, *Darwin and the Novelists: patterns of science in Victorian fiction*, Cambridge Mass., 1988.

Levine, George (ed.), *Constructions of the Self*, New Brunswick, 1992.

Lewis, Allan, *American Plays and Playwrights of the Contemporary Theater*, New York, 1970.

Lewis, R.W.B., *The Picaresque Saint: representative figures in contemporary fiction*, Philadelphia, 1958.

Lovejoy, A.O., *The Great Chain of Being: a study of the history of an idea*, London, 1936.

Marcuse, Herbert, *One-Dimensional Man: the ideology of industrial society*, London,1968.

Margolies, Edward, *Native Sons: a critical study of twentieth-century Negro American writers*, Philadelphia, 1968.

Marsden, Malcolm (ed.), *'If You Really Want to Know': a Catcher casebook*, Chicago, 1963.

McEwan, Neil, *Graham Greene*, London, 1988.

Mesnet, Marie B., *Graham Greene and the Heart of the Matter*, Westport, 1954.

Miller, Karl, *Doubles: studies in literary history*, Oxford, 1985.

Morrell, David, *John Barth: an introduction*, London, 1976.

Morrison, Blake, *The Movement: English poetry and fiction of the 1950s*, Oxford, 1980.

Morton, Peter, *The Vital Science: biology and the literary imagination, 1860–1900*, London, 1984.

Newman, Charles (ed.), *The Art of Sylvia Plath: a symposium*, Bloomington, 1970.

Nicholls, Peter, *Modernisms: a literary guide*, Berkeley, 1995.

O'Daniel, Therman B. (ed.), *James Baldwin: a critical evaluation*, Washington D.C., 1977.

O'Prey, Paul, *A Reader's Guide to Graham Greene*, London, 1988.

Olderman, Raymond M., *Beyond the Waste Land:, a study of the American Novel in the 1960s*, New Haven, 1972.

Ortega y Gasset, Eduardo, *The Dehumanization of Art*, Madrid,1925.

Orwell, George, *Collected Essays* New York, 1957.

Pearson, Sidney A. Jr., *Arthur Koestler*, Boston, 1978.

Pilling, John (ed.), *The Cambridge Companion to Beckett*, Cambridge, 1995.

Pinsker, Sanford, *The Schlemiel as Metaphor: studies in the Yiddish and American Jewish novel*, Carbondale, 1971.

Pinsker, Sanford (ed.), *Critical Essays on Philip Roth*, Boston, 1982.

Porter, Roy, *Mind Forg'd Manacles: a history of madness in England from the Restoration to the Regency*, London, 1987.

Quinones, Ricardo J., *Mapping Literary Modernism*, Princeton, 1985.

Rodgers, Bernard F., Jr, *Philip Roth* Boston, 1978.

Romanes, G J., *A Candid Examination of Theism*, London, 1892.

Rose, Jonathan, *The Edwardian Temperament, 1895–1919*, London, 1986.

Rosenblatt, Roger, *Black Fiction*, Cambridge, Mass., 1976.

Rovit, Earl (ed.), *Saul Bellow: a collection of essays*, Englewood Cliffs, 1970.

Salzberg, Joel (ed.), *Critical Essays on Salinger's 'Catcher in the Rye'*, Boston, 1990.

Salzman, Jack (ed.), *New Essays on 'The Catcher in the Rye'*, Cambridge, 1991.

Sass, Louis A., *Madness and Modernism: insanity in the light of modern art, literature, and thought*, New York, 1992.

Schwarz, Daniel R., *The Transformation of the English Novel, 1890–1930*, London, 1989.

Schwarz, Daniel R., *Reconfiguring Modernism*, New York, 1997.

Schwarz, Sanford, *The Matrix of Modernism*, Princeton, 1985.

Scott, Nathan A., Jr., *Mirrors of Man in Existentialism*, Abingdon, 1978.

Sharrock, Roger, *Saints, Sinners, and Comedians: the novels of Graham Greene*, Notre Dame, 1984.

Shelden, Michael, *Graham Greene: the enemy within*, New York, 1994.

Sinfield, Alan (ed.), *Society and Literature, 1945–1970*, London, 1983.

Smith, Barbara Herrnstein, *Poetic Closure: a study of how poems end*, Chicago, 1968.

Smith, Grahame, *The Achievement of Graham Greene*, Brighton, 1986.

Sperber, Murray (ed.), *Arthur Koestler: a collection of critical essays*, London, 1977.

Standley, F L. and Burt, N.V. (eds), *Critical Essays on James Baldwin*, Boston, 1988.

Steiner, George, *The Death of Tragedy*, London, 1956.

Stevenson, Anne, *Bitter Fame: a life of Sylvia Plath*, London, 1989.

Sypher, Wylie, *Loss of the Self in Modern Literature and Art*, New York, 1964.

Tanner, Tony, *City of Words: American fiction 1950–1970*, London, 1971.

Taylor, Charles, *Sources of the Self: the making of the modern identity*, Cambridge, Mass., 1989.

Taylor, John Russell, *Anger and After: a guide to the new British drama*, London, 1962.

Taylor, John Russell, (ed.), *Look Back in Anger: a casebook*, London, 1968.

Tharpe, Jac, *John Barth: the comic sublimity of paradox*, Carbondale, 1974.

Thody, Philip, *Twentieth-Century Literature: critical issues and themes*, London, 1996.

Trussler, Simon, *The Plays of John Osborne: an assessment*, London, 1969.

Wagner-Martin, Linda, *Sylvia Plath: a biography*, London, 1987.

Waldmeir, Joseph J. (ed.), *Critical Essays on John Barth*, Boston, 1980.

Walkiewicz, E.P., *James Baldwin*, Boston, 1986.

Wellwarth, George E., *The Theater of Protest and Paradox: developments in the avant-garde drama*, New York, 1964.

Wheeler, Michael, *Heaven, Hell and the Victorian*, Cambridge, 1994.

Wilde, Alan, *Horizons of Assent: modernism, postmodernism, and the ironic imagination*, Baltimore, 1981.

Wilson, Colin, *The Outsider: an enquiry into the sickness of mankind in the twentieth century*, London, 1967.

Wisse, Ruthe P., *The Schlemiel as Modern Hero*, Chicago, 1971.